Collins

KS3
English
Revision Guide

Paul Burns and Ian Kirby

About this Revision & Practice book

When it comes to getting the best results, practice really does make perfect! Experts have proved that repeatedly testing yourself on a topic is far more effective than re-reading information over and over again. And, to be as effective as possible, you should space out the practice test sessions over time.

This Revision & Practice book is specially designed to support this approach to revision and includes seven different opportunities to test yourself on each topic, spaced out over time.

*Covers spelling, punctuation and grammar.

Revise

These pages provide a recap of everything you need to know for each topic.

You should read through all the information before taking the Quick Test at the end. This will test whether you can recall the key facts.

> **Quick Test**
> 1. Name the two different ways of referring to the text.
> 2. What is meant by 'paraphrasing'?
> 3. When you are quoting, what goes inside the inverted commas?
> 4. What does PEE stand for?

Practise

These topic-based questions appear shortly after the revision pages for each topic and will test whether you have understood the topic. If you get any of the questions wrong, make sure you read the correct answer carefully.

Review

These topic-based questions appear later in the book, allowing you to revisit the topic and test how well you have remembered the information. If you get any of the questions wrong, make sure you read the correct answer carefully.

Mix it Up

These pages feature a mix of questions for all the different topics, just like you would get in a test. They will make sure you can recall the relevant information to answer a question without being told which topic it relates to.

Test Yourself on the Go

Visit our website at **collins.co.uk/collinsks3revision** and print off a set of flashcards. These pocket-sized cards feature questions and answers so that you can test yourself on all the key facts anytime and anywhere. You will also find lots more information about the advantages of spaced practice and how to plan for it.

Workbook

This section features even more topic-based and test-style questions, providing two further practice opportunities for each topic to guarantee the best results.

ebook

To access the ebook visit **collins.co.uk/ebooks** and follow the step-by-step instructions.

QR Codes

Found throughout the book, the QR codes can be scanned on your smartphone for extra practice and explanations.

A QR code in the Revise section links to a Quick Recall Quiz on that topic. A QR code in the Workbook section links to a video working through the solution to one of the questions on that topic.

Contents

Key Stage 2

Read the story below, taken from Aesop's Fables, and answer the questions that follow.

These questions will test how well you have remembered key ideas from Key Stage 2.

The Wind and the Sun

The wind and the sun got into an argument one day about which of them was the stronger. The argument turned into a quarrel and the quarrel almost into a fight. There seemed to be no way of settling the dispute. But suddenly they saw a young man walking down the road beneath them. He was obviously on a long journey and was well wrapped-up in a thick coat, a long scarf and a woolly hat.

'Here's our chance,' said the sun.

'What do you mean?' the wind asked.

'We can use that traveller to prove which of us is the stronger. Whichever of us can make him take off his hat and coat must be the stronger. You go first.'

So the sun hid behind a cloud and the wind started to blow. Nothing happened. So he blew harder. The wind was icy. The traveller fastened his coat. He blew even harder. Now the wind was fierce and rough. But the man pulled up his collar, wrapped his scarf more tightly round his neck and pulled down his hat over his ears. At last the wind ran out of breath and gave up in despair.

Then the sun came out from behind the cloud and shone. He shone on the traveller with all the power he had. The man felt the warmth of the kind sun beating down on him. As he grew warmer, he took off his hat and scarf. Then he unfastened his coat. Finally, he was so warm that he had to take off his coat altogether. He even stopped walking and sat down for a rest in the welcoming shade of an ancient tree.

So the sun was proved right and won the argument.

1 What are the sun and the wind arguing about? [1]

2 What is it about the young man that would make us think it is a cold day? [1]

3 Find and write two words which describe how unpleasant the wind is. [1]

4 Match each of the following nouns to an adjective used to describe it. One has been done for you. [1]

Nouns		Adjectives
The journey		icy
The man's hat		kind
The wind		long
The shade		welcoming
The sun		woolly

5 Why do you think the sun hid behind a cloud before the wind started to blow?
Tick (✓) the correct answer. [1]

a) Because he is frightened of the wind. ☐

b) Because he wants the traveller to feel only the wind and not the sun. ☐

c) Because he does not want to know what the wind is doing. ☐

d) Because he enjoys playing hide and seek. ☐

6 Look at the paragraph beginning: 'So the sun hid…'

How does the writer make this paragraph exciting?

Give **two** ways. [2]

7 Fables are stories designed to teach us about life. What message do you think this story is trying to give? Explain as fully as you can. [3]

Selecting Key Words and Ideas 1

You must be able to:

- Understand, describe, find and select information and ideas in texts
- Answer 'Who? What? Where? When? How? Why?' questions appropriately.

Finding and Selecting Information and Ideas

- You need to be able to find and identify key points in a **text**.
- You should be able to **select** relevant points from different parts of the text.
- An important skill is **skim reading**. Having already carefully read the text once, you should be able to read it again quickly, using your memory to help you find the part of the text you need.
- Sometimes you will be given an idea of where to find the information, for example, 'the first paragraph' or 'lines 1 to 6'.
- The most important thing to remember is that all the answers are there for you in the text.
- You can **paraphrase** (see page 8) or quote directly from the text, but you must not guess or make things up.

> ### Key Point
>
> You may need to refer to material from different parts of the text to answer one question.

Who, What, Where and When

- Questions that require you to select material from the text might begin with 'who', 'what', 'where' or 'when'.
- Look at the extract below and ask yourself:
  - **Who** alerts the writer to the danger?
  - **What** is the cause of the noise?
  - **Where** is the family staying when the flood happens?
  - **When** does the flood take place?

> ### Key Point
>
> These questions are designed to show that you understand what the writer is saying.

We were all exhausted by the time we got to bed that night. The journey from Birmingham had been long and tedious, with lengthy delays on the M6. It's always like that on Christmas Eve. It was already dark when we arrived at my mother's cottage and the children – Joey, Amelia and Tom – were in bed by eight o'clock. I stayed up for another hour, talking to Mum and putting the presents under the tree. I must have fallen asleep as soon as we got to bed.

The first indication that anything was wrong was when I heard a little voice saying 'Dad, Dad,' over and over again, and woke to find Tom pulling at my arm. It was almost midnight. He said that he had heard a strange noise and was frightened. I listened. I could hear the whoosh of rushing water coming from downstairs. I opened the bedroom door and saw that the water was already halfway up the stairs.

- **Who?** The person who alerts the writer to the danger is Tom. You know that Tom is the writer's son because he calls him 'Dad', so you could say, 'the writer's son, Tom'. However, it would not be enough to say 'the writer's son', as Joey might also be his son.
- **What?** The cause of the noise is the water. Rather than just 'the water', it would be better to say 'water rushing into the house' or 'water coming up the stairs', as it is the movement of the water that makes the noise.
- **Where?** The family are staying at the writer's mother's cottage. 'In a cottage' might get a mark but is not as good an answer.
- **When?** The flood takes place on Christmas Eve. 'At Christmas' would be too vague, as the writer is quite precise about the time, saying he was woken before midnight.

How and Why

- Questions that start with 'how' and 'why' often require you to do more than find something in the text – you have to work out for yourself how or why something happened.
- To say 'how' or 'why', you might have to 'read between the lines' (see page 10).
- Sometimes the writer clearly states how or why, in which case you might get a question like, 'According to the writer, how/why…' or, 'According to the text, how/why…'.
- You may be asked, 'How does the writer feel…' or, 'What does the character think…' You can only answer with what the writer or character actually *says* he or she thinks or feels.
- How and why questions about the text opposite could include:
    - How does the writer feel about the journey from Birmingham?
    - According to the text, why is the family exhausted?
    - According to the writer, how does Tom feel when he wakes his father?
- Appropriate answers would be:
    - He feels that the journey was tedious/tiresome.
    - They have had a long and tiring journey.
    - He feels frightened.

Key Point

You must not *guess* what the writer or anyone else *might* think.

Key Point

An answer to this sort of question must only contain what is actually in the text.

Quick Test

1. What is skim reading?
2. If a question starts, 'According to the text...' should you give your opinion about the text?
3. If a question asks you to find something 'in the first paragraph', should you use information from other paragraphs?

Key Words

text
select
skim reading
paraphrase

Selecting Key Words and Ideas 2

Quick Recall Quiz

You must be able to:

- Refer to a text using quotations
- Use paraphrasing where appropriate
- Use PEE effectively.

Referring to a Text and Using Quotations

- Some questions ask you to 'find and copy' or 'identify' a word or phrase from the text. Sometimes questions ask you to 'list' things. You need to find the answer in the text and write it without explanation.
- You could be given words or phrases from the text and be asked to explain or interpret them. In such a case no further **reference** to the text is required.
- You might be asked to find a word or phrase and give an explanation of it, or to match a word or phrase to an explanation, perhaps by drawing a line.
- Some questions ask you to support your answer with evidence from the text. This means that you answer the question in your own words, making sure you refer to the text.

Paraphrasing

- **Paraphrasing** means referring to the text but without using the exact words from the text.
- Paraphrasing is useful for summarising. For example, if you were asked to pick out the main points of a paragraph, you would need to pick out the important points and put them in your own words, perhaps including a few short quotations (see page 9).
- Unless the question specifically asks you to pick out words or phrases from the text or to quote from the text, you will still be rewarded for paraphrasing. (But, usually it is better to quote.)
- Look at the passage on page 6 again:
  - The question 'What is the cause of the noise?' does not ask for a direct quotation, so you can paraphrase, for example: 'Water bursting into the house and up the stairs.'
  - For a question such as, 'What does the family do on Christmas Eve?' you would have to pick out the main points and put them in your own words, summarising the passage in a shorter form:

> The family arrives to visit the writer's mother. The children go to bed about eight o'clock. The adults talk, put presents under the tree, and then go to bed. The writer falls asleep but just before midnight he is woken up by his son. There is water coming up the stairs.

← This tells us clearly what happened, leaving out unnecessary detail. (It is less than a third of the length of the original text.)

> **Key Point**
>
> All questions in a reading test involve referring to the text.

Quoting from the Text

- A **quotation** is a word or phrase taken directly from the text.
- When you quote from the text, put inverted commas (quotation marks) around the quotation.
- Answers to 'find and copy' questions are quotations. You only get a mark if you use the exact words used in the text.
- You should try to use a lot of very short quotations, and 'embed' them in your answer, for example:

> The writer emphasises how young and vulnerable Tom is by mentioning his 'little voice'.
>
> He is very tired after a 'long and tedious' journey from Birmingham.

PEE

- In longer answers you should get into the habit of using **PEE**:
  1. Make your **point**, saying what you want to about the text.
  2. Give your **evidence**, either as a quotation or by paraphrasing.
  3. **Explain** or explore the evidence you have given.

P → point
E → evidence
E → explanation

- Here is an example of the use of PEE to answer the question, 'What effect does the flood have on Tom?'

> Tom is afraid but does not understand what is happening. He tells his father that 'he had heard a strange noise', which suggests that it is something that he has never heard before and this is what scares him.

Reading 1: Revise

Key Point

When you quote, all the words that are taken from the text and are within the quotation marks have to be exactly as they are in the original text – even if you think the writer might have misspelt something! This applies to punctuation marks too.

Key Point

In longer answers, use PEE.

The first part of this answer makes the **point** – 'Tom is afraid but does not understand what is happening.'

The second part gives us the **evidence** in a quotation. The words taken from the text are in quotation marks.

The third part picks up on the word 'strange' to **explain** why the reader thinks it is the fact that the noise is unfamiliar that frightens him.

Key Words

reference
paraphrase
quotation
PEE
point
evidence
explain

Quick Test

1. Name the two different ways of referring to the text.
2. What is meant by 'paraphrasing'?
3. When you are quoting, what goes inside the inverted commas?
4. What does PEE stand for?

Inference, Deduction and Interpretation 1

Quick Recall Quiz

You must be able to:

- Deduce, infer or interpret information from texts
- Deduce, infer or interpret ideas from texts.

Reading 'Between the Lines'

- To **infer** means to understand something that is not directly stated. For example:
  - 'I inferred from her telling me to work on my own that she was accusing me of distracting the others.'
- When people want you to understand something beyond their actual words they **imply** it, for example:
  - 'By telling me I would work better on my own, she implied that I had been distracting the others.'
- To **deduce** is to work something out from information you are given. Detectives are often said to deduce things:
  - 'From the muddy footprint, I deduced that the thief had big feet and had entered from the garden.'
- To **interpret** means to explain the meaning of something. When you interpret something you make it easier to understand:
  - 'The article was full of technical language. Luckily, Anya is an expert at science and she interpreted it for me.'
- Questions which require you to 'deduce, infer or interpret' information or ideas are designed to see if you can do more than just find information in a text.
- Different people infer or deduce different things from the same text. Because of this, there can be more than one acceptable answer to a question.
- You need to support your answer with evidence from the text to show that your inference/deduction/interpretation is reasonable and makes sense.
- You may have heard the expression 'reading between the lines'. This is what you are doing when you are inferring, deducing and interpreting. It is a normal part of reading and listening – you do it all the time!

> ### Key Point
>
> The writer implies something; the reader infers something.

> ### Key Point
>
> To show that you have really understood a text you need to demonstrate that you are able to 'read between the lines'.

Information and Ideas

- Read the following text and then look at the examples that follow.

> Everybody knows that dogs make great companions. They're friendly, playful and loyal. But they require work and puppy-training can be frustrating. Sometimes with a puppy, it's one step forward and two steps back.

Example 1

- You could be asked to explain what something means in your own words.
- Think about the question, 'What does the writer mean by "sometimes with a puppy, it's one step forward and two steps back"?'
- You are being asked to interpret or explain the phrase used by the writer. Look at these students' answers:

> He's saying that if you go forward one step you will go back two. ✗

- You need to show that you understand what the phrase means in the context of the passage about puppies:

> He thinks it is frustrating. ✗

- A better answer would be:

> According to the writer, every time you make some progress with a puppy's training, something happens that makes you think you are not doing so well. ✓

Example 2

- You could be asked to find evidence in the text to support a general statement that has been inferred from the text.
- Think about the question:
  - 'Find two pieces of evidence in the text that suggest not all people are suited to owning dogs. Describe the sort of people the writer might be thinking about.'
- Look at this student answer:

> The writer says that puppies 'require work', which suggests that lazy people who do not like hard work should not have puppies. He also says 'puppy-training can be frustrating'. This implies that if you are not very patient and get frustrated easily, you should not have a puppy. ✓

> **Key Point**
>
> Writers do not always explain everything. They sometimes leave it up to us to work things out for ourselves.

> You must not simply repeat the phrase in slightly different words.

> Simply repeating a phrase from the passage is not enough.

> This answer explains what the writer means clearly.

> This student has made an inference or deduction from what the writer says about puppy-training, and although the writer has not mentioned lazy or impatient people, has come to a logical conclusion based on evidence.

Quick Test

1. Who 'implies' something – the writer or the reader?
2. What do we do when we interpret something?
3. Can there be more than one correct answer to a question?
4. How can you show that your inference or interpretation is a reasonable one?

>
>
> **Key Words**
>
> infer
> imply
> deduce
> interpret

Inference, Deduction and Interpretation 2

You must be able to:

- Use inference, deduction or interpretation to answer questions about events
- Use inference, deduction or interpretation to answer questions about characters.

Events

- Writers might leave you to draw your own conclusions about the reasons for events or the effect of them.
- Look at the passage below.

> Kezia just could not get to sleep that night. She kept going over and over what had happened in the practice: how heavy her legs had felt; how she missed an open goal and how the other girls seemed to be talking about her afterwards. She woke up feeling nervous and a little bit sick. It would be the most important match of her life but she had a very bad feeling about it.

Example 1

- Answer the question, 'Why did Kezia have "a bad feeling" about the match?'
  - This question requires you to identify the reasons for Kezia's feelings.
  - If you wrote 'she had a bad feeling because she woke up feeling sick,' you would not get a mark because 'feeling sick' is the result of her worry about the match, not the cause of it.
  - Similarly not being able to sleep is a result, not a cause.
  - A good answer might be:

> Kezia has a 'bad feeling' because the practice went badly for her. She had not felt well, her legs feeling 'heavy' and she 'missed an open goal'. She must be worried that she will play as badly in the match.

Example 2

- Answer the question, 'What effect does the practice have on Kezia?':
  - A good answer might be:

> Her bad experience at the practice worries Kezia so much that she cannot get to sleep and when she wakes up she feels sick.

- Often what you infer about events will be based on what has happened earlier in the text. For example, the writer might have told us something about Kezia that would affect our understanding of what is happening now.
- If you were asked 'Why was the match so important to Kezia?' you could not base your answer on the paragraph given above.

> **Key Point**
>
> Whatever the answer is, you cannot guess it. It is in the text somewhere.

You need to look back over the text for clues:

- Perhaps the coach has told her that she is in danger of losing her place on the team if she does not play well
- Maybe she has heard a scout from a professional team is coming
- Possibly her grandparents are coming to see her play.

- You might have to think about the whole story before making a deduction.

Characters

- Whether a text is fiction or non-fiction, it will usually be about people and, as a reader, you will be thinking about what those people are like – their characters.
- You might be asked questions about character, for example:
  - 'What do we learn about Mr Hardacre in this extract?'
- Sometimes a writer will describe a person's character, or you might be left to work this out for yourself from clues in the text, such as:
  - What the character does.
  - How others react to him or her.
  - What characters say, and how they speak.
- Read this passage about a character, Mr Hardacre:

> Mr Hardacre never smiled in class.
>
> Every time you were late, you were punished. He never listened to excuses and he never let you off.
>
> I was terrified of Mr Hardacre and would never have asked him for help with my work.
>
> "You can rest assured, Jenkins," he said, "that you will be punished for this and that the crime will remain on your record forever."

- If the writer were to add something about how Mr Hardacre spoke, it could be interpreted in a different way:

> "You can rest assured, Jenkins," he said, trying hard to suppress a smile, "that you will be punished for this and that the crime will remain on your record forever."

Key Point

You need to consider the **context** and think about the text as a whole when answering this sort of question.

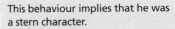

Key Point

We can get clues about characters from what they do, what they say and how others react.

This behaviour implies that he was a stern character.

You could interpret this as meaning he is unforgiving.

You could infer from this that Mr Hardacre is intimidating.

Most readers would infer from this that he is stern and unforgiving.

Think about what the barely suppressed smile could imply.

Quick Test

1. State four ways in which we can learn about characters.
2. If you are asked why something happens in a text, can you guess the answer?
3. How can you show that your answer is based on the text?
4. Should you give more than one interpretation of something?

Key Words

context
fiction
non-fiction
character

Read the passage below, from a tourist guide to Lisbon, and answer the questions that follow.

These questions will test your understanding of these topics.

○ ○ ○
◀ ▶ | www.lisbon.az

Lisbon: City of contrasts

Over the last fifty years, Portugal has become an increasingly popular holiday destination for Britons. Most flock to the sunny beaches of the Algarve in southern Portugal, but how many have considered a short break in the capital, Lisbon?

Just a couple of hours away, and served by budget airlines from all the UK's main airports, Lisbon is an ideal city for a relaxing weekend. It's warm, welcoming, inexpensive and full of surprises.

Lisbon is comparatively compact for a capital city, and has a cosy laid-back charm about it, but it was once one of Europe's wealthiest and most powerful cities. In the eighteenth century, Portugal possessed a huge empire, stretching from Macau, off the coast of China, to Brazil, in South America, where Portuguese is still spoken.

Although it's an ancient city, founded by the Romans, you won't find many really old buildings in Lisbon as much of the city was destroyed by the Great Earthquake in 1755. This was a huge disaster for the city and the country, but it did give architects and planners the opportunity to develop the smart and elegant Baixa district, which is today the lively heart of Lisbon, filled with restaurants, cafés and shops, and enlivened by street traders and entertainers. You can while away hours sitting in a pavement café with a coffee or one of the tasty local snacks, while you take in the sights and sounds of this lively, cosmopolitan city.

But don't spend all your time in the cafés, however tempting, as there's plenty more to explore. You'll need to be quite fit to negotiate all the hills, but the narrow, winding streets of Alfama, the oldest district of Lisbon, which miraculously survived the Great Earthquake, are full of atmosphere and interest. You might prefer to travel by one of Lisbon's ancient trams, go further afield using the efficient underground system, or take a bracing trip on the ferry across the Tagus River. At night, you'll find plenty to entertain you, from the haunting voices of the singers in the traditional Fado clubs to lively bars playing sounds from Brazil and Africa.

If you've got a little longer, you might want to venture further afield. A short train journey away you will find the old town of Sintra, full of stunning royal palaces and surrounded by beautiful countryside. Or you could head for the beach. In less than an hour you could be sunning yourself on the beach in elegant Estoril, enjoying a drink in its younger neighbour Cascais, or walking the coastal paths where huge Atlantic waves crash against the rocks.

There's a lot to see and do in a short time and, however much you manage to pack into your long weekend, we can guarantee it won't be enough and you'll soon be coming back for more.

1. Of which country is Lisbon the capital? [1]

2. According to the text, what was the positive result of the Great Earthquake for Lisbon? [1]

3. Pick out two words or phrases used to show that a trip to Lisbon will not cost a lot of money. [1]

4. How does the writer give the impression that Estoril might appeal to older tourists? [1]

5. Identify and explain a phrase which describes what is enjoyable about each of the following activities: [2]

   a) eating or drinking in a pavement café

   b) going to a Fado club

   c) a visit to Sintra

   d) a walk around Alfama.

6. The article is trying to attract a wide range of people to Lisbon.

   Explain how it tries to appeal to:

   a) people who want a quiet, relaxing weekend [2]

   b) people who prefer something a bit more lively. [2]

How Ideas are Organised 1

You must be able to:

- Identify and comment on the organisation of texts
- Comment appropriately on the opening of a text
- Comment appropriately on the ending of a text.

Structure and Organisation

- When you look at the **structure** of a text you are looking at:
  - the order in which ideas and events are mentioned
  - why the writer has chosen to arrange things in a certain way.

> **Key Point**
>
> Different texts have different structures.

Openings

- The opening of a text usually tries to draw you in so that you want to read on. It might introduce characters, settings or ideas.
- Here is the opening of a short story:

> It was a hot afternoon, and the railway carriage was correspondingly sultry, and the next stop was at Templecombe, nearly an hour ahead. The occupants of the carriage were a small girl, and a smaller girl, and a small boy. An aunt belonging to the children occupied one corner seat, and the further corner seat on the opposite side was occupied by a bachelor who was a stranger to the party, but the small girls and the small boy emphatically occupied the compartment.
>
> *From* **The Story-Teller** *by Saki*

> You are given a certain amount of information but you might still have a lot of questions, for example: 'Where are the children going?', 'Why are they with their aunt?' and, perhaps most importantly, 'Who is the bachelor?'

- You are told when and where the story takes place and introduced to the main characters and the relationship between them. This is quite a gentle opening.
- Sometimes writers prefer to plunge straight into the story with a dramatic opening, for example:

> "There's a wild creature in your house," said Max, as he walked across the road with Mr Tisdale.

> **Key Point**
>
> The opening of a text can give important information, arouse the reader's interest, or both.

- Non-fiction texts can also start with dramatic statements, designed to shock, surprise or intrigue the reader, for example:

> Are you bored with your life? Do you yearn for excitement and adventure?

> Rhetorical questions are often used to make the reader start thinking about the subject.

> Last year we threw away more than two hundred thousand tonnes of unwanted food.

> Both these openings would make the reader wonder what was coming next.

Endings

- Endings of a text can vary:
  - Some stories end with a neat **conclusion**, tying up loose ends.
  - Detective stories usually end with the crime being solved.
  - Other stories can leave the reader with a sense of mystery.
- Sometimes the end of a story will remind us of the beginning, making us reflect on how things have changed during the story:

> Taking all the evidence into account, there is no doubt in my mind that Horace was right about the treasure; it is now lost forever.

This text uses the final paragraph to sum up what has gone before and perhaps come to a conclusion.

- Other texts, especially persuasive texts, such as advertisements or charity appeals, end with an imperative/instruction:

> Get down to Salter's now for the bargain of a lifetime!

The purpose of this text is to get readers to act.

Turning Points

- You could be asked to explain how a story develops or how characters change over the course of a story.
- You should be able to pick out significant points in the text – **turning points** – where things happen to change the direction of the story or the feelings and attitudes of the characters.
- You could be asked a question like: 'When do Jane's feelings about Martin change? How does this affect the band?'

> Jane's feelings about Martin change when she hears the song he has written for Jo. Before this she thinks he is arrogant and insensitive. She realises that she has misjudged him and from now on treats him with respect.

This student has explained the turning point in Jane's feelings for Martin by stating her feelings before explaining what made her feelings change and the change in her behaviour as a result.

- Some questions focus on the **development** of the story, for example: 'Explain how the sequence of events builds up tension.' To answer, you need to pick out points when something happens that increases tension and excitement:

> At the beginning of the story everything is calm, but this changes when Dan hears a noise behind him. The writer does not explain what this is, which creates tension. A little later, the sky darkens and the noises increase, making the reader worried that something bad might happen. When the stranger appears suddenly, the story seems to be reaching a climax.

This student has picked out three turning points when the tension is increased and has explained their effect on the character and the reader.

Quick Test

1. Why might a text start with a rhetorical question?
2. Why might an advertisement or appeal end with an instruction?
3. What is a turning point?

How Ideas are Organised 2

You must be able to:

- Show that you understand different ways of ordering a text
- Comment appropriately on the use of stanzas or paragraphs
- Comment effectively on a range of presentational features.

Quick Recall Quiz

Chronological Order and Flashbacks

- **Chronological** order mentions events in the order in which they happen. This is the most straightforward and most common way to tell a story.
- A story may start with the end or somewhere in the middle. These parts of the story are often called 'flashbacks'.
- A text that is in reverse chronological order has the most recent events first. If you look at a blog or a discussion forum online you will often see this.

> **Key Point**
>
> A flashback might be used to explain the reasons for something happening or it could be a 'story within a story', told by one of the characters.

Other Ways of Ordering Information

- Texts (especially non-fiction) can be organised in these ways:
  - Information can be arranged in **alphabetical** order, as in a dictionary or encyclopaedia.
  - The most important or useful information may come first and the least important last.
  - A text that ranks things or people in order of achievement or popularity – for example a pop chart – can start with the most popular and work down (say from number one to number 100), or start with the least popular and work up (from 100 to one).

Paragraphs and Stanzas

- Most texts are set out in **paragraphs**.
  - In non-fiction, paragraphs often start with a 'topic sentence', which gives us an idea what the paragraph is about.
  - Paragraphs vary in length. Some paragraphs need to be long to describe or explain things in detail. Sometimes writers use short paragraphs for impact.
  - Prose writers write in paragraphs.
- Poems are often divided into **stanzas,** which are sometimes referred to as verses.
  - Sometimes all the stanzas are the same length; sometimes they differ. Similarly, all the lines in a poem might be the same length or there might be some short and some long lines.
  - There are even poems that look like their subject – these are called 'shape poems' or 'concrete poems'.

> **Key Point**
>
> A new paragraph is started when there is a change of time, place or subject matter, or when a new person speaks.

– Sometimes poets repeat important lines or phrases at the beginning or end of stanzas. Look out for repeated lines that change slightly and think about what this might mean.

Presentational Features

- Writers use a wide variety of presentational features to make their texts easier to understand or more attractive to readers.
- If you are asked a question about a presentational feature, think about what it adds to the text and the effect it has on the reader.

Headlines	Can tell us what the text is going to be about, for example, 'Everything You Need to Know about Beetles' or they may be jokey or intriguing, making us wonder what the text is going to be about: 'It's a Dog's Life for Carl the Cat'.
Sub-headings	Can be used to break up the text into sections. They tell us what the next section is about, so that we can find information easily by scanning the page.
Bullet points, numbers etc.	Are used to break up text into more easily digested chunks, sometimes instead of paragraphs.
Text boxes	Are common on websites, leaflets and posters. They might draw attention to a specific aspect of the subject or they might contain information such as prices, dates, etc.
Font style and size	Can make a difference. Some fonts or typefaces look like handwriting, making the message more personal. Key words are sometimes shown in bold.
Colour	Can be important both in text and background. Certain colours have **connotations**. For example, red is often associated with danger, while green makes us think of the environment, and yellow is associated with the sun.
Illustrations (e.g. diagrams, graphs, photos)	Provide information visually and can explain some ideas more clearly. Pictures can complement the text, making its meaning clearer, and can also be very emotive.

Quick Test

1. What sort of text might be in reverse chronological order?
2. What is a 'shape poem'?
3. How could a sub-heading save time for the reader?
4. Why might a text include diagrams or graphs?

Key Point

Presentational features can help the reader in many different ways, making the text clearer and more interesting.

Key Point

You can mention presentational features in answers to longer questions, such as 'How does the leaflet try to persuade readers to contribute to the charity?'

Key Words

chronological
alphabetical
paragraphs
stanzas
headline
sub-heading
text box
font
connotation
illustration

Exploring Language Choices 1

Quick Recall Quiz

You must be able to:

- Explain and comment on writers' choice of words
- Explain and comment on writers' use of literary features.

Choice of Words

- You could be asked why a writer uses a particular word or phrase, or you could be expected to comment on the writer's choice of words throughout the whole text.
- A word might have been chosen because it has a precise meaning:
   1 If a writer tells us that a man 'walked down the street', we know what he did but we do not know *how* he did it.
  2 If you look in a thesaurus, you will find a lot of different words under 'walk', such as stride, strut, toddle, waddle, limp and trudge. They all mean slightly different things.
  3 So if the writer told you that the man 'strode down the street' and you were asked why the writer used the word 'strode' or what the word 'strode' tells you about the man, you could answer:

> *'Strode' means he walked using long steps, which makes him seem determined and confident.*

- Think about connotation. A connotation is an association – the word or phrase reminds you of something. For example, the word 'heart' has connotations of love; the word 'dove' has connotations of peace.
- A writer's choice of words might depend on the subject matter. For example, a scientific article would use a lot of technical words. If these words were not explained, we could deduce that the texts were aimed at readers with some knowledge of the subject.

Standard English and Dialects

- Most texts used in tests are written in Standard English, as it is important that all students can understand them.
- Some texts include **dialect** words – words from a particular region or country. Writers use dialect to distinguish different speakers, giving a sense of their background.
- **Slang** might also be used. You would normally find slang words in dialogue, telling you something about the speaker's background.

>
> **Key Point**
> Writers choose words carefully. Think about meaning and connotation.

> This answer shows that the student understands the meaning of the word and has inferred from it something about the man's mood or character.

>
> **Key Point**
> A word or phrase might have different connotations for different people.

>
> **Key Point**
> Slang words are words which are used in particular groups, and are often associated with young people.

Literary Features

- The phrase 'literary features' refers to ways of using language to make meaning clear and provide interest to readers.
- Writers often use comparisons to 'paint pictures' for readers. You may be asked to explain why a writer uses a particular comparison.
- **Similes** and **metaphors** are commonly used comparison techniques:

Simile	Metaphor
Directly compares the thing or person being described to something it is not, using the words 'like', 'as' or 'than'.	Compares one thing with another but does not tell us it is doing so. It describes something as if it were something else.
Example 'She sat in the corner trembling like a mouse that has just seen a cat.' Mice are small, timid animals and this simile gives the impression that the girl is small and frightened. They are especially scared of cats, which kill and eat them, so mentioning the cat implies that there is someone or something that makes her extremely scared.	**Example** 'The soldiers were lions led by donkeys'. Lions are associated with courage and pride, while donkeys are traditionally thought to be stupid animals, so the idea of donkeys being in charge of lions is ridiculous. By using the metaphor the writer shows his admiration for the soldiers and contempt for their leaders.

- When looking at texts, think about how words sound if spoken:
  - **Onomatopoeia** is the use of a word that sounds like its meaning, usually words for sounds themselves, such as 'fizz', 'pop', 'crackle' or 'splash'. These words can help make the description come alive.
  - **Alliteration** is the use of the same sound at the beginning of a string of words, such as 'Pollution is a dirty and disgusting disgrace.' It is used to emphasise a certain phrase and create rhythm.
  - **Assonance** is the repetition of vowel sounds in a string of words, for example, 'How now, brown cow'?'
  - **Rhyme** can be used for comic effect or to emphasise certain words. Many poems use rhyme.

> **Key Words**
>
> dialect
> slang
> simile
> metaphor
> onomatopoeia
> alliteration
> assonance
> rhyme

> **Quick Test**
>
> Which literary device is being used in each of these sentences?
> 1. Happy Harry hates horses.
> 2. You're an angel, Amara.
> 3. It hit me like a ton of bricks.
> 4. The fireworks popped and fizzed in the sky.

Exploring Language Choices 2

Quick Recall Quiz

You must be able to:

- Explain and comment on writers' use of rhetorical devices
- Explain and comment on writers' use of grammar and punctuation.

Rhetorical Devices

- Rhetorical devices are techniques that speakers and writers use to influence their readers and listeners.
- They are used very often in texts which are written to persuade or argue.

Key Point

Writers use words to play on our emotions.

Rhetorical Device	Example
Rhetorical questions are questions which do not demand an answer. A writer might use them to make you think, providing your own answer in your head.	'Why is it that so many small shops are closing?' Writers usually know the answer they expect to a rhetorical question: 'The answer is obvious – it's the fault of the supermarkets.' But sometimes, especially at the end of a text, they might not offer an answer and the question is there to make you think about the issue and come to your own conclusions: 'We've looked at a lot of evidence and heard a lot of opinions, but the question remains. Why are so many small shops closing?'
Lists, often lists of three, are used to emphasise a point being made, to show there are several aspects to something or to build up to a climax.	'This issue affects the most vulnerable in our society: children, the elderly and the disabled.' This list is used to explain what the writer means by 'the most vulnerable' and, by providing three examples, show that many people are affected. 'This decision is unthinking, uncaring and downright cruel.' The writer builds up to the word 'cruel', playing on readers' emotions.
Repetition emphasises important points. Throughout a text, a writer may come back to the same point. There might be slight variations in the phrase used.	A writer might repeat the phrase, 'and still nobody knew the answer' at the end of each paragraph, but end the final paragraph with, 'and now everybody knew the answer.'
Hyperbole (exaggeration) emphasises opinions or feelings, either positive or negative.	'That building is surely the ugliest and most monstrous ever inflicted on the people of Puddington.' This example exaggerates in order to make the point of how ugly the building is.

- Writers use language to play on readers' emotions. This is **emotive** language.
- Emotive language can appeal to all sorts of emotions, for example sympathy, pity, anger.
- Read these newspaper headlines:

Council closes children's playground

This version lets us make up our own minds about how to react.

Cruel council closes heartbroken kids' playground

A few extra words means this version influences our emotions.

Grammar and Punctuation

- Most texts use the grammar of **Standard English**. So, when writers use non-standard grammar, just as when they use slang or dialect words, it is for a purpose.
- Non-standard English is most likely to be used in speech. Someone might say, 'She don't like them shoes no more,' rather than Standard English, 'She doesn't like those shoes anymore.'
- Non-standard grammar is rarely used for a whole text. In a story, it might reflect the character and background of the narrator. In a leaflet or advertisement, it might be trying to sound chatty and informal.
- Texts can be written in the first person (I or we), the second person (you) or the third person (he, she or they).
- The **tense** a text is written in can make a difference to its tone and its effect on readers.
  - The past tense is used for things that have happened and is usual in stories.
  - The present tense can make the story or description more vivid.
- Longer, complex sentences are used to convey complicated information or to describe something in detail. Short sentences can emphasise an important point by stating it simply.
- Exclamation marks (!) indicate shock, surprise or excitement. They can follow **imperatives** (commands), which address readers directly.
- Question marks, unless they are used in speech, indicate that writers are asking rhetorical questions.
- An **ellipsis** (…) can show that words have been missed out, or speech trailing off ('I was just wondering whether…Oh, never mind.'), or leave readers wondering what is going to happen next.

Key Point

How writers use grammar and punctuation contributes to the effect of texts on readers.

Key Point

The first person makes the text more personal. The second person addresses readers directly and makes them feel involved. The third person is more detached and neutral.

Key Point

A series of short sentences could be used to give a sense of excitement or anxiety.

Key Words

rhetorical questions
lists
repetition
hyperbole
emotive
Standard English
tense
imperative
ellipsis

Quick Test

Which rhetorical device is being used in each sentence?
1. He said it again. And again. And again.
2. I was so happy, happier than the happiest people who ever lived!
3. Is this the sort of future you want for your children?
4. They taunted the poor innocent creature heartlessly.

Read the extract below and answer the questions that follow.

These questions will test how well you have remembered key points from the previous topics.

From **A Christmas Carol**

by Charles Dickens

Once upon a time – of all the good days in the year, on Christmas Eve – old Scrooge sat busy in his counting-house. It was cold, bleak, biting weather: foggy withal: and he could hear the people in the court outside, go wheezing up and down, beating their hands upon their breasts, and stamping their feet upon the pavement stones to warm them. The city clocks had only just gone three, but it was quite dark already – it had not been light all day – and candles were flaring in the windows of the neighbouring offices, like ruddy smears upon the palpable brown air. The fog came pouring in at every chink and keyhole, and was so dense without, that although the court was of the narrowest, the houses opposite were mere phantoms. To see the dingy cloud come drooping down, obscuring everything, one might have thought that Nature lived hard by, and was brewing on a large scale.

The door of Scrooge's counting-house was open that he might keep his eye upon his clerk, who in a dismal little cell beyond, a sort of tank, was copying letters. Scrooge had a very small fire, but the clerk's fire was so very much smaller that it looked like one coal. But he couldn't replenish it, for Scrooge kept the coal-box in his own room; and so surely as the clerk came in with the shovel, the master predicted that it would be necessary for them to part. Wherefore the clerk put on his white comforter, and tried to warm himself at the candle; in which effort, not being a man of strong imagination, he failed.

'A merry Christmas, uncle! God save you!' cried a cheerful voice. It was the voice of Scrooge's nephew, who came upon him so quickly that this was the first intimation he had of his approach.

'Bah!' said Scrooge, 'Humbug!'

He had so heated himself with rapid walking in the fog and frost, this nephew of Scrooge's, that he was all in a glow; his face was ruddy and handsome; his eyes sparkled, and his breath smoked again.

'Christmas a humbug, uncle!' said Scrooge's nephew. 'You don't mean that, I am sure?'

'I do,' said Scrooge. 'Merry Christmas! What right have you to be merry? What reason have you to be merry? You're poor enough.'

'Come, then,' returned the nephew gaily. 'What right have you to be dismal? What reason have you to be morose? You're rich enough.'

Scrooge having no better answer ready on the spur of the moment, said, 'Bah!' again; and followed it up with 'Humbug!'

'Don't be cross, uncle.' said the nephew.

'What else can I be,' returned the uncle, 'when I live in such a world of fools as this? Merry Christmas! Out upon merry Christmas. […] If I could work my will,' said Scrooge indignantly, 'every idiot who goes about with "Merry Christmas" on his lips, should be boiled with his own pudding, and buried with a stake of holly through his heart. He should!'

1 Name two things that the people in the street do to try to keep warm. [1]

2 Why does Scrooge keep the door of his counting-house open? [1]

3 What do we learn about Scrooge's character in the second paragraph?

   Support your answer with evidence from the text. [2]

4 What is the effect of his walk on Scrooge's nephew's appearance? [2]

5 What do you think Scrooge means when he says that Christmas is 'humbug'? [1]

6 What impression do you get of Scrooge's nephew from the extract?

   Support your answer with evidence from the text. [3]

Read the leaflet below and answer the questions that follow.

The questions will test your understanding of these topics.

Step Back into History at Brokling Hall

Standing on top of Brokling Hill, commanding a view of four counties, Brokling Hall has dominated the landscape for five centuries. Built in the sixteenth century to impress – and sometimes repel – the neighbours, it now welcomes thousands of visitors through its doors every year. Brokling isn't a dusty, musty museum, though. When you walk through the doors, it's as if you've stepped out of your very own Tardis, having travelled back hundreds of years.

Every room in the Hall has been designed to recreate a day in its history. As you walk around, you will learn about everyday life in the past and meet some of the characters who lived here long ago (don't worry – they're not ghosts – just very convincing actors).

- **Trouble for the Tudors**

  It's 1585 and Sir Henry Brokling and Lady Anne, have been living at the Hall for less than a year. They've spent a small fortune on the best oak furniture and beautiful wall hangings, so why do they seem so worried? It seems they've had a letter from the Queen. She's planning to drop in for a few days – or weeks – with her huge entourage. And, of course, being the Queen, she'll expect nothing but the best.

- **Cavaliers and Roundheads**

  Brokling Hall finds itself in the middle of the English Civil War. It's 1648 and Parliament's army (the Roundheads) is fighting the King's supporters (the Cavaliers) for control of the country. Sir Richard Brokling is away fighting for the King when the local Roundheads attack Brokling Hall. How will Lady Henrietta, barricaded in the Hall with her children, manage to fend off the attackers?

- **Home for Christmas?**

  Fast-forward to 1914. The peace of a weekend party at luxurious Brokling Hall, which has been decorated in the latest style by Sir Alfred's new wife (former music-hall artiste Elsie Flanagan), is interrupted by the news that Britain is at war with Germany. Sir Alfred is determined to do his bit for King and Country. Downstairs, in the servants' hall, valet George and gardener Tom are just as keen, egged on by housemaids Ruby and Grace. None of them knows what to expect, but they're all sure of one thing: they'll be home for Christmas.

You can hire Brokling Hall for special occasions throughout the year.

We welcome bookings for weddings and conferences and can provide for all your catering and entertainment needs.

Call us to discuss a tailor-made package for your event.

Events management: 01347 789 02

Open every day except Tuesday, including bank holidays, from March to October.
Open from 9.00 a.m. until 7.00 p.m.
Adults £12.00 **Children** £6.00 **Senior Citizens** £6.00
Group bookings by arrangement
Phone 01347 789 01 for more details

1 In what order are the bullet-pointed paragraphs arranged? [1]

    a) Alphabetical order

    b) Chronological order

    c) Order of importance

2 How does the content of the two boxes differ from the rest of the text? [1]

3 Each of the bullet-pointed paragraphs gives the beginning of a story.

Why does the writer not give the whole story? [2]

4 Why does the writer compare going into the hall to stepping out of 'your very own Tardis'? [2]

5 In the last paragraph the writer tells us that Sir Alfred is 'determined to do his bit'?

What does this mean? [2]

6 The performances described in the text are set in the past but the present tense is used to describe them.

Why? [2]

Explaining Purposes and Viewpoints 1

You must be able to:

- Identify writers' purposes
- Comment effectively on writers' purposes.

Purpose

- People write texts for all sorts of reasons. You need to be able to identify the purpose(s) of the texts you are given.
- When you read a text, think about what the writer is trying to achieve.
- You can understand the purpose of a text by:
  - its content (what it is about)
  - its tone (e.g. serious, humorous, argumentative)
  - the kind of language used
  - its presentation.

> **Key Point**
>
> A text can have more than one purpose.

Entertain	Novels and stories are written to **entertain**, but may also want to make us think about ideas and issues. Many non-fiction writers also entertain. They also want us to enjoy reading what they have written.
Describe	Both fiction and non-fiction texts **describe** people, places and experiences. Biographies and travel writing are often very descriptive.
Inform	To **inform** simply means to tell people about something. Textbooks inform you. Many texts – from adverts to magazine articles – include information.
Instruct	To **instruct** is to tell someone how to do something. Again, textbooks do this but so do recipes and manuals that come with products like computers and washing machines.
Advise	If a text is giving advice, it suggests ways of dealing with problems. A careers booklet **advises** you about possible jobs. 'Problem pages' in magazines give advice to readers.
Argue	Some texts give a point of view and **argue** in support of it, or argue against someone else's opinion. Columnists in newspapers often do this. Sometimes a writer tries to give a balanced view of an issue and puts forward arguments on both sides.
Persuade	Some texts are designed to **persuade** you to support a point of view (so texts often argue and persuade) or to do something, such as buy a product or give to charity.

Questions about Purpose

- Questions about purpose normally require you to look at the text as a whole.
- You could be asked to identify the purpose or purposes of a text, for example:
  - 'What is Mary Spencer trying to achieve in her article about neglected donkeys?'
- The answer might be:

> She is informing readers about the terrible life of the donkeys and trying to persuade readers to send money to help them.

This answer shows the reader understands that the text has more than one purpose and clearly identifies both purposes.

- The question could identify the purpose and ask you to comment on how the writer tries to achieve that purpose, for example:
  - 'How does Mary Spencer try to persuade readers to support her campaign?'
- This would require quite a long answer:

> Mary Spencer tells us about how the donkeys have worked all their lives. She also tells us that many of them have been beaten and neglected. She says that they live 'in appalling conditions' and have a lot of disease.

Content Think about what she tells us about the donkeys. You might say: 'She persuades us by telling us about the donkeys' lives'. This is a better answer as it gives more detail and uses evidence from the text.

> The tone of the article is very serious and quite sad because of the subject, but she also seems quite angry at times, especially when she describes the ill treatment the donkeys have received.

Tone Try to describe the overall tone of the piece.

> She uses a lot of emotive words to describe the donkeys, like 'innocent', 'ill-treated' and 'tragic'. This makes us see the donkeys as victims and feel sorry for them. She uses a lot of rhetorical questions, such as, 'How can this be allowed to happen?' to make us think about the situation and what we can do about it.

Language Think about her choice of words and how the language she uses might support her purpose.

> The black and white picture of the donkey is very dramatic. It is so horrible that you might not want to look at it, but it brings home the reality of what she is saying.

Presentation Think about any presentational features that are used in the text.

Key Words

entertain
describe
inform
instruct
advise
argue
persuade
content
tone
language
presentation

Quick Test

Identify the main purpose of each of the following:
1. A leaflet advertising a pizza restaurant.
2. A recipe for a birthday cake.
3. A letter to the local paper disagreeing with something the council has done.
4. A booklet telling you how to take care of a guinea pig.

Explaining Purposes and Viewpoints 2

You must be able to:

- Identify writers' viewpoints
- Comment effectively on writers' viewpoints
- Comment on the overall effect of the text on the reader.

Writers' Viewpoints

- Writers do not express a point of view in all texts, for example a text which just gives a list of facts or a collection of recipes, but it is possible in most texts to deduce or infer the writer's viewpoint, even if it is not immediately obvious.
- Questions about viewpoint do not always use the word 'viewpoint'. You could be asked questions like:
  - 'How does the writer feel about living on the island?'
  - 'What is the writer's **attitude** to the plight of the donkeys?'
- In these cases, all you are being asked to do is find the writer's viewpoint in the text.

> **Key Point**
>
> Writers do not always state their opinions or feelings. You need to infer them from the text.

> I loved living on the island and was really sad when we had to leave.

> I am shocked and saddened by the treatment these animals receive. It makes me really angry to think that such suffering still exists.

Sometimes the writer's feelings or attitudes are expressed quite clearly as in these passages.

- If the writer does not express his/her **opinions** openly, you have to approach the questions differently, using inference, deduction or interpretation. Read the paragraph below.

> Looking back I see the time we spent on the island as a golden age. It was a time of innocence and great fun. The island was full of fascinating wildlife and larger-than-life characters. We were free to roam and felt that there was adventure waiting around every corner. When the time came to leave, after five wonderful years, I refused to go with my family. I said they could go if they wanted to but I would stay, living off what I could pick or catch and sleeping under the stars. I was nine years old.

- Consider the question, 'How does the writer feel about living on the island?'
- You could answer the question like this:

> It is obvious that the writer enjoyed life on the island, as she calls it a 'golden time' and 'wonderful', and says she had 'great fun'. She mentions 'adventure waiting around every corner', which suggests it was an exciting place to live. She liked it so much that she did not want to leave, even imagining that she could stay on without her family.

This is a good answer because it makes more than one point about the writer's feelings: she enjoyed life; she found it exciting; and she did not want to leave. Each of these points is backed up with evidence from the text, so it is clear that the student's understanding of the writer's feelings is based firmly in the text.

The Effect of the Text on the Reader

- Writers want a **reaction** from their readers.
- When you are asked about the **effect** of the text on the reader, you are usually being asked how it makes *you* feel and what it makes *you* think.
- Questions about the effect on the reader are very similar to questions about purpose. If a writer were successful in achieving his or her purpose, this would be reflected in the reader's reaction.

> *The text makes me feel sorry for the donkeys and want to give money.*

This reader's reaction shows that the writer has been successful in achieving her purpose.

- You also need to think about the writer's viewpoint.
- A text which argues a point of view might convince the reader of the argument:

> *I learned a lot that I did not know before from the article and the writer's arguments convinced me that we should keep the school uniform.*

- In a longer answer you have to take into account content, language, tone and presentation.
- Look again at the paragraph on page 30 about leaving the island and consider the question:
  - 'What effect does this passage have on the reader?'

> *This passage gives the reader a picture of what was so good about living on the island at that age. I was a bit jealous of the freedom and 'adventure' she describes. I could understand why it would be hard to leave, as a 'golden age' sounds like a perfect time, and because of this I felt sorry for her. Although the tone was quite sad, I also thought it was funny that she 'refused to go' and it made me realise just how young and innocent she was, because a nine-year old could not possibly stay there on her own.*

Discusses the effect of the content.

Discusses the language and tone.

There are no comments on presentation, because the text does not contain any interesting presentational devices.

All the points made are supported by short quotations.

Quick Test

1. What is meant by a person's 'attitude'?
2. What is meant by the 'effect' of a text on readers?
3. If you are 'convinced by her argument', do you agree or disagree with the writer?
4. Is it always necessary to comment on presentational devices when commenting on the effect of a text on the reader?

Key Words

attitude
opinion
reaction
effect

Structuring a Longer Response 1

Quick Recall Quiz

You must be able to:

- Write longer responses to questions where they are needed
- Understand what the question is asking you to do
- Support your answers with evidence from the text.

What Are 'Longer Responses'?

- Different schools set different types of tests and exams, and allocate marks in different ways.
- Whatever kind of test you do, however, you will find that not all questions attract the same number of marks. It is important to take this into account.
- The more marks there are for a question, the more time you need to spend answering it. A two-mark answer will probably be about twice as long as a one-mark answer, a four-mark answer twice as long as a two-mark answer, and so on.
- When you answer a longer response question, you need to make sure that your ideas are properly organised and answer the question as fully as possible.

> **Key Point**
>
> The more marks a question attracts, the longer the answer should be.

Reading the Question

- You must read the question properly, so you understand exactly what you have to do.
- You may be able to tell what the focus of the question is straightaway by identifying key words:

> **Key Point**
>
> Make sure you understand the **focus** of the question and follow the **instructions** carefully.

> How does the writer's choice of language create an impression that climbing the mountain is a strange but exciting experience?

Here the key word is 'language', so you know you will have to consider all the aspects of language you have studied.

> What impression do you get of the boy's character from his relationship with his parents and his attitude towards the horse?

This question focuses on character. To answer this successfully, you have to consider what sort of person the boy is and the methods the writer uses to convey this.

> How does the leaflet encourage readers to give up their time to help others?

To answer this question well, you should consider content, language and presentation.

Understanding the Question

- Some questions, particularly those requiring longer answers, will include a brief explanation of what you should do in the form of **bullet points**, for example:

> How does the writer's choice of language create an impression that climbing the mountain is a strange but exciting experience?
>
> You should comment on the writer's choice of words and phrases to describe:
>
> - the mountain and its surroundings
> - the different sights and sounds
> - the narrator's feelings.

> **Key Point**
>
> If a question includes bullet points, make sure you cover all of them.

> **Key Point**
>
> Try to use two or three quotations in each paragraph. Keep them short and use PEE (see page 9).

- The question above asks you about the writer's use of language. If that were all you were given, you might find it quite intimidating, but you are actually given quite a lot of help.
  - First, you are given a hint that you should pick out words and phrases from the text to comment on.
  - Then you are told which aspects of the text you should write about.
- Here is another example of a question including bullet points:

> Explain how the leaflet encourages readers to give up their time to help others. Write about:
>
> - the information you are given
> - the language used
> - the way the text is organised.

These bullet points guide you to consider the content ('the information you are given'), language ('the language used') and presentation ('the way the text is organised').

- Not all questions will give you bullet points, though. For example:

> What impression do you get of the boy's character from his relationship with his parents and his attitude towards the horse?
>
> Support your ideas with quotations from the whole text.

There are hints in the question about what you should look at. You need to focus on 'his relationship with his parents' and 'his attitude towards the horse'. You need to write about both of them to achieve a good mark.

Quick Test

1. If you are given three bullet points, how many should you write about?
2. Which of the following will require the longest answer?
   a) a three-mark question
   b) a two-mark question
   c) a five-mark question
3. If the question doesn't mention quotations, should you use them?

> **Key Words**
>
> focus
> instructions
> bullet points

Structuring a Longer Response 2

You must be able to:

- Approach longer answers with confidence
- Respond appropriately to the question and bullet points
- Write fluently, in good English.

Approaching the Question

- Here is a poem with a question that requires a longer response.

Sea Fever

I must go down to the seas again, to the lonely sea and the sky,
And all I ask is a tall ship and a star to steer her by,
And the wheel's kick and the wind's song and the white sail's shaking,
And a grey mist on the sea's face, and a grey dawn breaking.   4

I must go down to the seas again, for the call of the running tide
Is a wild call and a clear call that may not be denied;
And all I ask is a windy day with the white clouds flying,
And the flung spray and the blown spume, and the sea-gulls crying.   8

I must go down to the seas again, to the vagrant gypsy life,
To the gull's way and the whale's way where the wind's like a whetted
knife; And all I ask is a merry yarn from a laughing fellow-rover
And quiet sleep and a sweet dream when the long trick's over.   12

John Masefield

Question

How does the **language** of the poem express the poet's feelings about
the sea?

You should **comment** on the poet's **choice** of words and phrases to describe:

- the **experience** of being on a ship
- the sea and the weather
- what he wants from the experience.

Reading the Question

- First, look at the question itself and decide what you are being
  asked to focus on.
- There are two key words in the question above. The first is
  'language' and the second is 'feelings'. So you will have to discuss
  the language the writer uses and what it tells us about his feelings.
- If you look at the poem, you will see that these bullet points
  correspond roughly to the three stanzas of the poem, so the
  best way to organise your answer will be to write one paragraph
  about each bullet point, focusing on the appropriate stanza.

> **Key Point**
>
> This question gives you
> three bullet points, so
> you know that you have
> to cover all three to get
> good marks.

- You might want to add a short **introductory** paragraph, making a general point, a **concluding** paragraph, summing up your ideas, or both.
- Before you start writing, you could highlight or underline some words or phrases which strike you as worth commenting on, because they tell us something about the poet's feelings, for example: 'I must go down to the sea again' (line 1); 'lonely' (line 1); 'wheel's kick' (line 3); 'may not be denied' (line 6); 'the vagrant gypsy life' (line 9); 'a merry yarn' (line11); 'sweet dream' (line 12).

Key Point

Don't let yourself down by having great ideas but poor accuracy in spelling and grammar.

Model Answer

- Here is a model answer to the question opposite:

The poet starts by saying 'I must go down to the sea again.' This is repeated at the beginning of each stanza, showing how important it is to him. He uses the word 'must', suggesting that he cannot help himself. The feeling that pulls him to the sea is much stronger than just wanting to go there.

Explains the effect of the use of repetition, while focusing on the feelings of the poet.

Analyses the use of a single word – 'must'.

The first stanza describes some of the excitement of being on a ship. He says the sea and sky are 'lonely', which might mean that he is lonely when he is at sea, but this does not make him sad. He wants something simple to make him happy: 'all I ask is a tall ship'. 'The wheel's kick' and 'the white sail's shaking' show that it is quite exciting but it does not seem frightening. Sailing brings him hope. At the end of the stanza, it is dawn, which symbolises hope.

Focuses on the first bullet point and explains how being on a ship makes the poet feel.

The weather is also quite exciting and wild, and he feels as if it is calling him: 'a wild call and a clear call that may not be denied'. This suggests that nature itself is telling him what to do and he has no power to resist. He asks for a 'windy day', and the wildness of the weather and the sea seem to make him feel alive.

Shows understanding of the poet's use of symbolism.
Focuses on the second bullet point.

In the last stanza he calls being at sea a 'vagrant gypsy life', which makes me feel he does not want to be settled. He wants adventure and to be more like the birds and the animals: 'the gull's way and the whale's way.' He might be envious of their freedom.

Infers the poet's feelings from the way he describes nature.

Although he seems to be 'lonely' at first, he does not want to be completely alone, as he enjoys company. A 'merry yarn from a laughing fellow-rover,' gives us a picture of friendship and warmth. Finally, he wants 'a quiet sleep and a sweet dream,' which contrasts with life at sea. When he has had his adventures, he is satisfied and peaceful.

Key Words

language
comment
choice
experience
introductory
concluding
repetition
symbolism

Quick Test

1. According to the answer above, which of the following statements describe the poet's feeling about the sea?
   a) It excites him.
   b) He cannot resist it.
   c) It makes him feel free and alive.
   d) It frightens him.

Read the following extract and answer the questions that follow.

These questions will test how well you have remembered the key points from the previous topics.

From **The Adventures of Tom Sawyer**

by Mark Twain

'TOM!'

No answer.

'TOM!'

No answer.

'What's gone with that boy, I wonder? You TOM!'

No answer.

The old lady pulled her spectacles down and looked over them about the room; then she put them up and looked out under them. She seldom or never looked *through* them for so small a thing as a boy; they were her state pair, the pride of her heart, and were built for 'style', not service—she could have seen through a pair of stove-lids[1] just as well. She looked perplexed for a moment, and then said, not fiercely, but still loud enough for the furniture to hear:

'Well, I lay if I get hold of you I'll—'

She did not finish, for by this time she was bending down and punching under the bed with the broom, and so she needed breath to punctuate the punches with. She resurrected nothing but the cat.

'I never did see the beat of that boy!'

She went to the open door and stood in it and looked out among the tomato vines and 'jimpson' weeds that constituted the garden. No Tom. So she lifted up her voice at an angle calculated for distance and shouted:

'Y-o-u-u TOM!'

There was a slight noise behind her and she turned just in time to seize a small boy by the slack of his roundabout[2] and arrest his flight.

'There! I might 'a thought of that closet. What you been doing in there?'

'Nothing.'

'Nothing! Look at your hands. And look at your mouth. What IS that truck?'

'I don't know, aunt.'

"Well, I know. It's jam—that's what it is. Forty times I've said if you didn't let that jam alone I'd skin you. Hand me that switch[3]."

The switch hovered in the air—the peril was desperate—

'My! Look behind you, aunt!'

The old lady whirled round, and snatched her skirts out of danger. The lad fled on the instant, scrambled up the high board-fence, and disappeared over it.

His aunt Polly stood surprised a moment, and then broke into a gentle laugh.

'Hang the boy, can't I never learn anything? Ain't he played me tricks enough like that for me to be looking out for him by this time? But old fools is the biggest fools there is. Can't learn an old dog new tricks, as the saying is. But my goodness, he never plays them alike, two days, and how is a body to know what's coming? He 'pears to know just how long he can torment me before I get my dander up, and he knows if he can make out to put me off for a minute or make me laugh, it's all down again and I can't hit him a lick. I ain't doing my duty by that boy, and that's the Lord's truth, goodness knows. Spare the rod and spile the child, as the Good Book⁴ says. I'm a-laying up sin and suffering for us both, I know. He's full of the Old Scratch⁵, but laws-a-me! He's my own dead sister's boy, poor thing, and I ain't got the heart to lash him, somehow. Every time I let him off, my conscience does hurt me so, and every time I hit him my old heart most breaks. Well-a-well, man that is born of woman is of few days and full of trouble, as the Scripture says, and I reckon it's so. He'll play hookey⁶ this evening, I'll just be obleeged to make him work, tomorrow, to punish him. It's mighty hard to make him work Saturdays, when all the boys is having holiday, but he hates work more than he hates anything else, and I've GOT to do some of my duty by him, or I'll be the ruination of the child.'

1 *stove-lids* – thick, round metal covers on the top of a cooking stove
2 *roundabout* – a type of jacket
3 *switch* – a thin rod or stick used for punishment
4 *the Good Book* – the Bible
5 *Old Scratch* – an American folk name for the Devil
6 *play hookey* – truant

1 At the beginning of the passage, Tom's name is printed three times in capital letters and followed by an exclamation mark.

What is the effect of this on the reader? [2]

2 In the last paragraph, Twain writes 'spile' instead of 'spoil' and 'obleeged' instead of 'obliged'.

Explain why he does this. [1]

3 Aunt Polly says, 'Can't learn an old dog new tricks, as the saying goes.'

What does she mean by this? [2]

4 How does the mood and tone of the passage change with the sentence, 'His Aunt Polly stood surprised a moment…'? [2]

5 This passage opens the novel. What does it lead the reader to expect from the rest of the book?

Explain as fully as you can and support your answer with references to the text. [3]

Read the text below, from a leaflet about a cat rescue centre, and answer the questions that follow.

The questions will test your understanding of the topics.

Adopt a Cat and Find a Friend

Hope Hill Cat Rescue is a centre for abandoned cats and kittens, dedicated to rescuing and re-homing unloved and unwanted animals.

At Hope Hill all our rescued cats are examined by qualified vets and treated for any medical problems. They are well-fed and groomed and given the affection so many of them have missed out on. Kittens are kept for a few weeks longer than adult cats and are looked after in foster homes, where they learn to trust humans.

When we think they are ready, we invite members of the public who are willing to give them a good home to come and look at them and find a cat that suits them.

CASE HISTORY: BIFFY

BIFFY was found abandoned by the side of a busy road by one of our volunteers. Only four weeks old, she was completely alone. Our volunteers searched for hours but could find no trace of her mum. Perhaps she had been ill or injured by a car – or perhaps her kittens had been taken from her by humans.

Biffy was underweight and covered in fleas – a sad little bundle of fur and bones. Luckily, Meghan, our volunteer, noticed her in the gutter – she could so easily have been run over or just left to die.

Fortunately, our vet Kanwal found that she had no major health issues and, after a few weeks of tender loving care, Biffy is ready for a new home. She is a short-haired tabby with an adorable face. She has totally regained her confidence and is an inquisitive kitten, who loves exploring and playing with her toys, but she also likes being petted and cuddled.

When you adopt one of our cats, you know you are getting a healthy, well-cared for animal. You will also get expert after-care, as we make regular checks on adopted cats and are always happy to answer any queries or deal with any problems you may have once you have taken your cat home.

You can now see Biffy on our website, together with more than 50 other cats and kittens who are just waiting for new homes.

At Hope Hill we rely on volunteers and donations. If you would like to volunteer – either at the centre or in one of our charity shops – call us now for details. All donations, however small, are welcome. We do ask adopters for a donation of around £50 to help pay for injections and neutering, as well as the administration involved in re-homing.

In return, you will get the joy of a cat's companionship. If you have already cared for a cat, we don't need to say any more. If you haven't, you have a lot to look forward to. Cats are independent and adventurous pets but they are also good companions and return your affection with interest. If you choose to adopt one of our rescue cats, you will not only be helping to reduce the number of abandoned pets and giving a happy life to one lucky animal; you will also be improving the quality of your own life. As we say at Hope Hill, a house isn't a home without a cat!

1 According to the text, kittens 'learn to trust humans' in foster homes.

Explain why the writer tells us this. [2]

2 There are two people mentioned by name in the leaflet, Meghan and Kanwal.

What is the effect on the reader of referring to Meghan as 'our volunteer' and Kanwal as 'our vet'? [3]

3 How does the leaflet try to persuade readers to adopt a cat?

You should comment on how the writer:

- describes the work of the rescue centre
- tells the story of Biffy
- describes the benefits of adopting a cat.

You should aim to write about one side of A4 when answering this question. [10]

Purpose, Audience and Form

Quick Recall Quiz

You must be able to:

- Deconstruct the question so you know what is expected of you
- Direct your reading at the correct purpose, audience and form.

Purpose

- You may be expected to write to persuade, argue, advise inform, explain or describe.
- You need to make sure that the features of your writing match the **purpose** that you have been given.

Audience

- You need to direct your writing towards a specific **audience**. This might be students at your school, or your head teacher; it could also be the general public, readers of a specific magazine, town councillors or the managers of a business.
- You need to think about how you can change your choice of words to match your audience, for example:
  - If your audience is young, you might include some more modern words and references in order to engage them (your accuracy should still be perfect though!).
  - If the audience is older, or in a position of authority, you might use more **formal**, sophisticated and respectful words.

Form

- You will need to write in a particular **form**, for example:
  - a newspaper article
  - a magazine column
  - an email
  - a formal letter
  - a report
  - a short story.
- You should think about the form when you are writing. For example, if you are asked to write a newspaper article, you will write in the past **tense** and you will need to include:
  - a headline
  - short paragraphs that include the 5Ws (who, what, where, when, why)
  - brief interviews with people linked to the story.

> ### Key Point
>
> Make sure you know how you would address different age groups and how to structure different forms. If you are unsure, look at the examples in this book and around your school or home.

- If, for example, you are writing a letter, you should remember to use:
  - a formal opening (Dear...)
  - a formal closing (Yours sincerely/faithfully)
  - tenses that are appropriate to the content.

Deconstructing the Question

- In order to successfully identify the purpose, audience and form you need to spot key words in the questions.
- Read this question:

> You want to organise a non-uniform day at school, but your head teacher thinks that this will distract students from their classes. On behalf of your year group, you need to write a letter that persuades your head teacher to let the day go ahead. You have already been given some ideas by your classmates:
>
> - Mention that everyone brings £1 and it's for charity.
> - Say why we deserve it.
> - Promise we'll still work hard.
>
> Write your letter, persuading the head teacher to let the non-uniform day go ahead.

- In the question above, the purpose (persuade) is mentioned at the start and again at the end. This should get you thinking about the different persuasive techniques you could include in your writing.
- The audience (your head teacher) is also mentioned three times. This should tell you that you need to be formal and respectful in your writing, trying to look at the issue from the head teacher's point of view, rather than that of the students.
- The form (a letter) is also mentioned twice. This should remind you that you need to start and end your writing in a specific way.
- You should make use of the present tense (for example, 'This event is for a good cause...') and the future tense ('We will behave perfectly.') as you are talking about a future event.

Key Point

When you are writing a formal letter, you need to sign off using 'Yours sincerely' or 'Yours faithfully'. If you know the name of the person you are writing to (e.g. Mr Martin) use 'Yours sincerely'; if you don't know their name (e.g. Sir/Madam) use 'Yours faithfully'.

Quick Test

1. List six different purposes of writing.
2. How might you use words differently when talking to teenagers compared with addressing a head teacher?
3. List some different forms of writing.

Key Words

purpose
audience
formal
form
tense

Paragraphs and Connectives

You must be able to:

- Break your written work into appropriate and useful paragraphs
- Use connective words and phrases to orientate the reader.

Paragraphing

- **Paragraphs** make your writing easier to understand. They show that you are structuring your work and help you to develop your work.
- You should use paragraphs in your writing to show changes in:
  - time
  - place
  - focus.
- Most paragraphs contain several sentences, as they should develop an idea fully.
- You can use short paragraphs for effect:
  - to surprise the reader in a descriptive piece
  - to emphasise a point in some argumentative writing.
- Read these two paragraphs of a text:

> The moon shone down on the silent street. Shadows of trees swayed across the pavement, moving swiftly like thieves in the night. The ground glittered with frost.
>
> In the old house at the end of the road, nothing could be heard except the ticking of an old grandfather clock. Cobwebs stretched across the walls and ceilings, and dust lay grey and thick on all the surfaces.

- Read this paragraph:

> I'm here to talk about something that affects us all: pollution. It surrounds us constantly; it pumps out of our cars, drifts out of our chimneys, and stacks up in our bins. But should we bother trying to solve the problem? I am going to persuade you that we should.

- Read this paragraph:

> To begin with, we all need to think about exactly how our daily lives pollute the world around us. Start with when you wake up in the morning, and work through your usual actions until you go to bed at night.

> **Key Point**
>
> Use paragraphs to make different ideas in your writing easier to follow.

A paragraph is used here to show that the writer is moving their focus to a different place.

The writer could also have started a new paragraph with the second sentence. This would create emphasis by adding a dramatic pause to show the severity of pollution. This would be appropriate because the first sentence is an introduction, while the next three explore the problem of pollution.

In this persuasive text, the paragraph shows that the writer is moving from explaining about the problem to focusing on things that can be done.

Connectives

- **Connectives** are words and phrases that link ideas, sentences and paragraphs.
- Connectives are used to orientate the reader, showing how the writing is progressing or developing.
- Here are some examples:

There are different groups of connectives:
- – temporal / time connectives
- – place connectives
- – sequence connectives
- – compare / contrast connectives.

Temporal (time)	Place	Sequence	Compare/ Contrast
The following morning,	Across town,	First,	In contrast,
Two hours later,	25 miles away,	Next,	However,
In 1984,	Leaving her house,	After this,	On the other hand,
The previous week,	Downstairs,	Finally,	Similarly,
Suddenly,	Tamina was at work,	In conclusion,	Furthermore,

- Different connectives will suit different types of writing. For example:
  - – Argue or persuade – sequence, compare/contrast
  - – Advise – sequence
  - – Inform – place, sequence
  - – Explain – time, place, sequence, compare/contrast
  - – Describe – time, place

> **Key Point**
>
> When you start a new paragraph, you should always use a connective word or phrase.

> **Quick Test**
>
> 1. Why are paragraphs helpful to the reader?
> 2. When should you start a new paragraph?
> 3. Why do you need connectives in your writing?
> 4. What four groups can you organise connectives into?

> **Key Words**
>
> paragraphs
> emphasis
> connective

Grammar

You must be able to:

- Construct a range of sentences
- Use tenses correctly.

Sentences

- You should try to use a range of **sentence** structures, in order to keep your writing varied and interesting.
- Simple sentences contain just one main clause (including a subject and a verb), for example, 'The bus was old.' You should not use too many of these in your writing because they can seem quite childish. However, they are good for presenting an idea in a dramatic way.
- Compound sentences are two main clauses joined by a **conjunction** such as 'and' or 'but'. For example, 'The bus was old and it was dirty.' This is useful when you want to link two important ideas together.
- Complex sentences are the main type of sentence that should appear in your writing.
  - Complex sentences have a **main clause** (your central idea) and a **subordinate clause** (extra information), separated by a comma. For example, 'The bus was old, its paint peeling away to leave patches of dark rust.'
  - In a complex sentence, the main clause should make sense on its own but the subordinate clause will not (because it is not a complete sentence, it just adds extra detail).
  - When using complex sentences, the subordinate clause can go before, after, or in the middle of the main clause.

> **Key Point**
>
> Vary your sentences to keep your writing varied and interesting.

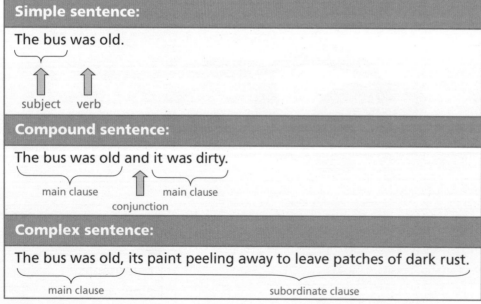

Simple sentence:

The bus was old.

subject   verb

Compound sentence:

The bus was old and it was dirty.

main clause   conjunction   main clause

Complex sentence:

The bus was old, its paint peeling away to leave patches of dark rust.

main clause   subordinate clause

- Depending on your style of writing, you could also include a list in order to illustrate an idea.

Tenses

- You need to choose a tense that matches the purpose and form of your writing. For example:
  - A descriptive story could be in the past or the **present tense**.
  - A description of a childhood memory would only work in the **past tense**.
  - If you are informing someone about a travel destination, you might use the present tense to tell people where things are, but the past tense to relate the history of the place.
  - If you were informing your audience about a forthcoming event, you would mainly use the **future tense**.
- Whichever tense you use, you need to make sure that your words all 'agree'. This means that, if you are writing in one tense, you must not use some words in a different tense.
- The table shows some examples of verbs in different tenses.

Revise

Key Point

The subordinate clause will not make sense on its own ('his eyes burning with desire').

Verb	Present	Past	Future	Conditional
	Things that are happening right now.	*Things that have already happened.*	*Things that will definitely happen.*	*Things that could happen, or could have happened, in the right circumstances.*
To eat	I eat I am eating	I ate I was eating I had eaten	I will eat I will be eating	I would eat I would have eaten
To go	I go I am going	I went I was going I had gone	I will go I will be going	I should go I should have gone
To have	I have I am having	I had I was having I had had	I will have I will be having	I might have I might have had
To play	I play I am playing	I played I was playing I had played	I will play I will be playing	I could play I could have played
To take	I take I am taking	I took I was taking I had taken	I will take I will be taking	I ought to take I ought to have taken

Quick Test

1. What are the three main types of sentence?
2. What are the three positions in which you can place a subordinate clause in relation to the main clause?
3. What is the difference between the past and the present tense?
4. What is the difference between the future and the conditional tense?

Key Words

sentence
conjunction
main clause
subordinate clause
present tense
past tense
future tense
conditional

Punctuation and Spelling

Quick Recall Quiz

You must be able to:

- Punctuate a range of sentences accurately
- Spell most words accurately.

Apostrophes

- **Apostrophes** are used to show **ownership** (possession) and **abbreviation** (omission):

Apostrophes to Show Ownership/Possession	Examples
If you are writing about a single person or object that owns something you add an apostrophe and then an 's'.	The dog's kennel; the boy's coat; the dress's washing instructions
If you are writing about more than one person or object that owns something, you just add the apostrophe.	The three dogs' kennel; the four boys' coats; the two dresses' washing instructions
If you are writing about a person who owns something and their name ends in an 's', you still use an apostrophe and an 's'. *The only exception is if their name ends with an –iz sound, in which case you just add the apostrophe.*	Jess's house; Mr Santos's house; Mrs Bridges' house
Apostrophes to Show Abbreviation/Omission	**Examples**
The apostrophe is used to show that words are run together or that a letter or a few letters are missed out. For example, when writing informally, you might use apostrophes to show abbreviation.	could have → could've would have → would've did not → didn't he is → he's they are → they're

Commas

- When you write a list, remember to put **commas** between each item. You do not need a comma before the last item in a list; instead, you should write 'and' or 'or'. For example:
  - 'This was a land of volcanic peaks, scorching lava, ash clouds and burning sands.'
- In a complex sentence, you should use a comma to separate your main **clause** from your subordinate clause. Try to move the subordinate clause around to add variety:
  - At the start: 'His face red with anger, the teacher shouted at the noisy class.'
  - At the end: 'The teacher shouted at the noisy class, his face red with anger.'
  - In the middle (remember you need two commas): 'The teacher, his face red with anger, shouted at the noisy class.'

> **Key Point**
>
> Phrases like 'should have' (sometimes abbreviated to 'should've') are not spelled 'should of' or 'shoulda'.

> **Key Point**
>
> The main clause should always make sense on its own ('The teacher shouted at the noisy class').

Punctuation for Effect

- Use a **colon** to start a list or to emphasise a point. For example: 'It's obvious what you should do: talk to your friend and resolve this problem.'
- Use **exclamation marks** sparingly (or they will lose their impact).
- Remember to use question marks for questions.
- Put **speech marks** around speech.
- Do not use a dash as a single punctuation mark. You can use two, like brackets or commas, to separate a subordinate clause in the middle of a main clause.

Spelling

- You cannot suddenly learn how to spell perfectly; this skill is learned over years by reading a lot and checking words regularly in a dictionary.
- Learn the **plural** forms of familiar words. Do you add an –s or an –es?
- Learn the endings of words when they are used in different tenses, such as 'playing', 'running', 'gained', 'banned'. Should you just add –ing or –ed, or do you need to double the consonant as well?
- Learn how to spell the sounds that often occur at the end of words. For example:
  - –tion (in attention, mention, creation)
  - –ble (in horrible, miserable, stable)
  - –ous (in marvellous, gorgeous, momentous).

> **Key Point**
>
> Do not misspell words that you've already been given in the question.

> **Key Words**
>
> apostrophe
> ownership
> abbreviation
> comma
> clause
> colon
> exclamation mark
> speech mark
> plural

> **Quick Test**
>
> 1. When should you use apostrophes?
> 2. What do you use a comma for in a complex sentence?
> 3. What is the difference between a main clause and a subordinate clause?
> 4. What can you use a colon for in a sentence?

Read the extract below and answer the questions that follow.

These questions will test how well you have remembered the key points from the previous topic.

Treasure Island

by Robert Louis Stevenson

The narrator, Jim Hawkins, describes the appearance of a mysterious sailor at his father's inn, The Admiral Benbow.

I remember him as if it were yesterday, as he came plodding to the inn door, his sea-chest following behind him in a hand-barrow – a tall, strong, heavy, nut-brown man, his tarry pigtail falling over the shoulder of his soiled blue coat, his hands ragged and scarred, with black, broken nails, and the sabre cut across one cheek, a dirty, livid white. I remember him looking round the cove and whistling to himself as he did so, and then breaking out in that old sea-song that he sang so often afterwards:

'Fifteen men on the dead man's chest –

Yo-ho-ho, and a bottle of rum!'

in the high, old tottering voice that seemed to have been tuned and broken at the capstan bars. Then he rapped on the door with a bit of stick like a handspike that he carried, and when my father appeared, called roughly for a glass of rum. This, when it was brought to him, he drank slowly, like a connoisseur, lingering on the taste and still looking about him at the cliffs and up at our signboard.

'This is a handy cove,' says he at length; 'and a pleasant sittyated grog-shop. Much company, mate?'

My father told him no, very little company, the more was the pity.

'Well, then,' said he, 'this is the berth for me. Here you, matey,' he cried to the man who trundled the barrow; 'bring up alongside and help up my chest. I'll stay here a bit,' he continued. 'I'm a plain man; rum and bacon and eggs is what I want, and that head up there for to watch ships off. What you mought call me? You mought call me captain. Oh, I see what you're at- there'; and he threw down three or four gold pieces on the threshold. 'You can tell me when I've worked through that,' says he, looking as fierce as a commander.

And, indeed, bad as his clothes were and coarsely as he spoke, he had none of the appearance of a man who sailed before the mast, but seemed like a mate or skipper accustomed to be obeyed or to strike. The man who came with the barrow told us the mail had set him down the morning before at the Royal George, that he had inquired what inns there were along the coast, and hearing ours well spoken of, I suppose, and described as lonely, had chosen it from the others for his place of residence. And that was all we could learn of our guest.

He was a very silent man by custom. All day he hung round the cove or upon the cliffs with a brass telescope; all evening he sat in a corner of the parlour next the fire and drank rum and water very strong. Mostly he would not speak when spoken to, only look up sudden and fierce and blow through his nose like a fog-horn; and we and the people who came about our house soon learned to let him be. Every day when he came back from his stroll he would ask if any seafaring men had gone by along the road. At first we thought it was the want of company of his own kind that made him ask this question, but at last we began to see he was desirous to avoid them. When a seaman did put up at the Admiral Benbow (as now and then some did, making by the coast road for Bristol) he would look in at him through the curtained door before he entered the parlour; and he was always sure to be as silent as a mouse when any such was present. For me, at least, there was no secret about the matter, for I was, in a way, a sharer in his alarms. He had taken me aside one day and promised me a silver fourpenny on the first of every month if I would only keep my 'weather-eye open for a seafaring man with one leg,' and let him know the moment he appeared. Often enough, when the first of the month came round and I applied to him for my wage, he would only blow through his nose at me and stare me down; but before the week was out, he was sure to think better of it, bring me my four-penny piece, and repeat his orders to look out for 'the seafaring man with one leg.'

1 *Treasure Island* is written from the viewpoint of a young boy, Jim Hawkins.

Why do you think this is? Give **two** reasons. [2]

2 This extract is taken from the first chapter of *Treasure Island*. What is the purpose of these opening pages? Tick (✓) three answers.

a) To introduce the narrator

b) To explain what the stranger is doing there

c) To create an atmosphere of mystery around the man with one leg

d) To indicate that it will be a story about the sea

e) To persuade the reader to visit the Admiral Benbow

f) To warn children not to speak to strangers [3]

3 What impression do we get of the mysterious stranger? You should comment on:
* the way the narrator describes his appearance
* the way the stranger talks
* the way the stranger acts.

Support your ideas with quotations from the text.

You should aim to write about one side of A4 answering this question. [10]

Look at this writing task.

Your school has set up a student magazine, and you have been put in charge of the advice page. One week, you receive the following message from a student.

> Dear Student Help
>
> I'm in year 8 and I'm being bullied by someone in year 10. It's making me really miserable. I must have done something wrong but I'm not sure what! I don't know what to do and I feel so alone. Please help!
>
> From
> Feeling Scared

Write your response for the Student Help page, advising this student on how to deal with bullying.

1. **a)** What is your purpose, audience and form for this piece of writing to advise? [3]

   b) What will you need to use to separate your writing? [1]

   c) What types of connectives do you need for this piece of writing? [1]

   d) What three types of sentence structure should you make use of to keep your writing varied? [3]

2. Read the student's response opposite. The content is good, but the organisation and accuracy is not. Rewrite the answer, correcting any errors in:

   - paragraphing [2]
   - connectives [2]
   - punctuation [10]
   - spelling [10]
   - grammar [5]

Dear Feeling Scared,

Understand that its not your fault. You is not a bad person: the bully is. No one should be able to treat you like this you are a victim and their are lots of people who can help you. Keep that in your mind, rather than worrying that you are to blame. Secondly do something about the bullying. Don't just except it; you need to talk to someone. This mite be your form tutor the school counsellor, or your head of year. I know youre feeling scared and maybe embarrased, but don't you think it's better to get this in the open. If you do, it will made you feel much better and show you that you're not alone. Once you had done this, you need to try to avoid the bully until the issue is dealt with. Try to get on with life rather than focusing on this problem its important that you spent time with your freinds, as this will make you feel safe and remind you that your not alone. It would also be a good idea to tell your best mates so they understand what you've been feeling and can look out for you while you get over this horrible experiance.

You could speak to the teacher whos been helping you about arranging a meeting with the bully. It can help to talk things over, so the bully knew how bad they've made you feel. This is also a chance to get over any misunderstanding, in case the bully has felt you've wronged them in some little way. Siting down and talking like adults is always a good way too clear the air and move on.

Youll soon be enjoying life again and feeling safe around school.

Thanks four your letter,
Student Help

Plan, Structure and Develop your Response

Quick Recall Quiz

You must be able to:

- Plan and order your ideas quickly so you know how your writing will progress
- Know how to build up the level of detail in your writing.

Planning your Response

- Once you have read the question and understood your purpose, audience and form, you need to **plan** your response.
- You can sketch your ideas out quickly using a list of bullet points, a flow diagram or a spidergram.
- You only need to write brief notes to outline your thoughts about the topic.
- Here is an example of a question and the sort of plan that a student might create.

> **Key Point**
>
> You should practise making plans so that you can do it quickly and effectively.

> **Key Point**
>
> Remember to look for purpose, audience and form in the question.

Your local newspaper is running a writing competition. Your piece must be entitled 'A Lasting Memory'. This is what the competition asks for:

Describe a memorable point in your life. You should include details about:

- where and when this took place
- what happened and how you felt
- why the memory is still important to you.

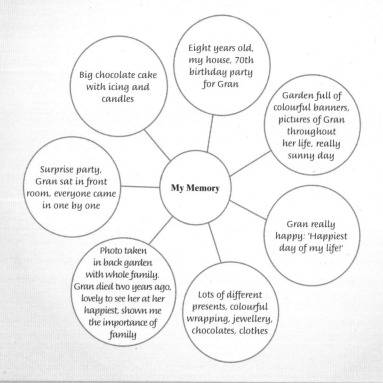

Structuring your Response

- Once you have noted your basic ideas, you should read them through and put them into a logical order, perhaps by numbering them.
- Treat each number as a paragraph; this will ensure that your ideas have a sensible **structure** and will allow you to build up your written response.

Developing your Response

- Your plan and structure only give you the bare bones of your writing, and the order in which you will organise it.
- You need to make sure that you **develop** each paragraph in full.
- In the question on page 52, you would be writing to describe, so you would have to include lots of descriptive detail. For example:
  - you would mention the different colours (trying to use interesting vocabulary, rather than basic primary colours) and the patterns of the banners
  - you could incorporate a simile or metaphor
  - you could then describe the pictures of Gran, showing her getting younger as they change from recent colour photos to old black and white pictures, perhaps mentioning the different styles of fashion
  - you could mention the weather, using different images to link the sunny day to everyone's happiness.
- If the task was writing to explain, you would develop your paragraphs by making your views clear, perhaps giving an example to support your meaning.
- If you had a question on writing to persuade, you would make your point and then use different persuasive techniques to really convince the reader, perhaps backing your comments up with statistics or examples so the reader is confident that you know what you are talking about and trusts your opinion.

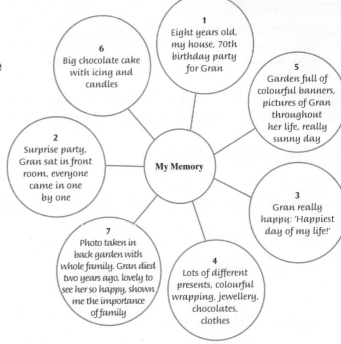

1
Eight years old, my house, 70th birthday party for Gran

6
Big chocolate cake with icing and candles

5
Garden full of colourful banners, pictures of Gran throughout her life, really sunny day

2
Surprise party, Gran sat in front room, everyone came in one by one

My Memory

3
Gran really happy: 'Happiest day of my life!'

7
Photo taken in back garden with whole family. Gran died two years ago, lovely to see her so happy, shown me the importance of family

4
Lots of different presents, colourful wrapping, jewellery, chocolates, clothes

Quick Test

1. What do you need to understand before you can start doing your planning?
2. Do your planning notes need to be very detailed?
3. Why is it important to structure your writing?
4. How should you develop your writing?

Key Words

plan
structure
develop

Writing to Persuade

You must be able to:

- Come up with a number of persuasive ideas
- Use different persuasive techniques to make your ideas effective.

Getting Started

- Before you plan your ideas for a writing to persuade question, you need to be clear about your form, your audience, and what you are persuading your readers about.
- When you plan your work, you should not just look at the issue from your own point of view, for example, if you are trying to persuade your local MP to support the building of a new leisure complex, think about how it would benefit the community and the MP, as well as you:
  - You could suggest that it would keep young people busy doing something fun and useful, so that they will not hang around on the street being a nuisance or even committing petty crime.
  - You could say that increased leisure activities would keep young people healthy and happy, and that the complex would help provide much needed employment in the area.
  - You could even suggest that the complex might appear on the national news and show how hard-working and committed to the town the MP is, making their re-election more likely.

Persuasive Techniques

- It is important that, as well as achieving a high level of accuracy in your spelling, grammar and punctuation, you use a range of persuasive devices.
- The following persuasive devices are arranged as a mnemonic: FORESTRY.
  - **Facts.** Always support your argument with plenty of facts, to convince the reader that you know what you are talking about.
  - **Opinions.** Get your views across in a powerful way. In order to sound convincing, state your opinions as facts, rather than writing 'I think' or words like 'perhaps' and 'maybe'.
  - **Rhetorical questions.** These are questions that you ask to get your readers thinking. For example, if you are trying to encourage people to vote, you might ask this rhetorical question: 'Don't you want to have your say about your own future?'

> **Key Point**
>
> Think about the views of the people you are trying to persuade.

> **Key Point**
>
> A mnemonic is a word to aid your memory, so you can remember the devices more easily.

- **Emotive language** and **empathetic** language. Try to use powerful words or images that make your readers feel something, such as pride, sympathy or guilt.
- **Statistics**. Include statistics to make yourself sound well informed. This is a test of your writing (not your statistical knowledge and research) so, as long as they sound realistic, you can make them up.
- **Triplets**. Organising ideas and examples into lists of three, or triplets, is a good way to really emphasise a point. For example, if you are persuading people to eat less junk food, you might write: 'These foods are full of the things that destroy your health: they are high in salt, high in calories, and high in saturated fat.'
- **Repetition**. In the example above, as well as putting the three unhealthy factors into a triplet, the writer has repeated 'high' three times, to get across just how bad these foods are. Repetition is an effective way to emphasise a point.
- **You (second person)**. When writing to persuade, it is a good idea to address the audience (using 'you', also known as the second person). People are much more likely to be persuaded by you if they think they are being targeted directly, because it makes them feel special and valued.

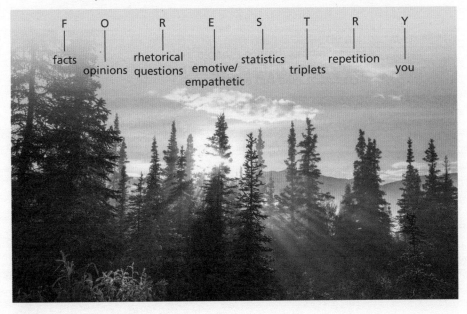

F O R E S T R Y
facts opinions rhetorical questions emotive/empathetic statistics triplets repetition you

Quick Test

1. As well as your own opinions, what do you need to consider when trying to persuade someone?
2. Which mnemonic will help you remember different persuasive techniques?
3. What are the different persuasive techniques mentioned in the mnemonic?
4. As well as using your persuasive techniques, what else must you remember in order to get good marks?

Writing 7

Writing to Argue

Quick Recall Quiz

You must be able to:

- Come up with a balanced argument
- Use different techniques to make your ideas clear and effective.

Getting Started

- Before planning your ideas for a writing to argue question, you need to be clear about your form, your audience, and the argument you are going to present.
- Writing to argue is similar to writing to persuade, in that you are presenting your views about an issue. There is one major difference: you need to present a **balanced argument** (you need to present both sides of the issue).
- For example, you could be asked to argue whether a new supermarket should be built in your local high street. Here is a simple way to structure your argument:

> **Key Point**
>
> Always include both sides of the argument, but make sure you give a final decision as well.

Using a short, introductory paragraph, state the issue being debated.

Write a series of paragraphs arguing for or against the issue. Make your views varied and offer clear reasons or evidence.

Write several paragraphs looking at the alternative views. For each one, unless it has been covered already, offer your counter argument.

In your final paragraph, you should present your conclusion and summarise why you are for or against the idea.

Features of Writing to Argue

- As well as remembering the need for accuracy in your spelling, punctuation and grammar and structuring a clear argument, you must include specific features in your writing to help make it effective.
- Do not lose sight of the fact that you are looking at *both sides of the argument*, not just your own viewpoint.
- You will need to use a lot of **connectives** of comparison and contrast. For example:
  - You will need words like 'similarly' and 'furthermore' when building up your argument.
  - You will need phrases like 'on the other hand' and 'in contrast' when arguing the view against or when you are countering these ideas.
- In addition, you will need to use some connectives of cause and effect to show why you think the way you do.

Connectives of Cause and Effect	
As a result	Due to
Because of this	Therefore
Consequently	Thus

- You should use a connective at the end of your writing to signal to the audience that you are bringing your argument to its **conclusion**. For example: 'In conclusion', 'To summarise', 'Overall'.
- You should use **topic sentences** at the start of your paragraphs. For example: 'In addition to this, a new supermarket in the High Street would damage small businesses like the newsagent and the greengrocers.'
- Topic sentences set out your point clearly to the audience, before you spend the rest of the paragraph explaining or justifying it.

> **Quick Test**
>
> 1. How is writing to argue different from writing to persuade?
> 2. What should you include in your final paragraph in writing to argue?
> 3. What different connectives will you need to use in writing to argue?
> 4. What is a topic sentence used for?

> **Key Words**
>
> balanced argument
> connectives
> conclusion
> topic sentence

Writing to Advise

You must be able to:

- Come up with a number of clear suggestions
- Use different techniques to make your advice effective.

Getting Started

- As always, before doing any planning for a writing to advise question, you need to be sure about the form, your audience, and the issue about which you are offering advice.
- Writing to advise is a little like writing to persuade and argue. You are getting across your point of view about what someone should do and trying to encourage the reader to follow your advice.
- Your use of **tone** will be different when writing to advise; you need to sound firm but also friendly and supportive in your writing.

> ### Key Point
>
> 'Advice' (spelt with a 'c') is a noun, e.g. 'Give some advice'. 'Advise' (spelt with an 's') is a verb, e.g. 'I will advise her about it.'

Features of Writing to Advise

- You should try to learn some key phrases that you can use to show you understand and are being helpful:

- Notice that many of these phrases use the **second person** ('you'). This is important to make the reader feel that you are talking directly to them about an issue with which they need help.

- As well as using 'you', there are other techniques from the FORESTRY mnemonic (pages 54–55) that you can use:
  - opinions
  - rhetorical questions
  - empathy
  - triplets
  - repetition.
- You are advising the reader about taking different steps that will help them with one issue. For this reason, you need to **order** your ideas logically in the planning stage and then, when writing, use connectives of sequence.
- Try not to be too mechanical (just writing: first, second, third, etc.). Try to use a variety of connectives, for example: 'after this', 'next', 'once this has been achieved'.
- You need to use two different sentence functions:
  - When showing empathy with the reader, include statements that show you understand the issue.
  - However, when you offer specific advice, use instructions (also called **imperatives**). This is vital, to encourage the reader to follow your advice. A friendly tone is important, so that the reader does not feel they are being told off.
  - To make an order seem kinder, begin it with a friendly subordinate clause, for example: 'Although it might be hard at first…'
- Because you need to make suggestions and give orders, you need to learn a variety of **modal verbs**. These are verbs that affect other verbs by adding a suggestion of possibility or necessity. For example:

Key Point

'Imperatives' are also known as 'commands'. They are instructions; for example, 'stay calm', 'talk to someone you trust'.

Modal Verb	Used in a sentence to advise
Could	You could speak to a friend.
Must	You must prove to the people at work that you know what you are talking about.
Need	You need to build up your self-confidence.
Ought	You ought to get out more and try to meet new friends.
Should	You should ignore what she says about you and get on with your life.

Key Point

Use modal verbs to urge your audience to follow your advice while also creating some sense of choice.

Quick Test

1. Why is tone important in writing to advise?
2. What sort of phrases can you use when giving advice to appear friendly and supportive?
3. Why is the second person important in writing to advise?
4. What are modal verbs and why are they useful in writing to advise?

Key Words

tone
second person
order
imperative
modal verb

Look at this writing task.

You have been invited to enter a competition being run by a travel magazine. The challenge is to complete a piece of persuasive writing, encouraging people to travel to a particular destination. The competition details are below:

> **Travel Writing Competition**
>
> Think of somewhere you have visited and enjoyed. This could be somewhere in Britain or abroad. For example, it could be a busy city, a peaceful beach resort or an area full of forests and wildlife.
>
> Write an article persuading people to visit. Try and get across how amazing the place is and why others will enjoy it too.
>
> Write your entry for the travel magazine, persuading the magazine's readers to visit the destination you have chosen.

1   **a)** What is the purpose, audience and form for this piece of writing?   [3]

    b) What will you need to use to separate your different ideas?   [1]

    c) What types of connectives do you need for this piece of writing?   [1]

    d) What three types of sentence structure should you make use of to keep your writing varied?   [3]

2   Read the student's response opposite. The content is good, but the organisation and accuracy is not. Rewrite the answer, correcting any errors in:

- paragraphing   [2]
- connectives   [2]
- punctuation   [10]
- spelling   [10]
- grammar   [5]

There's Nowhere Like Newquay!

Are you looking for an amazing beach resort in England. Then look know further than Newquay in Cornwall. This amazing town is home to beautifull beaches lots of leisure activitys exciting entertainment, and friendly locals.

The main reason to come to Newquay is its nine amazing beaches. The warm, golden sands stretch for miles, providing the perfect place to relaxing and get a tan. Youll see clear blue waters lapping hypnotically against the shore and beckoning you to come in for a swim. As well as being famously stuning Newquays coastline is also well-known for attracting surfers from all over the globe. You can join in, or just sit back and watch people tackling waves of up to six metres high. Watching the colourfull boards ride the waves or dissapear in the crashing foam can be almost as exhilarating as trying it yourself!

If you venture beyond the beachs there's still plenty to do. You can visit the zoo take a ride on the miniature railway, or play a round of mini-golf. There are also plenty of walks along the South West Coast Path (the longest in England) where you will be rewarded with picturesque views and lots of nature, from rare migrating birds to cute seals and sunbathing lizards. Furthermore the old town was a joy to walk around. The quaint streets are lined with pretty houses and gardens. There is also lovly arts and crafts shops, so you can buy something unique to remind you of your fantastic holiday. It's also a great opportunity to enjoy a traditional english cream tea, with home-baked scones fresh strawberry jam, and lashings of Cornish cream.

Theres no reason to get bored. The town boasts lots of freindly pubs, tasty restaurants and lively clubs. There are also theatres, cinemas, bingo halls, and amusement arcades, not forgeting the chance to watch a match at Newquay FC's home ground.

Come to Newquay and you'll never wanted to leave!

1 **Look at this task on writing to persuade. Give yourself 45 minutes (including 10 minutes planning time).**

> The school librarian has asked your year group to take part in a project encouraging the younger students to read more. As part of the project, you've been asked to write the text for a leaflet that will persuade students to visit the library and get reading.
>
> Below are some ideas that members of the Read Now! Project have suggested:
>
> - Books are exciting and entertaining.
> - There's a book to suit everyone's interests (fiction and non-fiction).
> - Reading improves literacy which will improve all your grades.
> - It's fun to read a book amongst a group of friends and talk about it.
>
> Using these ideas as a starting point, write your persuasive leaflet.

    a) Create a plan for your leaflet, using the following ideas as a guide: **[6]**

- Why books are enjoyable
- Why books are educational
- Persuasive techniques to include in the leaflet

    b) Now write the text for your leaflet.   **[30]**

2 **Look at this task on writing to argue. Give yourself 45 minutes (including 10 minutes planning time).**

> Your headteacher is considering banning films from being shown in lessons at school. You have been asked to write an article for the school magazine, arguing the issues around the proposed ban.
>
> You have spoken to the headteacher, other teachers, and groups of pupils to get different points of view. Below are some of their comments:
>
> - For the ban: it's a waste of teaching time; students can watch any educational films in their own time; films are so full of historical inaccuracies, etc. that they're not educational anyway; students learn much better from books not films.
> - Against the ban: there are lots of great educational films which are a useful, alternative way to learn or reinforce understanding; educational films help to bring subject content to life; educational films are good at presenting different sides of an issue; films are also a good treat for when classes have worked really well.
>
> Using these ideas as a starting point, write your article.

a) Create a plan for your article, using the following ideas as a guide: [6]

- The argument in support of the ban
- The argument against the ban
- Techniques to highlight the arguments, and a conclusion presenting your own opinion

b) Now write your article. [30]

3 **Look at this task on writing to advise. Give yourself 45 minutes (including 10 minutes planning time).**

You work for the local newspaper, and you've been asked to write a weekly column advising readers. This week you've had a letter asking for different ideas about a surprise birthday celebration that a group of friends want to organise.

They would like some ideas about:

- Good places to go for a fun day out.
- A memorable present that they could get (they have about £50 to spend).
- Where they could go for a meal afterwards.
- Other ways in which they can make the day a fun, memorable celebration.

Using these ideas as a starting point, write the response for your advice column.

a) Create a plan for your advice column, using the following ideas as a guide: [6]

- Where to go and what to do
- What to buy and ways to make the birthday memorable
- Techniques to make your advice effective

b) Now write the text for your advice column. [30]

Vocabulary and Sentences

Quick Recall Quiz

You must be able to:

- Include a wide range of vocabulary that matches your purpose, audience and form
- Use a range of sentence structures to keep your writing varied and create different effects.

Varied Vocabulary

- To keep your writing lively and interesting, you need to vary your vocabulary.
  - Don't just use the first word that comes to mind.
  - Avoid using the same words over and over again.
- Try to think of more interesting words, particularly when choosing **verbs** and **adjectives**. For example, the sentence 'I went to the old shop and got some nice sweets,' could be written in many different ways:

I went to	the old shop	and got	some nice sweets.
I crept to	the ancient shop	and bought	some amazing sweets.
I raced to	the historic shop	and collected	some delicious sweets.
I ran to	the crumbling shop	and gathered	some gorgeous sweets.
I sidled to	the dilapidated shop	and grabbed	some sumptuous sweets.
I walked to	the run-down shop	and purchased	some tantalising sweets.
I wandered to	the unloved shop	and selected	some tasty sweets.

- Think about different words for colours, for example:
  - red scarlet, crimson
  - blue → navy, azure
  - green → emerald, jade
  - yellow → gold, lemon.

> **Key Point**
>
> You should not always use the first word that comes to you; can you use something more interesting and specific that is just as suitable?

Subject-specific Vocabulary

- You need to make sure that your vocabulary is appropriate to the subject. For example, when writing about the environment, you should not use vague terms about 'things harming the planet'. You need to use words and phrases like pollution, greenhouse gases, carbon footprint and recycling.
- Sometimes it can help, as part of your planning, to make a quick list of subject-specific words that you might include in your work.

> **Key Point**
>
> Reading widely different types of fiction and non-fiction will help to build up your knowledge of subject-specific vocabulary.

Varied Sentence Structures

- You should be using punctuation accurately to form a range of **simple**, **compound** and **complex sentences**.
- Simply by varying your sentences, you add variety to your writing and create different effects.
- You can use certain sentence structures to create specific effects:
  - short, simple sentences
  - compound sentences
  - complex sentences
  - lists.

Short, simple sentences

- To emphasise a point:
  - Reality television should be banned.
- To surprise your reader in fiction:
  - A man stepped out from the shadows.

Compound sentences

- To join two ideas together:
  - Homework is stressful and it reduces social interaction.
- To create a contrast:
  - Travelling by car is convenient but it causes extra pollution.

Complex sentences

- To build up a point:
  - We need police on the beat, making our streets safe for all.
- To add extra detail:
  - Despite the rain beating down, the bird took flight.

Lists

- To emphasise a point:
  - You are a good, kind-hearted, friendly and generous person.
- To build up a powerful image:
  - The fog came quickly, swirling through the streets, gardens, alleyways and back yards.

- Remember, where appropriate, to use sentences that carry a range of messages: statements, exclamations of emotion, questions and commands.

 Quick Test

1. Suggest two alternatives for the verbs 'to go' and 'to get'.
2. What subject-specific words might you use when writing about the environment?
3. What effects can you achieve by using a short sentence?
4. What are the different types of information or message that a sentence can convey?

Key Words

verb
adjective
simple sentence
compound sentence
complex sentence

Writing to Inform

Quick Recall Quiz

You must be able to:

- Come up with a range of information
- Use different features of writing to inform to make your work effective.

Getting Started

- Before you plan your ideas for a writing to inform question, you need to be clear about your form, your audience, and what you need to tell your reader.
- You need to present your reader with lots of information in the form of **facts** and **statistics**. Remember, you will have to make a lot of this information up!
  - If, for example, you were writing about a crime, you would have to make it all up.
  - If you were writing about your home town, there would be less to invent.
  - However, if you couldn't remember something and had to make it up, this would not matter: the question is testing your writing, not your general knowledge.

Features of Writing to Inform

- When writing to inform, you will usually use the third person and a combination of past and present tense.
- It is very important that you use plenty of **connectives** of time and place and try to order your ideas logically.
- If you are giving information about an event (such as an accident involving a lorry that has closed a motorway), you need to organise your ideas **chronologically**. For example:

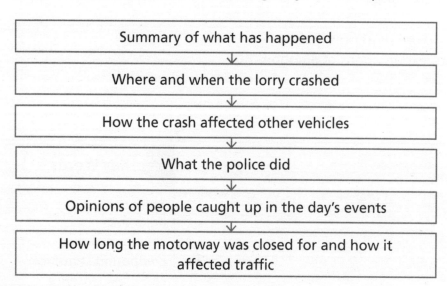

Summary of what has happened
Where and when the lorry crashed
How the crash affected other vehicles
What the police did
Opinions of people caught up in the day's events
How long the motorway was closed for and how it affected traffic

> **Key Point**
>
> The third person is 'he', 'she', 'they', 'it', 'Mrs Cook', 'the man', 'the child', etc.

> **Key Point**
>
> Connectives of time and place ensure that your audience can tell where and when things are happening.

- If you are giving information about a place (such as a new shopping centre) or an idea (such as a charity), you need to arrange your ideas **thematically**. For example:

The focus of the charity
↓
The history of the charity
↓
Celebrities who are involved in the charity
↓
Some of the charity's biggest successes
↓
The charity's current big project
↓
How the reader can get involved with the charity

- When you are writing to inform, you should focus on facts rather than feelings.
- Remember that a reader would be coming to your article to find information that they want to know.
- You may need to use a combination of positive and negative language. For example:
  - If you were informing people about a city break in London, you would mention all the great things that people can do there.
  - However, you may need to inform the audience that the restaurants in a particular area are very expensive, or that certain places are best avoided late at night.
- Writing to inform is different from a piece of writing intended to persuade, because you would give both the positives and negatives in writing to inform, but only one or the other in writing to persuade.

> **Key Point**
>
> Make sure that your ideas are clearly ordered, and focus on fact rather than opinion.

Quick Test

1. What type of information dominates in writing to inform?
2. What type of connectives should you use in writing to inform?
3. What are the two main ways in which you could organise your informative writing?
4. Why might a mix of positive and negative language be important in writing to inform?

Key Words

fact
statistic
connective
chronological
thematic

Writing to Explain

You must be able to:

- Get across to the audience how or why something happens or has happened
- Use different features of writing to explain to make your work clear.

Getting Started

- Before you plan your answer for a writing to explain question, you need to establish the form, audience, and what you need to explain.
- In a writing to explain task, you present the facts about something (rather like writing to inform) but then go into more detail about cause and effect.
- When explaining the **cause** and **effect** of something, you should also consider alternatives and try to explain what would happen if something were done differently. For example, you could be asked to write an article for a parenting magazine about the pressures on young people today.
  - First, you would plan your writing by thinking about what different pressures exist.
  - You could think about the causes of each pressure, the effect it has on young people, and how parents can help.
  - Your first two ideas might look something like this:

> **Key Point**
>
> Make sure that you explain the relationship between cause and effect clearly.

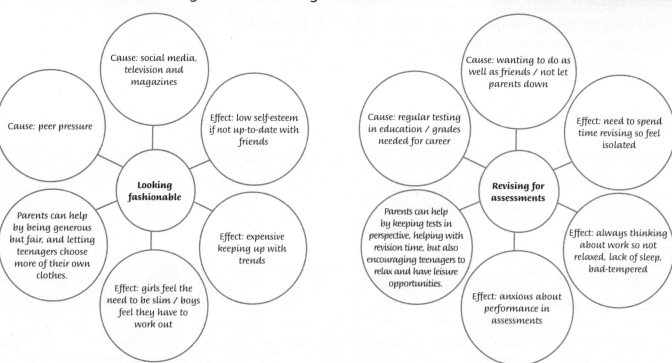

- You would then be able to start writing: explaining each pressure, along with its causes and effects, in individually themed paragraphs.

Features of Writing to Explain

- With writing to explain, you need to use connectives of cause and effect, for example:
    - as a result
    - because of this
    - consequently
    - due to
    - therefore
    - thus.
- You need to use some connectives of comparison in order to link your different points together.
- You should write in the **present tense** to explain a current issue (such as the problems affecting teenagers). However, you should use the **past tense** to explain how something happened.
- You should usually write in the third person. However, if you are asked to explain something about your age group, you might use the **pronoun** 'we'.
- You should try to include facts, offer a balanced view that is supported by evidence, and separate your ideas into clear paragraphs that start with topic sentences.

> **Key Point**
>
> Connectives are important in writing to explain as they link your points and show cause and effect.

Quick Test

1. What additional information do you need to focus on that makes explaining different from informing?
2. What type of connectives should you use when writing to explain?
3. What should you consider when deciding which tense to use in writing to explain?
4. Why do you need clear paragraphs and topic sentences in writing to explain?

> **Key Words**
>
> cause
> effect
> present tense
> past tense
> pronoun

Writing to Describe

Quick Recall Quiz

You must be able to:

- Use different descriptive techniques to build up vivid images for the reader.
- Develop your descriptions to maintain the attention of the reader.

Getting Started

- In order to start planning for a writing to describe task, you need to establish your form, your audience, and what you need to describe.
- A question could ask you to describe something completely imaginary (such as an alien world) or it could give you a particular scene (for example, a celebrity wedding).
- You still need to order your ideas carefully so that they make sense; this could be chronologically or thematically.
- You need to develop your descriptions so that the reader can really imagine what you describe.
- Try to establish settings (and character if necessary) and create a powerful atmosphere.

Descriptive Techniques

- You should always try to use a wide variety of interesting **verbs**, **adjectives** and **adverbs**. Do not limit yourself to the most obvious words: try to be creative.
- Include a range of descriptive techniques to keep your writing vivid and interesting. Avoid using the same technique repeatedly, as it will lose its impact.
- **Similes** and **metaphors** are types of imagery that compare someone or something with something else:
  - Similes are comparisons that use 'like' or 'as' (for example, 'The vampire had teeth like daggers.').
  - Metaphors are impossible comparisons that claim to be true (such as, 'The man's eyes were burning with anger.').
- **Personification** describes objects or abstract nouns in an interesting way by giving them human characteristics, for example: 'The charming cottage sat smiling in the middle of the countryside,' or 'Fear crept through the streets.'
- **Onomatopoeia**, **alliteration** and **sibilance** are ways in which you can help your readers to picture a scene or feel the atmosphere by using sound.
  - Onomatopoeic words sound like the sound they describe, for example, 'pop' or 'bang'.
  - Alliteration is the repetition of the same sound at the start of several words, for example, 'the rapidly rushing river'.

> **Key Point**
>
> Avoid describing everything in the same way; use a range of vocabulary, descriptive techniques, and sentence structure.

- Sibilance is a repetition of 's' sounds (often to create a creepy atmosphere), for example, 'The beast slithered silently through the silky darkness to its next victim.'

- When it comes to the **senses**, don't just include how things look. Describe smells, sounds, textures and tastes.

Keeping on Track

- Although writing to describe should be quite easy (it is something that you have been doing for many years), students often do this less well than they could.

- Don't forget about paragraphs and punctuation.

- Planning your descriptive writing is vital. Make sure you don't simply list objects and events without really developing their descriptions.

- One way to plan your description is in the form of a thought-shower that you then number into clear paragraphs. Here is an example for the task, 'Describe your dream world'.

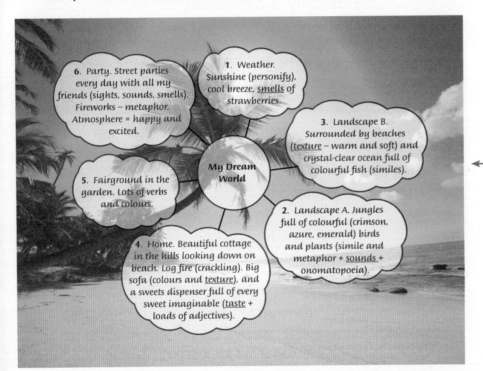

6. Party. Street parties every day with all my friends (sights, sounds, smells). Fireworks – metaphor. Atmosphere = happy and excited.

1. Weather. Sunshine (personify), cool breeze, smells of strawberries.

3. Landscape B. Surrounded by beaches (texture – warm and soft) and crystal-clear ocean full of colourful fish (similes).

My Dream World

5. Fairground in the garden. Lots of verbs and colours.

2. Landscape A. Jungles full of colourful (crimson, azure, emerald) birds and plants (simile and metaphor + sounds + onomatopoeia).

4. Home. Beautiful cottage in the hills looking down on beach. Log fire (crackling). Big sofa (colours and texture), and a sweets dispenser full of every sweet imaginable (taste + loads of adjectives).

This is a well thought-out plan with plenty of things to describe. The student has remembered to include descriptions of senses other than sight and has thought about effective descriptive techniques to use.

Quick Test

1. When you are writing to describe, what are you trying to give to the reader?
2. How can you order your ideas to make them clear?
3. What are some of the different techniques you can use to build up your descriptions?
4. What must you still remember to do, even when having fun describing something?

Key Words

verb
adjective
adverb
simile
metaphor
personification
onomatopoeia
alliteration
sibilance
senses

1 **Look at this task on writing to persuade. Give yourself 45 minutes (including 10 minutes planning time).**

> You have been asked to make a speech to the local council, persuading them to provide more facilities for young people in your local park. Your friends have already given you some ideas:
> - Better lighting for safety
> - A football pitch and tennis court
> - Some slides and swings for younger children
> - Bins for rubbish and a graffiti wall
>
> Write your persuasive speech ready for when you meet the local council.

a) Use boxes like the ones below to note your ideas. Try to find reasons to support each of your friends' ideas, and a persuasive technique you could use. [6]

Better lighting:	Football pitch and tennis court:	Slides and swings:	Bins and graffiti wall:
• Keeps us safe, especially in winter when it gets dark by 4pm • Makes it easier to play games like tennis and football • Use a rhetorical question			

b) Now write your speech. [30]

2 **Look at this task on writing to argue. Give yourself 45 minutes (including 10 minutes planning time).**

> You have been asked to write an article for the school magazine, arguing the pros and cons of the Internet. You have been asked to give a balanced argument while deciding whether the Internet is a good or a bad thing. Read the brief below:
>
> > This month the school magazine has the topic of technology. We want an article that debates the pros and cons of the Internet. Think about how it benefits people (from students to pensioners), but also how it can be a danger. Have a clear point of view but also provide a balanced argument.
>
> Write your argument for the school magazine.

a) First, create a table like the one below and note down some quick ideas about the Internet's good and bad points. Try to come up with three ideas for each column. [6]

Good	Bad
The Internet allows you to communicate with people all over the world.	People spend too much time online, talking to people on the Internet, rather than going out and actually meeting people.

b) Now write your article. [30]

3 **Look at this task on writing to advise. Give yourself 45 minutes (including 10 minutes planning time).**

Your pen-friend has written you a letter telling you that she is being bullied at school by a group of girls who used to be her friends. Here is part of her letter:

> It's been going on for a few months now. It started with just a bit of name-calling but now they try to trip me up in the corridors and gang up on me outside at lunchtime. I even got a nasty message on Facebook the other night. I just don't know what to do.

Write a letter to your pen-friend advising her what to do.

a) Create a plan for your letter, using the following ideas as a guide:

- Advice on how to cope with bullying
- Advice on telling people
- Modal verbs to include in the letter. [8]

b) Now write your letter. [30]

1 Look at this task on writing to inform. Give yourself 45 minutes (including 10 minutes planning time).

You are a reporter for a local newspaper. You have heard that there is a fire at a nearby school; it started in the cookery block, spread to the library and now the school has been evacuated whilst the fire brigade try to put out the fire.

Your editor sends you this message:

> I want the school fire to be today's front page story. Head to the school and find out what happened and what the current situation is. Remember to get opinions and comments from students, parents and the head teacher. Our readers will want to know how the fire started, why it spread so quickly and whether the school has an effective fire drill. Don't forget that they'll need to know how long the school will be closed for and how this will affect the community.

Write an article for the front page of the newspaper. (Do not write in columns.)

a) Create a plan for your news article using the following headings:

- What/when/where/how
- Three things the fire brigade have been doing
- Three different opinions [10]

b) Now write your article. [30]

2 Look at this task on writing to explain. Give yourself 45 minutes (including 10 minutes planning time).

You work for a company that makes mobile phones. You have been designing a new mobile that will be the most high-tech phone on the market. You receive this request from your manager:

> The first model of the fully working mobile phone should be nearly complete. Please write a detailed report, explaining:
> - What problems were encountered and how they have been sorted out (*e.g. battery not lasting long enough, camera not good enough, too heavy*).
> - Which functions are now working better than other phones on the market, and who these might appeal to (*e.g. ability to play games on your mobile, most up-to-date sat-nav, high-resolution video camera*).
> - What improvements still need to be made (*e.g. increase storage for music and video files*).
> Include anything else you need to update me on.

Write your report for your manager, remembering to explain the information he wants.

a) First, create a table like the one below and note down your ideas and explanations. Try to come up with four ideas for each prompt. [4]

Problems and solutions	
Best functions	
Necessary improvements	
Any other details	

b) Now write your report. [30]

3 **Look at this task on writing to describe. Give yourself 45 minutes (including 10 minutes planning time).**

You have been invited to enter a piece of descriptive writing for a magazine. This month's theme is contrasts. Read the writing brief below:

> Produce a piece of descriptive writing on the theme of contrasts. It's up to you how you approach the theme. You could describe two events with contrasting emotions, the same place but at two different times of the year, or you could describe a city followed by a description of the countryside.

Write your submission for the magazine, remembering to include lots of description.

a) Create a table like the one below and note down your ideas for your contrasting writing. Think about the things you'll describe, the different senses you can incorporate and the descriptive techniques you might use. Try to come up with six things for each column. [6]

Part 1	Part 2

b) Now write your description. [30]

As You Like It – Key Characters

Quick Recall Quiz

You must be able to:

- Explain what the main characters are like
- Explain how Shakespeare shows this through his writing.

Rosalind

- Rosalind is independent and mocks men who only pretend to be strong:

> ROSALIND   We'll have a swashing and a martial outside,
> As many other mannish cowards have
> That do outface it with their semblances.

- She is strong-willed, using rhetorical techniques of **repetition**, **rhetorical questions**, short sentences and (with the word Highness) **irony** to stand up to Duke Frederick:

> ROSALIND   So was I when your Highness took his dukedom,
> So was I when your Highness banish'd him.
> Treason is not inherited, my lord,
> Or if we did derive it from our friends,
> What's that to me? My father was no traitor.

Repetition.

Rhetorical question.

- She is clever. The use of list and repetition here shows her witty ability to see the truth of the world:

> ROSALIND   … your brother and my sister no sooner met but they looked, no sooner looked but they loved, no sooner loved but they sighed, no sooner sighed but they asked one another the reason, no sooner knew the reason but they sought the remedy.

- Rosalind uses her confidence and wit to teach Orlando to be a more attentive lover:

> ROSALIND   …men are April when they woo, December when they wed: maids are May when they are maids, but the sky changes when they are wives.

Orlando

- Orlando is kind-hearted and loyal. The **adjective** 'proud', his repetition of 'son' and the rejection of Frederick's status emphasise his loyalty to his father's memory:

> ORLANDO   I am more proud to be Sir Rowland's son,
> His youngest son, and would not change that calling
> To be adopted heir to Frederick.

> **Key Point**
>
> Use quotations from the text in order to justify your opinions about the characters.

- Although it is supposed to be funny that Orlando is a bad poet, the description of Rosalind's qualities through **simile** and **metaphor** show his romantic side:

> From the east to western Inde,
> No jewel is like Rosalind,
> Her worth being mounted on the wind,
> Through all the world bears Rosalind.

This simile suggests Rosalind is more precious than any jewel.

With this metaphor Orlando suggests that Rosalind is worth more than all the world.

- Orlando is uneducated. The lowly simile, coupled with the contrasting **verbs** ('charged' versus 'obscuring' and 'hiding') show his anger at his lack of refinement:

> ORLANDO   My father charged you in his will to give me good education: you have trained me like a peasant, obscuring and hiding from me all gentleman-like qualities.

- Rosalind later tells Orlando that he has proven himself a gentleman:

> ROSALIND   Know of me then – for now I speak to some purpose – that I know you are a gentleman of good conceit.

Jaques

- Jaques is perceptive and critical. The **extended** theatre **metaphor** shows his understanding of the world:

> JAQUES   All the world's a stage,
> And all the men and women merely players:
> They have their exits and their entrances;
> And one man in his time plays many parts,
> His acts being seven ages.

- He is **melancholy**. In this speech, repetition and metaphor are used to emphasise how he likes to wallow in his own misery:

> JAQUES   More, I prithee, more. I can suck melancholy out of a song, as a weasel sucks eggs. More, I prithee, more.

- At the end, he decides to retire to the monastery with Duke Frederick:

> JAQUES   To him I will. Out of these convertites,
> There is much matter to be heard and learn'd.

Key Point

Think about the ways in which different themes are explored through the characters.

Key Words

repetition
rhetorical question
irony
adjective
simile
metaphor
verb
extended metaphor
melancholy

Quick Test

1. What are some of Rosalind's most admirable characteristics?
2. What are Orlando's most admirable characteristics?
3. What does Orlando prove to himself and others by the end of the play?
4. How does Rosalind change Orlando during the play?

As You Like It – Themes

Quick Recall Quiz

You must be able to:

- Identify the key themes of the play
- Explain how Shakespeare uses characters and events to explore these themes.

Love

- The theme of love is portrayed through various characters.
- Love at first sight is presented through Rosalind and Orlando, and Celia and Oliver:

ORLANDO	What passion hangs these weights upon my tongue? I cannot speak to her, yet she urg'd conference.

- Through Rosalind, Shakespeare explores the idea that love should be realistic not idealistic:

ROSALIND	But these are all lies: men have died from time to time and worms have eaten them, but not for love.

- Romantic love is also **parodied** through Audrey and Touchstone:

AUDREY	I do not know what 'poetical' is. Is it honest in deed and word? Is it a true thing?
TOUCHSTONE	No truly; for the truest poetry is the most feigning, and lovers are given to poetry.

- The play ends with four marriages: Rosalind and Orlando, Celia and Oliver, Silvius and Phebe, and Touchstone and Audrey.

Injustice

- The theme of injustice is presented through Frederick's **usurpation** of Duke Senior, and his later banishment of Rosalind:

FREDERICK	You, niece, provide yourself. If you outstay the time, upon mine honour And in the greatness of my word, you die.

- Injustice is also explored through Oliver's unjust treatment of Orlando:

ORLANDO	He keeps me rustically at home, or, to speak more properly, stays me here at home unkept; for call you that keeping for a gentleman of my birth, that differs not from stalling of an ox?

> **Key Point**
>
> Think about how different themes are explored through the events of the play.

Orlando compares Oliver's treatment of him to someone keeping an ox. (An ox is an animal bred for work.)

Court Versus Country

- The court is presented as a place of **oppression** and injustice, while the country allows freedom:

> CHARLES He is already in the Forest of Arden, and a many merry men with him...and fleet the time carelessly as they did in the golden world.

- The country heals the problems of the city, with lovers united and the dukedom restored:

> DUKE SENIOR First, in this forest, let us do those ends
> That here were well begun and well begot:
> And after, every of this happy number
> That have endur'd shrewd days and nights with us,
> Shall share the good of our returned fortune.

Disguise

- The freedom of the country is also presented by Shakespeare through the way in which characters can transform themselves:
  - Rosalind into Ganymede
  - Celia into Aliena:

> ROSALIND I could find it in my heart to disgrace my man's apparel and to cry like a woman. But I must comfort the weaker vessel, as doublet and hose ought to show itself courageous to petticoat; therefore courage, good Aliena.

Regret and Restoration

- Frederick restores Duke Senior his position, and converts to a hermit, while Oliver regrets his mistreatment of Orlando:

> OLIVER 'Twas I. But 'tis not I. I do not shame
> To tell you what I was, since my conversion
> So sweetly tastes, being the thing I am.

Quick Test

1. Which key characters represent love?
2. Which characters are treated unjustly?
3. What is the importance of the countryside?
4. What themes do Oliver and Frederick help to present?

As You Like It – Language

Quick Recall Quiz

You must be able to:

- Analyse how Shakespeare uses language to present character and theme
- Analyse how Shakespeare uses language to achieve a response from his audience.

Rhetorical Speech

- Here is an example of **rhetorical** speech, when we first meet Duke Senior in the Forest of Arden:

DUKE SENIOR	Now, my co-mates and brothers in exile,
	Hath not old custom made this life more sweet
	Than that of painted pomp? Are not these woods
	More free from peril than the envious court?
	Here feel we not the penalty of Adam,
	The seasons' difference, as the icy fang ← Personification
	And churlish chiding of the winter's wind... ← Alliteration
	Sweet are the uses of adversity,
	Which like the toad, ugly and venomous, ← Simile
	Wears yet a precious jewel in his head;
	And this our life, exempt from public haunt,
	Finds tongues in trees, books in the running brooks, ← Metaphor
	Sermons in stones, and good in everything.

> **Key Point**
>
> Rhetorical speech is used to persuade, motivate or convey meaning.

- Duke Senior uses his speech to motivate his men to be optimistic about their exile.
- The rhetorical question and repetition draw a contrast between the freedom of the forest and the oppression of the court.
- Shakespeare then gives him powerful images, emphasised by **personification** and **alliteration**, to suggest they are better off in the forest.
- The final list of **similes** and **metaphors** focuses on optimism and the qualities of their new pastoral home.

Descriptive Speech

- One example of Shakespeare's **descriptive** language is Jaques's famous speech about the seven ages of man:

JAQUES	All the world's a stage,
	And all the men and women merely players: ← Metaphor
	They have their exits and their entrances;
	And one man in his time plays many parts,
	His acts being seven ages. At first the infant,
	Mewling and puking in the nurse's arms.
	And then the whining school-boy, with his satchel

> And shining morning face, creeping like snail
> Unwillingly to school. And then the lover,
> Sighing like furnace, with a woeful ballad
> Made to his mistress' eyebrow...

Similes

- Shakespeare gives Jaques striking **adjectives**, **verbs**, similes and metaphors that build up images of the different stages of life.
- The speech allows us to see Jaques's interest in human nature.
- The fourth line also introduces the idea that people are always changing, which is reflected in the progress of the characters throughout the play.

Emotive Speech

- An example of Shakespeare using **emotive** language is where Orlando pins poems about Rosalind to the trees:

ORLANDO	Hang there, my verse, in witness of my love:
	And thou, thrice-crowned queen of night, survey
	With thy chaste eye, from thy pale sphere above,
	Thy huntress' name, that my full life doth sway.
	O Rosalind! these trees shall be my books
	And in their barks my thoughts I'll character;
	That every eye which in this forest looks
	Shall see thy virtue witness'd everywhere.
	Run, run, Orlando; carve on every tree
	The fair, the chaste and unexpressive she.

- In the first four lines of this extract, Shakespeare uses images of the moon to compare its influence on the Earth with Rosalind's influence on Orlando.
- The exclamation as he says her name shows passion.
- The repetition of 'witness' suggests that he is so much in love that he wants everyone to know.
- The final **triplet** of adjectives ('unexpressive' means inexpressible) emphasises the perfection that he sees in Rosalind.

> ### Key Point
>
> Descriptive speech is used to help the audience imagine a scene or understand how a character sees a situation.

> ### Key Point
>
> Emotive speech is used to convey powerful emotions, either to show what a character is feeling or to get the audience to share a character's feelings.

> ### Key Words
>
> rhetorical
> personification
> alliteration
> simile
> metaphor
> descriptive
> adjective
> verb
> emotive
> triplet

> ### Quick Test
>
> 1. What does Shakespeare use rhetorical language for?
> 2. What is the point of descriptive language?
> 3. How is emotive language used by Shakespeare?
> 4. What different technical features of language should you look out for?

As You Like It – Performance

Quick Recall Quiz

You must be able to:

- Explain how characters' lines should be spoken in order to convey their meaning
- Explain how actors can perform in order to highlight the meaning of the lines.

Speaking the Lines

- When delivering their lines, actors can do various things with their voices in order to make Shakespeare's meaning clear. For example:
  - raise and lower volume
  - alter the tone of voice
  - speed up or slow down the pace
  - introduce dramatic pauses.

Acting the Lines

- Actors can use movement to highlight Shakespeare's meaning. This can include:
  - facial expressions
  - hand gestures
  - movement around the stage
  - interacting with other characters
  - using props.

> ### Key Point
>
> You need to show your understanding of Shakespeare's writing by explaining how it should be performed.

Writing about Performance

- It is vital, when explaining how an actor should perform, that you link your ideas closely to the text and provide clear, analytical reasons.

ROSALIND	[Aside to CELIA] I will speak to him, like a saucy lackey and under that habit play the knave with him. – Do you hear, forester?
ORLANDO	Very well: what would you?
ROSALIND	I pray you, what is't o'clock?
ORLANDO	You should ask me what time o'day: there's no clock in the forest.
ROSALIND	Then there is no true lover in the forest; else sighing every minute and groaning every hour would detect the lazy foot of Time as well as a clock.
ORLANDO	And why not the swift foot of Time? Had not that been as proper?
ROSALIND	By no means, sir: Time travels in divers paces with divers persons. I'll tell you who Time ambles withal, who Time trots withal, who Time gallops withal and who he stands still withal.

Rosalind addressing Celia is private, so she should use her normal voice. When speaking as Ganymede to Orlando, it should be exaggeratedly masculine (like a 'saucy lackey') to create humour. She could try to walk in a manly way, and clap her arm around Orlando's shoulders like mates when she asks him the time.

Orlando should seem surprised as Rosalind/Ganymede and Celia have been secretly watching him.

He should find Ganymede slightly strange or puzzling, to show that Rosalind's performance isn't perfect.

It should be clear to the audience that she is making fun of Orlando's romantic side. She could emphasise the verbs 'sighing' and 'groaning', perhaps looking over her shoulder at Celia to get a laugh. When she refers to there being 'no true lover', she could pause between each word, accompanied by a tap on his chest with her finger, as if she is challenging him (because Rosalind wants to test his love).

This could be at a fast pace, to build up the **witty repartee** between himself and Rosalind. The word 'swift' could be emphasised to show he is trying to contradict Ganymede's ideas.

Her final speech should be spoken at a quicker pace and with a smile, perhaps closer to her natural voice because she is showing us her witty side. To make it more comic and to portray Ganymede, she could also do a comic **mime** for the different ways time moves.

Quick Test

1. What is it possible for an actor do with his or her voice when performing lines?
2. How can he or she add movement in order to emphasise the meaning of their lines?
3. When writing about performance, what must you link all of your ideas closely to?
4. When writing about Performance, what are you trying to show you understand?

Key Words

pace
wit
repartee
mime

1 Look at this task on writing to inform. Give yourself 45 minutes (including 10 minutes planning time).

You work for the local tourist board. They want you to create a guide to the town, informing tourists about where they can go and what they can do. Read the memo sent to you by the head of the tourist board:

> Create a guide for the town so tourists know where to go and what to do. Try to include:
> - sites of historical or cultural interest
> - leisure activities
> - places to relax, eat and drink
> - places to stay.

Write your guide, informing tourists about what they can do in your local town.

a) First copy the boxes below and note the different information you want to give to tourists about the town. [8]

Sites of historical or cultural interest	
Leisure activities	
Places to relax, eat and drink	
Places to stay	

b) Now write your guide. [30]

2 Look at this task on writing to explain. Give yourself 45 minutes (including 10 minutes planning time).

Your school is holding an environment awareness week. You have been asked to give a speech in assembly, explaining how students contribute to the world's pollution and how they can reduce their impact. Read the details given to you by the head teacher:

> Thanks for taking part in the environment awareness week and agreeing to give the key speech in assembly. I want you to explain to the students how their daily lives pollute the planet, and how they can start helping the environment instead. Remember to give the students plenty of facts and details. They need to understand what causes pollution and how they can change their lives in order to have a more positive effect on the world.

Write your speech, explaining to the student body how they cause pollution and what they can do to change this.

a) First create a plan for your speech using the following headings:

1. Introduction
2. Point 1 (For example: Getting a lift to school when it would only take ten minutes to walk = pollution from car exhaust fumes and more use of the planet's natural resources.)
3. Point 2
4. Point 3
5. Point 4
6. End statement [10]

b) Now write your speech. [30]

3 **Look at this task on writing to describe. Give yourself 45 minutes (including 10 minutes planning time).**

The school recently took part in a local carnival in order to raise money for charity. One hundred students from the school dressed up, gave sweets to the people lining the streets, and collected money in charity buckets. The head teacher has asked you to describe the day's events for the school newsletter. He has given you this brief:

Describe the school's participation in the local carnival. It was a great day, so try to get across the fun atmosphere. Include what our students dressed up as, what other costumes people were wearing, how you felt handing out sweets and collecting for charity, and how you felt at the end of the carnival.

Write your article for the school newsletter, describing your experience at the carnival for students and parents.

a) Create a plan for your article using the following headings:

1. Three of the best costumes
2. Three different feelings I had during the day (and why)
3. Four interesting words or phrases to describe the carnival atmosphere [10]

b) Now write your article. [30]

Read this extract from *As You Like It*, Act 1 scene 2, after Orlando and Rosalind have met and become attracted to each other. She and Celia congratulate Orlando on his success in the wrestling match.

ORLANDO	I am more proud to be Sir Rowland's son,
	His youngest son; and would not change that calling,
	To be adopted heir to Frederick.
ROSALIND	My father loved Sir Rowland as his soul,
	And all the world was of my father's mind:
	Had I before known this young man his son,
	I should have given him tears unto entreaties,
	Ere he should thus have ventured.
CELIA	Gentle cousin,
	Let us go thank him and encourage him:
	My father's rough and envious disposition
	Sticks me at heart. Sir, you have well deserved:
	If you do keep your promises in love
	But justly, as you have exceeded all promise,
	Your mistress shall be happy.
ROSALIND	Gentleman, *[Giving him a chain from her neck]*
	Wear this for me, one out of suits with fortune,
	That could give more, but that her hand lacks means.
	Shall we go, coz?
CELIA	Ay. Fare you well, fair gentleman.
ORLANDO	Can I not say, I thank you? My better parts
	Are all thrown down, and that which here stands up
	Is but a quintain, a mere lifeless block.
ROSALIND	He calls us back: my pride fell with my fortunes;
	I'll ask him what he would. Did you call, sir?
	Sir, you have wrestled well and overthrown
	More than your enemies.
CELIA	Will you go, coz?
ROSALIND	Have with you. Fare you well.
	Exeunt ROSALIND and CELIA
ORLANDO	What passion hangs these weights upon my tongue?
	I cannot speak to her, yet she urged conference.
	O poor Orlando, thou art overthrown!
	Or Charles or something weaker masters thee.

Using the extract opposite, answer the following questions.

1 **Character**

   a) How can we tell that Rosalind is unhappy after the exile of her father? [2]

   b) Using a quotation as evidence, how is this extract typical of Orlando's loyalty? [2]

   c) Using a quotation as evidence, how is this extract typical of Orlando's romantic nature? [2]

   d) How can you tell that Celia dislikes her father's behaviour? [2]

2 **Themes**

   a) How does Rosalind's speech show the theme of love?

      Select a quotation as evidence and explain your choice. [2]

   b) How does Orlando's speech show the theme of love?

      Select a quotation as evidence and explain your choice. [2]

   c) Where does Orlando fail to speak when he should? [2]

   d) How does this extract show the theme of injustice? [2]

3 **Language**

   a) How is emotive language used to illustrate the feelings of Rosalind and Orlando towards their fathers? [2]

   b) How does Orlando use rhetorical speech to show the confusion caused by love? [2]

   c) What does Celia's descriptive speech show about her thoughts and feelings? [2]

   d) When Rosalind says, 'My pride fell with my fortunes,' which two situations is she talking about? [2]

4 **Performance**

   a) How could an actor playing Rosalind use her performance to convey the meaning of the lines in this scene? [4]

   b) How could an actor playing Orlando use his performance to convey the meaning of the lines in this scene? [4]

Romeo and Juliet – Key Characters

You must be able to:

- Explain what the main characters are like and how they change
- Explain how Shakespeare shows this through his writing.

Romeo

- Romeo is romantic, first falling in love with Rosaline and then moving on to Juliet. This **metaphor** suggests he worships love and Juliet:

> ROMEO   My lips, two blushing pilgrims, ready stand.

- He is uninterested in the Capulet–Montague feud, and reacts to the news of the fight with a weary attitude. He does not need an answer to his question because he is used to the violence between the families.

> ROMEO   What fray was here?
>
> Yet tell me not, for I have heard it all.

- He has visions of misfortune ahead. The stars are used to **symbolise** fate; the words 'fear' and 'consequence' sound ominous:

> ROMEO   I fear too early, for my mind misgives
>
> Some consequence yet hanging in the stars.

- He is devoted to Juliet and feels he cannot live without her. As he plans his suicide, he pledges to stay forever by Juliet's side:

> ROMEO   O here
>
> Will I set up my everlasting rest
>
> And shake the yoke of inauspicious stars
>
> From this world-wearied flesh.

- During the play, Romeo is full of conflicting feelings about love. These are sometimes conveyed through **oxymorons**:

> ROMEO   Feather of lead, bright smoke, cold fire, sick health...
>
> This love feel I that feel no love in this.
>
> How silver-sweet sound lovers' tongues by night,
>
> Like softest music to attending tears.

> **Key Point**
>
> Use quotations from the text in order to justify your opinions about the characters.

Juliet

- Juliet falls in love with Romeo. Using metaphor, she pledges herself to Romeo completely and offers to make him her master:

JULIET	And all my fortunes at thy foot I'll lay,
	And follow thee my lord throughout the world.

Alliteration highlights her commitment to Romeo.

- She worries things are happening too fast. The **repetition** of the **adverb** 'too' and the **simile** here emphasise the idea of rushing into things:

JULIET	It is too rash, too unadvis'd, too sudden,
	Too like the lightning.

With this simile, Juliet compares their love to lightning – quick, sudden and potentially dangerous.

- She is quite strong minded: getting married in secret, willing to face her father's anger by refusing to marry Paris, and faking her own death.
- Here she repeats her father's words, adding the negative 'not', to emphasise her refusal. This is added to by the cheeky religious exclamation 'and [Saint] Peter too':

JULIET	Now by Saint Peter's Church, and Peter too,
	He shall not make me there a joyful bride.

Key Point

Think about the ways in which different themes are explored through the characters.

- At the start, Juliet has a good relationship with her parents, especially her father:

CAPULET	She is the hopeful lady of my earth...
	My will to her consent is but a part.

Capulet clearly dotes on his daughter.

- However, by the middle of the play and her refusal to marry Paris, they treat her very badly:

CAPULET	Hang thee young baggage, disobedient wretch!
	... never after look me in the face.
	Speak not, reply not, do not answer me.
	My fingers itch.

Capulet's commands to Juliet highlight his anger.

Quick Test

1. How is Romeo different from the other Montagues?
2. What subject is Romeo often talking or thinking about?
3. What contrasts are there in Juliet's character?
4. How does Juliet's relationship with her parents change during the play?

Key Words

metaphor
symbolise
oxymoron
repetition
adverb
simile

Romeo and Juliet – Themes

You must be able to:

- Identify the key themes of the play
- Explain how Shakespeare uses characters and events to explore these themes.

Quick Recall Quiz

Love

- Love is portrayed in *Romeo and Juliet* through:
  - Romeo's early **melancholy** over his **unrequited** love for Rosaline:

ROMEO	Not mad but bound more than a madman is:
	Shut up in prison, kept without my food,
	Whipp'd and tormented…

Romeo compares his unrequited love for Juliet to being in prison and being tortured.

> **Key Point**
>
> Think about how different themes are explored through characters and events.

  - The way Romeo and Juliet fall in love at first sight, with their first lines together forming a sonnet (Act 1 scene 5, lines 92–105).
  - Their willingness to risk their family's anger for love:

JULIET	Deny thy father and refuse thy name.
	Or if thou wilt not, be but sworn my love
	And I'll no longer be a Capulet.

  - The idea that they are **fated** to love and die together:

CHORUS	From forth the fatal loins of these two foes
	A pair of star-cross'd lovers take their life.

Alliteration emphasises their love and fate.

  - The way they die for love:

JULIET	O happy dagger.
	This is thy sheath. There rust, and let me die.

Conflict

- The theme of conflict is presented through the Capulet and Montague families.
- The play begins by telling us the family feud has gone on for years:

CHORUS	From ancient grudge break to new mutiny,
	Where civil blood makes civil hands unclean.

- After the orders of Prince Escalus, the Capulet parents try to calm the situation down:

TYBALT	'Tis he, that villain Romeo.
CAPULET	Content thee, gentle coz, let him alone.

- Their failure to calm the situation is seen in the fight between Romeo, Tybalt and Mercutio, which has such terrible consequences for all three:

TYBALT	Boy, this shall not excuse the injuries
	That thou hast done me, therefore turn and draw.

- The death of Tybalt fills the Capulets with hatred:

LADY CAPULET	I beg for justice, which thou, Prince, must give.
	Romeo slew Tybalt. Romeo must not live.

- The conflict is only resolved through the loss of their children:

PRINCE	Capulet, Montague,
	See what a scourge is laid upon your hate,
	That heaven finds means to kill your joys with love.

Key Point

When analysing the text, remember to comment on the effects achieved by Shakespeare's language choices.

Short, simple sentences are used for effect and emphasis.

Time

- The whole storyline takes place in less than a week, and everything is rushed: Romeo and Juliet's wooing and wedding, the preparations for the marriage to Paris, and Juliet's funeral. Part of the effect of this is to suggest that these events are fated and unstoppable:

CHORUS	The fearful passage of their death-mark'd love.

- We also see time in terms of coincidence and error:
  - Romeo goes to the Capulet ball because Rosaline may be there but he meets Juliet instead.
  - The Friar's letter to Romeo goes astray.
  - Juliet does not wake until Romeo has killed himself:

FRIAR	Ah what an unkind hour
	Is guilty of this lamentable chance?

Quick Test

1. Which key characters represent love?
2. How is the theme of conflict represented?
3. How does the theme of time affect Romeo and Juliet's lives?
4. How does the idea of fate link to the themes of love, conflict and time?

Key Words

melancholy
unrequited
fate

Romeo and Juliet – Language

Quick Recall Quiz

You must be able to:

- Analyse how Shakespeare uses language to present character and theme
- Analyse how Shakespeare uses language to achieve a response from his audience.

Rhetorical Speech

- An example of rhetorical speech is where Lord Capulet tries to force Juliet to marry Paris:

> CAPULET   Soft! Take me with you, take me with you, wife.
>
> How! Will she none? Doth she not give us thanks?
>
> Is she not proud? Doth she not count her blest,
>
> Unworthy as she is, that we have wrought
>
> So worthy a gentleman to be her bridegroom?
>
> [...]
>
> How now, how now, chop-logic! What is this?
>
> 'Proud,' and 'I thank you,' and 'I thank you not;'
>
> And yet 'not proud,' mistress minion, you,
>
> Thank me no thankings, nor, proud me no prouds,
>
> But fettle your fine joints 'gainst Thursday next,
>
> To go with Paris to Saint Peter's Church,
>
> Or I will drag thee on a hurdle thither.

> **Key Point**
>
> Rhetorical speech is used to persuade, motivate or convey meaning.

Rhetorical questions are used to try to persuade Juliet to marry.

An imperative is used. This shows Capulet trying to control Juliet.

- The combination of exclamation marks and question marks shows Capulet's anger and confusion.
- Capulet uses rhetorical questions to suggest Juliet is ungrateful.
- He uses contrast (unworthy/worthy) to suggest Juliet should feel honoured to marry Paris.
- He repeats and **mimics** Juliet's words to suggest she is talking nonsense.
- **Repetition** and **imperatives** show that his word is final.
- Capulet uses threat and insult to scare and shame her.

Descriptive Speech

- One example of descriptive language in *Romeo and Juliet* is where Friar Lawrence is describing his plants:

> FRIAR LAWRENCE   Within the infant rind of this small flower
>
> Poison hath residence and medicine power:
>
> For this, being smelt, with that part cheers each part;
>
> Being tasted, slays all senses with the heart.

> **Key Point**
>
> Descriptive speech is used to help the audience imagine a scene or understand how a character sees a situation.

> Two such opposed kings encamp them still
> In man as well as herbs, grace and rude will;
> And where the worser is predominant,
> Full soon the canker death eats up that plant.

- Shakespeare uses the **extended metaphor** of the plant to explore the Capulet–Montague conflict.
- The Friar talks about two opposites: medicine and poison.
- Shakespeare is linking this to love and hate, as the Friar will come to hope that Romeo and Juliet's love will stop the family feud.
- The last line suggests that poison is stronger, however, reminding us that the lovers are fated to die.

Emotive Speech

- Here is an example of Shakespeare using emotive language, when Romeo enters Juliet's tomb:

ROMEO	For here lies Juliet, and her beauty makes
	This vault a feasting presence full of light.
	Death, lie thou there, by a dead man interr'd.
	[...] O, how may I
	Call this a lightning? O my love! my wife!
	Death, that hath suck'd the honey of thy breath,
	Hath had no power yet upon thy beauty:
	Thou art not conquer'd; beauty's ensign yet
	Is crimson in thy lips and in thy cheeks,
	And death's pale flag is not advanced there.

Personification of death.

Use of the word 'honey' emphasises Juliet's sweetness and beauty.

Personification of death.

- The repetition of 'beauty' shows his love and reluctance to accept that she is dead.
- This is emphasised by the use of metaphors to show the power of her beauty.
- Shakespeare uses **personification** of death to show Romeo's horror at Juliet's passing, but (with imagery of battle) also his belief that she is stronger than death.
- A **rhetorical question** and **exclamations** show his shock and grief, with repetition of 'my' to emphasise his feelings of loss.

> ### Key Point
>
> Emotive speech is used to convey powerful emotions, either to show what a character is feeling or to get the audience to share a character's feelings.

Quick Test

1. What does Shakespeare use rhetorical language for?
2. What is the point of descriptive language?
3. How is emotive language used by Shakespeare?
4. What different technical features of language should you look out for?

Key Words

mimicry
repetition
imperative
extended metaphor
personification
rhetorical question
exclamation

Romeo and Juliet – Performance

Quick Recall Quiz

You must be able to:

- Explain how characters' lines should be spoken in order to convey their meaning
- Explain how actors and actresses can perform in order to highlight the meaning of the lines.

Speaking the Lines

- When delivering their lines, actors can do various things with their voices in order to make Shakespeare's meaning clear. For example:
  - raise and lower volume
  - alter the tone of voice
  - speed up or slow down the pace
  - introduce dramatic pauses.

Acting the Lines

- Actors can also use movement to highlight Shakespeare's meaning. This can include:
  - facial expressions
  - hand gestures
  - movement around the stage
  - interacting with other characters
  - using props.

Key Point

You need to show your understanding of Shakespeare's writing by explaining how it should be performed.

Writing about Performance

- It is vital, when explaining how an actor should perform, that you link your ideas closely to the text and provide clear, analytical reasons:

LADY CAPULET	What noise is here?
NURSE	O lamentable day!
LADY CAPULET	What is the matter?
NURSE	Look, look! O heavy day!
LADY CAPULET	O me, O me! My child, my only life,
	Revive, look up, or I will die with thee!
	Help, help! Call help.
Enter CAPULET	
CAPULET	For shame, bring Juliet forth; her lord is come.

When Lady Capulet addresses the Nurse, she should sound annoyed, thinking that the Nurse is making a fuss as usual. To emphasise this, she could sweep into the room not really noticing Juliet.

When she realises what has happened, she could stop still to show her shock. She should put long pauses between the repeated exclamations to show her shock, then take hold of Juliet and add more desperation and urgency to her voice as she calls for help.

NURSE	She's dead, deceased, she's dead; alack the day!
LADY CAPULET	Alack the day, she's dead, she's dead, she's dead!
CAPULET	Ha! let me see her: out, alas! She's cold:
	Her blood is settled, and her joints are stiff;
	Life and these lips have long been separated:
	Death lies on her like an untimely frost
	Upon the sweetest flower of all the field.

Where she repeats 'she's dead', she should sound hysterical, perhaps even angry or guilty as she sees Lord Capulet or herself as partly to blame.

When Lord Capulet enters, he should seem dominant and angry (as we saw him when he ordered Juliet to marry Paris) as if he is worried that Juliet is going to disobey him. When he realises she is dead and exclaims 'Ha!' he could put his hand to his mouth and sound almost in pain. All his children are now dead. When he says 'let me see her,' he could gently move his wife away from Juliet's body.

His subsequent movements and voice could contrast with Lady Capulet's hysteria by being slower and quieter to show his shock.

Capulet should sound loving and sad as he describes Juliet's beauty, perhaps stroking her arms and face to emphasise the imagery in his words.

Quick Test

1. What can an actor or actress do with his or her voice when performing lines?
2. How can he or she add movement in order to emphasise the meaning of the lines?
3. When writing about performance, what must you link all of your ideas closely to?
4. When writing about Performance, what are you trying to show you understand?

Key Words

pause
exclamation
imagery

As You Like It, **Act 1 scene 1, lines 37–72. Act 4 scene 3, lines 131–162**

In the first extract, Orlando and Oliver argue. In the second extract, Oliver relates how his brother saved him from a lion.

1 In these extracts, how does the language used show the change that has taken place in the brothers' relationship during the play? Support your ideas by referring to both extracts.   **[18]**

Extract A: Act 1 scene 1, lines 37–72

ORLANDO	Shall I keep your hogs and eat husks with them? What prodigal portion have I spent, that I should come to such penury?
OLIVER	Know you where your are, sir? 40
ORLANDO	O, sir, very well; here in your orchard.
OLIVER	Know you before whom, sir?
ORLANDO	Ay, better than him I am before knows me. I know you are my eldest brother; and, in the gentle condition of blood, you should so know me. The courtesy of nations allows you my better, in that you are the first-born; but the same tradition takes not away my blood, were there twenty brothers betwixt us: I have as much of my father in me as you; albeit, I confess, your coming before me is 50 nearer to his reverence.
OLIVER	What, boy! *[Strikes him]*
ORLANDO	Come, come, elder brother, you are too young in this. *[Putting a wrestler's grip on him]*
OLIVER	Wilt thou lay hands on me, villain?
ORLANDO	I am no villain; I am the youngest son of Sir Rowland de Boys; he was my father, and he is thrice a villain that says such a father begot villains. Wert thou not my brother, I would not take this hand from thy throat till this other had pulled out thy tongue for saying so: thou hast railed on thyself. 60
ADAM	Sweet masters, be patient: for your father's remembrance, be at accord.
OLIVER	Let me go, I say.
ORLANDO	I will not, till I please: you shall hear me. My father charged you in his will to give me good education: you have trained me like a peasant, obscuring and hiding from me all gentleman-like qualities. The spirit of my father grows strong in me, and I will no longer endure it: therefore allow me such exercises as may become a gentleman, or 70 give me the poor allottery my father left me by testament; with that I will go buy my fortunes.

Extract B: Act 4 scene 3, lines 131–162

OLIVER	Twice did he turn his back and purposed so;
	But kindness, nobler ever than revenge,
	And nature, stronger than his just occasion,
	Made him give battle to the lioness,
	Who quickly fell before him: in which hurtling
	From miserable slumber I awaked.
CELIA	Are you his brother?
ROSALIND	Wast you he rescued?
CELIA	Was't you that did so oft contrive to kill him?
OLIVER	'Twas I; but 'tis not I. I do not shame
	To tell you what I was, since my conversion
	So sweetly tastes, being the thing I am.
ROSALIND	But, for the bloody napkin?
OLIVER	By and by.
	When from the first to last betwixt us two
	Tears our recountments had most kindly bathed,
	As how I came into that desert place:–
	In brief, he led me to the gentle duke,
	Who gave me fresh array and entertainment,
	Committing me unto my brother's love;
	Who led me instantly unto his cave,
	There stripp'd himself, and here upon his arm
	The lioness had torn some flesh away,
	Which all this while had bled; and now he fainted
	And cried, in fainting, upon Rosalind.
	Brief, I recover'd him, bound up his wound;
	And, after some small space, being strong at heart,
	He sent me hither, stranger as I am,
	To tell this story, that you might excuse
	His broken promise, and to give this napkin
	Dyed in his blood unto the shepherd youth
	That he in sport doth call his Rosalind.

140

150

160

Read this extract from *Romeo and Juliet*, Act 3 scene 5, after Romeo and Juliet have spent the night together. It is morning and the two lovers know that, as punishment for killing Tybalt, Romeo must leave Verona or be executed.

JULIET	Then, window, let day in, and let life out.
ROMEO	Farewell, farewell! one kiss, and I'll descend.
	He goeth down
JULIET	Art thou gone so? Love, Lord, ay, husband, friend!
	I must hear from thee every day in the hour,
	For in a minute there are many days:
	O, by this count I shall be much in years
	Ere I again behold my Romeo!
ROMEO	Farewell!
	I will omit no opportunity
	That may convey my greetings, love, to thee.
JULIET	O think'st thou we shall ever meet again?
ROMEO	I doubt it not; and all these woes shall serve
	For sweet discourses in our time to come.
JULIET	O God, I have an ill-divining soul!
	Methinks I see thee, now thou art below,
	As one dead in the bottom of a tomb:
	Either my eyesight fails, or thou look'st pale.
ROMEO	And trust me, love, in my eye so do you:
	Dry sorrow drinks our blood. Adieu, adieu!
	Exit
JULIET	O Fortune, Fortune! All men call thee fickle:
	If thou art fickle, what dost thou with him
	That is renown'd for faith? Be fickle, Fortune,
	For then, I hope, thou wilt not keep him long,
	But send him back.

Using the extract opposite, answer the following questions.

1 **Character**

    a) How can we tell that Romeo and Juliet are in love? [2]

    b) Using a quotation as evidence, how does this scene show Juliet will miss Romeo? [2]

    c) Using a quotation as evidence, how does this scene show that Romeo is confident they will be together? [2]

    d) How can you tell that Juliet is less optimistic about the situation than Romeo? [2]

2 **Themes**

    a) How does Romeo's speech illustrate the theme of love?

    Select a quotation as evidence and explain your choice. [2]

    b) How does Juliet's speech illustrate the theme of time?

    Select a quotation as evidence and explain your choice. [2]

    c) In this scene, Romeo suffers from conflicting feelings: he wants to stay, yet knows he must go.

    Where can you find evidence of this? [2]

    d) How does this scene illustrate the theme of fate? [2]

3 **Language**

    a) How is emotive language used to show Juliet's love for Romeo? [2]

    b) How does Juliet use rhetorical speech to show her feelings about her unfortunate relationship with Romeo? [2]

    c) How does Juliet's descriptive speech show her fears about the future? [2]

    d) When Romeo says, 'Dry sorrow drinks our blood,' what is Shakespeare trying to convey? [2]

4 **Performance**

    a) How could an actor use her performance of Juliet in order to convey the meaning of the lines in this scene? [4]

    b) How could an actor use his performance of Romeo in order to convey the meaning of the lines in this scene? [4]

Macbeth – Key Characters

You must be able to:

- Explain what the main characters are like and how they change
- Explain how Shakespeare shows this through his writing.

Macbeth

- Lady Macbeth tells us that Macbeth is a good man:

> LADY MACBETH ...thy nature:
> It is too full o' th' milk of human kindness.

- Macbeth's indecision about killing the King shows a **conscience**:

> MACBETH He's here in double trust:
> First as I am his kinsman and his subject,
> Strong both against the deed; then, as his host,

- Macbeth is very **ambitious**:

> MACBETH *[Aside]* Two truths are told,
> As happy prologues to the swelling act
> Of the imperial theme.

- He is easily **manipulated** by his wife:

> MACBETH Prithee, peace.
> I dare do all that may become a man.

- At the start of the play, Macbeth appears to be brave and is respected by others, but he later loses that respect:

> CAPTAIN For brave Macbeth (well he deserves that name).
> DUNCAN O valiant cousin! Worthy gentleman!

> MACDUFF I am not treacherous.
> MALCOLM But Macbeth is.

Here the **adjective** 'treacherous' is very different from adjectives like 'valiant' and 'worthy' from earlier in the play.

- Macbeth becomes cruel and vicious.
- In contrast to the 'milk of human kindness' **metaphor**, here Macbeth is vindictive: killing Macduff's whole family in revenge for him leaving Scotland:

> MACBETH The castle of Macduff I will surprise;
> Seize upon Fife; give to th'edge o' th' sword
> His wife, his babes, and all unfortunate souls
> That trace him in his line.

Macbeth's cruelty is emphasised by the **list** of his innocent victims.

Key Point

Use quotations from the text in order to justify your opinions about the characters.

- Macbeth begins to lose control of his mind. In contrast to his bravery on the battlefield, here the **repetition** of the exclamation 'Hence!' makes him seem terrified:

| MACBETH | If trembling I inhabit then, protest me The baby of a girl. Hence horrible shadow! Unreal mock'ry, hence! |

His terror is emphasised by comparing himself to a baby.

Lady Macbeth

- At the start of the play, Lady Macbeth seems to be confident and manipulative:

| LADY MACBETH | What beast was't then, That made you break this enterprise to me? When you durst do it, then you were a man. |

- She is ambitious and willing to be as cruel as is necessary to achieve her aims:

| LADY MACBETH | Come you spirits That tend on mortal thoughts, unsex me here, And fill me, from the crown to the toe, top-full Of direst cruelty. |

- Lady Macbeth loses control of her mind. Compared with earlier in the play, when she was direct in her aims, using repetition and metaphor to emphasise her points, by the end her mind is wandering. Her lack of mental control in emphasised by pauses and short sentences to show her sudden changes in thought.

| LADY MACBETH | One; two: why, then 'tis time to do't. – Hell is murky. – Fie, my Lord, fie! a soldier, and afeard? |

- She becomes tortured by the cruelty of her past actions:

| LADY MACBETH | Here's the smell of blood still: all the perfumes of Arabia will not sweeten this little hand. |

> **Key Point**
>
> Both Macbeth and Lady Macbeth change over the course of the play.

Where once she prayed to increase her 'cruelty', here she is horrified by the 'smell of blood' knowing that she is damned ('will not sweeten').

> **Key Words**
>
> **conscience**
> **ambition**
> **manipulate**
> **adjective**
> **metaphor**
> **list**
> **repetition**

> **Quick Test**
>
> 1. Suggest one of the good things about Macbeth's character at the start of the play.
> 2. In what ways does Macbeth's character deteriorate?
> 3. Where does Lady Macbeth seem stronger than Macbeth?
> 4. How is Lady Macbeth different by the end of the play?

Macbeth – Themes

You must be able to:

- Identify the key themes of the play
- Explain how Shakespeare uses characters and events to show these themes.

Quick Recall Quiz

Ambition and Power

- Macbeth and Lady Macbeth reveal their **ambition** through:
  - their reactions to the witches' prophesies:

MACBETH	The Prince of Cumberland! – That is a step On which I must fall down, or else o'erleap, For in my way it lies. Stars, hide your fires! Let not light see my black and deep desires.

  - the things they do to gain power:

LADY MACBETH	If he do bleed, I'll gild the faces of the grooms withal, For it must seem their guilt.

  - how they become **corrupted** by power and will do anything to keep it:

MACDUFF	Each new morn, New widows howl, new orphans cry, new sorrows Strike heaven on the face.

Evil and Witchcraft

- The theme of evil and witchcraft is presented through the witches:

FIRST WITCH	Round about the cauldron go; In the poison'd entrails throw.

- The theme is also explored through the way in which Macbeth and Lady Macbeth come under the witches' influence.
- When Macbeth says 'So foul and fair a day I have not seen' in Act 1 scene 3, he is repeating the witches' words from Act I scene 1.
- Lady Macbeth echoes the words of the second witch who says she has been 'killing swine' (Act 1 scene 3), in this speech:

LADY MACBETH	when in swinish sleep Their drenched natures lie, as in a death, What cannot you and I perform upon Th'unguarded Duncan?'

> ### Key Point
>
> When analysing text, remember to comment on the effects achieved by Shakespeare's language choices.

Manipulation

- Lady Macbeth's behaviour is an obvious example of **manipulation**:

> LADY MACBETH   Was the hope drunk,
>   Wherein you dress'd yourself? Hath it slept since?

- We also see this theme in the way the witches convince Macbeth to deceive himself:

> MACBETH   I will not be afraid of death and bane,
>   Till Birnam forest come to Dunsinane.

Madness

- The theme of madness is shown through Macbeth's disturbed mind on the night of the murder:

> MACBETH   Methought, I heard a voice cry, Sleep no more!
>   Macbeth does murder Sleep!

- Later, we see his erratic behaviour at the banquet:

> MACBETH   Avaunt! and quit my sight! let the earth hide thee!
>   Thy bones are marrowless, thy blood is cold;

- Lady Macbeth displays madness before her death:

> DOCTOR   Unnatural deeds
>   Do breed unnatural troubles: infected minds […]

Natural Order

- When Macbeth kills the King and takes his place (instead of Duncan's eldest son, Malcolm), he upsets the natural order and the '**Divine Right** of Kings'. This is seen in:
  - descriptions of the weather (the opening stage direction foreshadows the violent events: 'Thunder and lightning')
  - the powerful presence of the witches
  - the way in which Macbeth's and Lady Macbeth's minds are shown to be disturbed:

> LADY MACBETH   You lack the season of all natures, sleep.

> **Key Point**
>
> Think about how different themes are explored through characters and events.

> **Quick Test**
>
> 1. Which key characters represent ambition and power?
> 2. Which characters manipulate Macbeth?
> 3. What happens to Lady Macbeth at the end of the play?
> 4. In what way has the natural order been disturbed in the play?

> **Key Words**
>
> ambition
> corruption
> manipulation
> **Divine Right**

Macbeth – Language

You must be able to:

- Analyse how Shakespeare uses language to present character and theme
- Analyse how Shakespeare uses language to achieve a response from his audience.

Rhetorical Speech

- Lady Macbeth uses **rhetorical** speech when she tries to persuade Macbeth to kill the king:

MACBETH	We will proceed no further in this business: He hath honour'd me of late; and I have bought Golden opinions from all sorts of people, Which would be worn now in their newest gloss, Not cast aside so soon.
LADY MACBETH	Was the hope drunk Wherein you dress'd yourself? Hath it slept since? And wakes it now, to look so green and pale At what it did so freely? From this time Such I account thy love. Art thou afeard To be the same in thine own act and valour As thou art in desire? Wouldst thou have that Which thou esteem'st the ornament of life, And live a coward in thine own esteem, Letting 'I dare not' wait upon 'I would,' Like the poor cat i' the adage?

Rhetorical questions.

Simile used to mock Macbeth.

> **Key Point**
>
> Rhetorical speech is used to persuade, motivate or convey meaning.

- Macbeth begins with a clear statement to show he is in control.
- He uses formal but **euphemistic** phrasing ('this business') to suggest he is in charge and dislikes the plan.
- He uses an **extended metaphor** linked to wealth to suggest he is satisfied with the life he has.
- Lady Macbeth uses **personification** and rhetorical questions to display anger with Macbeth and to get him to think about his decision.
- She uses emotional blackmail ('Such I account thy love') and insults him ('afeard').
- She mocks him by comparing him to a fearful cat in a proverb.

Descriptive Speech

- One example of Macbeth using **descriptive** language occurs when he learns that Fleance has escaped:

MACBETH	Then comes my fit again: I had else been perfect, Whole as the marble, founded as the rock, As broad and general as the casing air:

Similes using imagery from the natural world to show strength.

> But now I am cabin'd, cribb'd, confined, bound in
> To saucy doubts and fears. But Banquo's safe?
> [...]
> There the grown serpent lies; the worm that's fled
> Hath nature that in time will venom breed,
> No teeth for the present.

Alliteration is used for emphasis.

Metaphor highlights Macbeth's paranoia.

- Shakespeare uses **similes** to show how important Banquo and Fleance's deaths are to his feeling of security.
- He then uses a list of **alliterated** verbs to emphasise how he feels at the idea of Fleance's escape.
- He believes Fleance will grow up to take the throne, and this paranoia is shown in the nightmarish metaphor where Fleance is transformed from a harmless worm into a deadly serpent.

Key Point

Descriptive speech is used to help the audience imagine a scene or understand how a character sees a situation.

Emotive Speech

- An example of Shakespeare using **emotive** language occurs when he makes us sympathise with Macduff's grief over the murder of his family:

MACDUFF	All my pretty ones? Did you say all? O hell-kite! All? What, all my pretty chickens and their dam At one fell swoop? [...] O, I could play the woman with mine eyes And braggart with my tongue! But, gentle heavens, Cut short all intermission; front to front Bring thou this fiend of Scotland and myself; Within my sword's length set him; if he 'scape, Heaven forgive him too!

Metaphor compares his wife and children to chickens.

- The repeated questions suggest Macduff cannot believe the news about his family.
- He compares his wife and children to birds, which suggests their vulnerability.
- He compares himself to a woman (rather than a soldier) to convey how weakened he feels.
- The exclamation marks show his feelings turning to anger as he calls Macbeth a fiend and pledges to kill him.

Key Point

Emotive speech is used to convey powerful emotions, either to show what a character is feeling or to get the audience to share a character's feelings.

Key Words

rhetorical
euphemism
extended metaphor
personification
descriptive
simile
alliteration
emotive

Quick Test

1. What does Shakespeare use rhetorical language for?
2. What is the point of descriptive language?
3. How is emotive language used by Shakespeare?
4. What different technical features of language should you look out for?

Macbeth – Performance

Quick Recall Quiz

You must be able to:

- Explain how characters' lines should be spoken in order to convey their meaning
- Explain how actors and actresses can perform in order to highlight the meaning of the lines.

Speaking the Lines

- When delivering their lines, actors can do various things with their voices in order to make Shakespeare's meaning clear. For example:
  - raise and lower volume
  - alter the tone of voice
  - speed up or slow down the **pace**
  - introduce dramatic pauses.

> **Key Point**
>
> You need to show your understanding of Shakespeare's writing by explaining how it should be performed.

Acting the Lines

- Actors can also use movement to highlight Shakespeare's meaning. This can include:
  - facial expressions
  - hand gestures
  - movement around the stage
  - interacting with other characters
  - using props.

Writing about Performance

- It is vital, when explaining how an actor should perform, that you link your ideas closely to the text and provide clear, analytical reasons.

LADY MACBETH Come on; Gentle my lord,

Sleek o'er your rugged looks; be bright and jovial
Among your guests tonight.

MACBETH   So shall I, love; and so, I pray, be you:

> When Lady Macbeth addresses Macbeth she should sound encouraging, as she is trying to get him to look less troubled in front of his guests.

> To emphasise this, she could smile, put her arms around him, and emphasise the **adjectives** 'bright' and 'jovial' to show how she wants him to behave.

> Macbeth should at first seem to follow Lady Macbeth's advice, speaking calmly and warmly as he says, 'So shall I, love'. His face should be more relaxed, in line with his wife's request.

Let your remembrance apply to Banquo;
Present him eminence, both with eye and tongue:
Unsafe the while, that we
Must lave our honours in these flattering streams,
And make our faces vizards to our hearts,
Disguising what they are.

> As his speech continues, he should again show anxiety in his face. This should also appear in his voice, sounding almost terrified in the line 'unsafe the while', then speeding up into a sharp whisper as he talks of how to treat Banquo.

LADY MACBETH   You must leave this.

> In her second speech she could move away from him to express her annoyance with him, and sound more firm and frustrated. She could raise her voice slightly and emphasise the modal verb 'must' to show that she is trying to force him to do what she wants.

MACBETH   O, full of scorpions is my mind, dear wife!
Thou know'st that Banquo, and his Fleance, lives.

> He should sound a little uncontrolled to emphasise how his paranoia about Banquo is affecting him. This should be evident in the metaphor 'full of scorpions is my mind'. He should put his fists to his temples to show mental agony, while raising his voice (particularly the horrible 'scorpions'; perhaps pausing dramatically before this word as he struggles to describe his unnatural feelings) in a way that will worry Lady Macbeth about being overheard. He could look around the room, as if surrounded by enemies, to emphasise his paranoia.

> In his last line, he could turn back to Lady Macbeth and grip her, as if desperate for her to empathise with his fears. He could emphasise 'thou know'st', as if he can't believe she is so calm.

Quick Test

1. What can an actor or actress do with his or her voice when performing lines?
2. How can he or she add movement in order to emphasise the meaning of their lines?
3. When writing about performance, what must you link all of your ideas closely to?
4. When writing about performance, what are you trying to show you understand?

Key Words

pace
adjective
modal verb
metaphor

Romeo and Juliet, Act 1 scene 2, lines 7–34. Act 3 scene 5, lines 158–168 and 175–196

In the first extract, Lord Capulet and Paris are discussing the request that Paris has made to marry Juliet. In the second extract, Lord Capulet is angry with Juliet for refusing to marry Paris.

1 In these extracts, how does the language used show the changes in Lord Capulet's feelings about his daughter, Juliet? Support your ideas by referring to both extracts. **[18]**

Extract A: Act 1 scene 2, lines 7–34

CAPULET   But saying o'er what I have said before:
            My child is yet a stranger in the world;
            She hath not seen the change of fourteen years,
            Let two more summers wither in their pride,   10
            Ere we may think her ripe to be a bride.
PARIS   Younger than she are happy mothers made.
CAPULET   And too soon marr'd are those so early made.
            The earth hath swallow'd all my hopes but she,
            She is the hopeful lady of my earth:
            But woo her, gentle Paris, get her heart,
            My will to her consent is but a part;
            An she agree, within her scope of choice
            Lies my consent and fair according voice.
            This night I hold an old accustom'd feast,   20
            Whereto I have invited many a guest,
            Such as I love; and you, among the store,
            One more, most welcome, makes my number more.
            At my poor house look to behold this night
            Earth-treading stars that make dark heaven light:
            Such comfort as do lusty young men feel
            When well-apparell'd April on the heel
            Of limping winter treads, even such delight
            Among fresh female buds shall you this night
            Inherit at my house; hear all, all see,   30
            And like her most whose merit most shall be:
            Which on more view, of many mine being one
            May stand in number, though in reckoning none,
            Come, go with me.

Extract B: Act 3 scene 5, lines 158–168 and 175–196

JULIET	Good father, I beseech you on my knees,	
	Hear me with patience but to speak a word.	
CAPULET	Hang thee, young baggage! disobedient wretch!	160
	I tell thee what: get thee to church o' Thursday,	
	Or never after look me in the face:	
	Speak not, reply not, do not answer me;	
	My fingers itch. Wife, we scarce thought us blest	
	That God had lent us but this only child;	
	But now I see this one is one too much,	
	And that we have a curse in having her:	
	Out on her, hilding!	
	[...]	
LADY CAPULET	You are too hot.	
CAPULET	God's bread! it makes me mad:	
	Day, night, hour, tide, time, work, play,	
	Alone, in company, still my care hath been	
	To have her match'd: and having now provided	
	A gentleman of noble parentage,	180
	Of fair demesnes, youthful, and nobly train'd,	
	Stuff'd, as they say, with honourable parts,	
	Proportion'd as one's thought would wish a man;	
	And then to have a wretched puling fool,	
	A whining mammet, in her fortune's tender,	
	To answer 'I'll not wed; I cannot love,	
	I am too young; I pray you, pardon me.'	
	But, as you will not wed, I'll pardon you:	
	Graze where you will you shall not house with me:	
	Look to't, think on't, I do not use to jest.	190
	Thursday is near; lay hand on heart, advise:	
	An you be mine, I'll give you to my friend;	
	And you be not, hang! Beg! Starve! Die in the streets!	
	For, by my soul, I'll ne'er acknowledge thee,	
	Nor what is mine shall never do thee good:	
	Trust to't, bethink you; I'll not be forsworn.	
	Exit	

Read this extract from *Macbeth*, Act 3 scene 4, in which Macbeth is confronted by the ghost of Banquo at the banquet.

The GHOST OF BANQUO enters, and sits in MACBETH's place

MACBETH	Here had we now our country's honour roof'd,
	Were the graced person of our Banquo present;
	Who may I rather challenge for unkindness
	Than pity for mischance!
ROSS	His absence, sir,
	Lays blame upon his promise. Please't your highness
	To grace us with your royal company.
MACBETH	The table's full.
LENNOX	Here is a place reserved, sir.
MACBETH	Where?
LENNOX	Here, my good lord. What is't that moves your highness?
MACBETH	Which of you have done this?
LORDS	What, my good lord?
MACBETH	Thou canst not say I did it: never shake
	Thy gory locks at me.
ROSS	Gentlemen, rise: his highness is not well.
LADY MACBETH	Sit, worthy friends: my lord is often thus,
	And hath been from his youth: pray you, keep seat;
	The fit is momentary; upon a thought
	He will again be well: if much you note him,
	You shall offend him and extend his passion:
	Feed, and regard him not. Are you a man?
MACBETH	Ay, and a bold one, that dare look on that
	Which might appal the devil.
LADY MACBETH	O proper stuff!
	This is the very painting of your fear:
	This is the air-drawn dagger which, you said,
	Led you to Duncan. O, these flaws and starts,
	Impostors to true fear, would well become
	A woman's story at a winter's fire,
	Authorized by her grandam. Shame itself!
	Why do you make such faces? When all's done,
	You look but on a stool.
MACBETH	Prithee, see there! Behold! Look! Lo!
	How say you?
	Why, what care I? If thou canst nod, speak too.
	If charnel-houses and our graves must send
	Those that we bury back, our monuments
	Shall be the maws of kites.

GHOST OF BANQUO vanishes

Using the extract opposite, answer the following questions.

1 Character

a) Using a quotation as evidence, how is this scene typical of Lady Macbeth's character?   [2]

b) How does Macbeth seem changed from how he is presented in Act 1?   [2]

c) Select two quotations and explain how they show this changed image of Macbeth.   [2]

d) What emotions are making him react as he does towards Banquo's ghost?   [2]

2 Themes

a) How might this scene show the theme of madness?

Select a quotation as evidence and explain your choice.   [2]

b) How might this scene show the theme of manipulation?

Select a quotation as evidence and explain your choice.   [2]

c) How does this scene include the theme of natural order being disturbed?   [2]

d) How does Macbeth's speech suggest power at the very start of the scene?   [2]

3 Language

a) How is emotive language used to show Macbeth's terror?   [2]

b) How does Lady Macbeth use rhetorical speech when trying to stop Macbeth's outburst?   [2]

c) What does Macbeth's descriptive speech at the end of the scene show about his thoughts and feelings?   [2]

d) How does the language of the noblemen at the banquet show their respect for Macbeth?   [2]

4 Performance

a) How could an actor use her performance of Lady Macbeth in order to convey the meaning of the lines in this scene?   [4]

b) How could an actor use his performance of Macbeth in order to convey the meaning of the lines in this scene?   [4]

Macbeth, Act 1 scene 3, lines 83–107. Act 4 scene 3, lines 1–21 and 31–50

In the first extract, Macbeth and Banquo have just heard the witches' prophecies when Ross and Angus arrive with praise from the king. In the second extract, Malcolm and Macduff are in England discussing how Macbeth is ruining their beloved Scotland.

1 In these extracts, how does the language used show how people's views of Macbeth change during the play? Support your ideas by referring to both extracts. [18]

Extract A: Act 1 scene 3, lines 83–107

BANQUO	Were such things here as we do speak about?
	Or have we eaten on the insane root
	That takes the reason prisoner? 85
MACBETH	Your children shall be kings.
BANQUO	You shall be king.
MACBETH	And thane of Cawdor too: went it not so?
BANQUO	To the selfsame tune and words. Who's here?

Enter ROSS and ANGUS

ROSS	The king hath happily received, Macbeth, 90
	The news of thy success; and when he reads
	Thy personal venture in the rebels' fight,
	His wonders and his praises do contend
	Which should be thine or his: silenced with that,
	In viewing o'er the rest o' the selfsame day, 95
	He finds thee in the stout Norweyan ranks,
	Nothing afeard of what thyself didst make,
	Strange images of death. As thick as hail
	Came post with post; and every one did bear
	Thy praises in his kingdom's great defence, 100
	And pour'd them down before him.
ANGUS	We are sent
	To give thee from our royal master thanks;
	Only to herald thee into his sight,
	Not pay thee.
ROSS	And, for an earnest of a greater honour, 105
	He bade me, from him, call thee thane of Cawdor:
	In which addition, hail, most worthy thane!
	For it is thine.

Extract B: Act 4 scene 3, lines 1–21 and 31–50

MACDUFF   Let us rather
Hold fast the mortal sword, and like good men
Bestride our down-fall'n birthdom: each new morn
New widows howl, new orphans cry, new sorrows
Strike heaven on the face, that it resounds   5
As if it felt with Scotland and yell'd out
Like syllable of dolour.

MALCOLM   What I believe I'll wail,
What know believe, and what I can redress,
As I shall find the time to friend, I will.   10
What you have spoke, it may be so perchance.
This tyrant, whose sole name blisters our tongues,
Was once thought honest: you have loved him well.
He hath not touch'd you yet. I am young;
but something
You may deserve of him through me, and wisdom   15
To offer up a weak poor innocent lamb
To appease an angry god.

MACDUFF   I am not treacherous.

MALCOLM   But Macbeth is.   20
A good and virtuous nature may recoil
In an imperial charge.
[...]

MACDUFF   Bleed, bleed, poor country!
Great tyranny! lay thou thy basis sure,
For goodness dare not cheque thee: wear thou
thy wrongs;
The title is affeer'd! Fare thee well, lord:
I would not be the villain that thou think'st   35
For the whole space that's in the tyrant's grasp,
And the rich East to boot.

MALCOLM   Be not offended:
I speak not as in absolute fear of you.
I think our country sinks beneath the yoke;   40
It weeps, it bleeds; and each new day a gash
Is added to her wounds: I think withal
There would be hands uplifted in my right;
And here from gracious England have I offer
Of goodly thousands: but, for all this,   45
When I shall tread upon the tyrant's head,
Or wear it on my sword, yet my poor country
Shall have more vices than it had before,
More suffer and more sundry ways than ever,
By him that shall succeed.   50

Reading

1. The text below is a leaflet introducing children to gardening. Read the text and answer the questions that follow.

Gardening for Kids

You're never too young to start gardening. It's healthy, it's fun and it's educational.

Getting Kids Involved

If your children are showing an interest in gardening and you want to encourage them, here are some tips for getting them involved:

- Give them their own space – just a small corner of the garden, a few plant pots or a window box will do to start with. The important thing is that it's theirs and they're in charge.
- Let them get dirty! In fact, encourage them. Gardening is all about the earth and kids love digging holes and making mud pies.
- Get the right equipment. Young children won't be able to handle a lot of adult-sized tools, so get them light-weight, smaller tools that they can manage.
- Help them to choose attractive, interesting plants – flowers such as sunflowers or sweet peas, which are easy to grow and colourful, or maybe fruit such as strawberries, which they'll enjoy eating.
- Think about making a scarecrow, digging a pond or putting up a bird table. These all add to the fun of gardening.

Safety First

Children love adventures and we should encourage them to be adventurous, but gardens can be dangerous places. Here's how to keep gardening safe as well as fun.

- Make sure your children wear suitable clothing, including wellies. Hats and sunscreen are absolute essentials on hot summer days.
- Avoid using chemicals. Keep all fertilisers and sprays out of reach of small children and make sure older kids are properly supervised when using them.
- The same goes for tools. Make sure all equipment is stored properly in a locked shed when not in use.
- Make sure all fences and gates are secure.

Fun and Educational Too!

Gardening is fun for all age groups and we never stop learning. Children have a lot to gain from working outdoors and watching things grow:

- **Exercise** – gardening is brilliant physical exercise and you're so busy you hardly notice you're doing it.
- **Discovery** – they'll learn about plants, the weather, the Earth, the environment, nutrition and much more.
- **Creativity** – what could be more creative than planting a tiny seed and helping it to grow into something beautiful?
- **Self-confidence** – their self-confidence will grow with their gardens, as they achieve their goals and enjoy (literally!) the fruits of their labours.

a) Why does the leaflet suggest that children might like to grow:

    i) sunflowers [1]

    ii) strawberries? [1]

b) Why does the writer say that tools should be kept in a locked shed? [2]

c) **i)** What is meant by the expression 'enjoy…the fruits of their labours'? [2]

    ii) Why does the writer add 'literally!' in brackets? [2]

d) The leaflet is divided into three parts ('Getting Kids Involved', 'Safety First' and 'Fun and Educational Too!').

If the following bullet points were added, which sub-heading would each relate to?

Give the sub-heading and explain why you have chosen it.

    i) Cover ponds and pools.

    ii) Responsibility – they'll learn a lot from caring for plants.

    iii) Take them to parks and garden centres to get ideas. [3]

e) How would 'Gardening for Kids' help parents who want to encourage their children to learn about gardening?

You should comment on:

- the sort of advice the leaflet gives
- the language used in the leaflet
- the way the leaflet is organised and presented.

You should aim to write about one side of A4 when answering this question. [10]

Mixed Test-Style Questions

2 Read the text below and answer the questions that follow.

In this extract from *The Secret Garden* by Frances Hodgson Burnett, Mary is playing alone in the garden of the big house where she is living. She is fascinated by a walled garden where nobody has been for ten years. Yesterday she found a key on the ground but could not find a door.

From **The Secret Garden**

by Frances Hodgson Burnett

Mary skipped round all the gardens and round the orchard, resting every few minutes. At length she went to her own special walk and made up her mind to see if she could skip the whole length of it. It was a good long skip and she began slowly, but before she had gone half-way down the path she was so hot and breathless that she was obliged to stop. She did not mind much, because she had already counted up to thirty. She stopped with a little laugh of pleasure, and there, lo and behold, was the robin swaying on a long branch of ivy. He had followed her and he greeted her with a chirp. As Mary skipped toward him she felt something heavy in her pocket strike against her at each jump, and when she saw the robin she laughed again.

'You showed me where the key was yesterday,' she said. 'You ought to show me the door today; but I don't believe you know!'

The robin flew from his swinging spray of ivy on to the top of the wall and he opened his beak and sang a loud, lovely trill, merely to show off. Nothing in the world is quite as adorably lovely as a robin when he shows off – and they are nearly always doing it.

Mary Lennox had heard a great deal about Magic in her Ayah's[1] stories, and she always said that what happened almost at that moment was Magic.

One of the nice little gusts of wind rushed down the walk, and it was a stronger one than the rest. It was strong enough to wave the branches of the trees, and it was more than strong enough to sway the trailing sprays of untrimmed ivy hanging from the wall. Mary had stepped close to the robin, and suddenly the gust of wind swung aside some loose ivy trails, and more suddenly still she jumped toward it and caught it in her hand. This she did because she had seen something under it—a round knob which had been covered by the leaves hanging over it. It was the knob of a door.

She put her hands under the leaves and began to pull and push them aside. Thick as the ivy hung, it nearly all was a loose and swinging curtain, though some had crept over wood and iron. Mary's heart began to thump and her hands to shake a little in her delight and excitement. The robin kept singing and twittering away and tilting his head on one side, as if he were as excited as she was. What was this under her hands which was square and made of iron and which her fingers found a hole in?

It was the lock of the door which had been closed ten years and she put her hand in her pocket, drew out the key and found it fitted the keyhole. She put the key in and turned it. It took two hands to do it, but it did turn.

And then she took a long breath and looked behind her up the long walk to see if anyone was coming. No one was coming. No one ever did come, it seemed, and she took another long breath, because she could not help it, and she held back the swinging curtain of ivy and pushed back the door which opened slowly – slowly.

Then she slipped through it, and shut it behind her, and stood with her back against it, looking about her and breathing quite fast with excitement, and wonder, and delight.

She was standing inside the secret garden.

[1]*Ayah – a nurse or nanny, who looks after children, in India. Mary was brought up in India before being sent to live in England.*

a) How would you describe Mary's mood in the first paragraph?

   Support your answer with evidence from the text.   [3]

b) i) Which **two** things about the robin give the impression that he recognises Mary?   [2]

   ii) Explain how each of these would give that impression.   [2]

c) i) Why has Mary not been able to find the door before now?   [2]

   ii) How is the door knob revealed to her?   [2]

d) How does Frances Hodgson Burnett build up a sense of mystery and excitement in this extract?

   You should comment on:

   * The part played by the robin in finding the door
   * Mary's reaction to finding the door
   * How the writer describes her opening the door and entering the garden.

   You should aim to write about one side of A4 when answering this question.   [10]

Mixed Test-Style Questions

Writing

1 **Spend 45 minutes (including 10 minutes planning time) on this writing task.**

The First Day at School

Your school will be sending home a booklet to all parents of new students who are about to join the school. The head teacher would like it to contain a letter from an older student to new students, advising them on how to settle in at the school.

Below is a brief from the head teacher, outlining what should be included:

> Thank you for agreeing to write to new students. They would benefit from advice on:
> - how to be prepared for school,
> - how to make new friends,
> - how to make a good impression on the first day.

Write your letter.   [30]

2 **Spend 45 minutes (including 10 minutes planning time) on this writing task.**

Anecdote Competition

A creative writing magazine is holding a competition for the best anecdote: a short story about an interesting or funny experience in your life.

Below are the competition details:

> Tell us your best anecdote!
>
> Include plenty of description that allows the reader to imagine people, places, thoughts and feelings.
>
> It can be funny, sad, exciting, scary – anything that will be an interesting read.
>
> As it's an anecdote, don't forget to include lots of your thoughts and feelings at the time.

Write your anecdote.   [30]

You can use this page to make notes for question 2.

(This page will not be marked.)

Time, Place, People

Sequence of events

Things you thought and felt

Shakespeare

Spend 45 minutes on ONE of the Shakespeare tasks below.

1 *Romeo and Juliet,* Act 1 scene 5, lines 53–91 and Act 3 scene 1, lines 55–92

In the first extract, Tybalt wants to start a fight with Romeo at the Capulet party, but is prevented by Lord Capulet. In the second extract, Tybalt tries to start a fight with Romeo. Mercutio gets involved and is killed.

In these extracts, how does Shakespeare present the theme of conflict?

Support your ideas by referring to both of the following extracts. [18]

Act 1 scene 5, lines 53–91

TYBALT	This, by his voice, should be a Montague.
	Fetch me my rapier, boy. What dares the slave
	Come hither, cover'd with an antic face,
	To fleer and scorn at our solemnity?
	Now, by the stock and honour of my kin,
	To strike him dead, I hold it not a sin.
CAPULET	Why, how now, kinsman! Wherefore storm you so?
TYBALT	Uncle, this is a Montague, our foe,
	A villain that is hither come in spite,
	To scorn at our solemnity this night.
CAPULET	Young Romeo is it?
TYBALT	'Tis he, that villain Romeo.
CAPULET	Content thee, gentle coz, let him alone;
	He bears him like a portly gentleman;
	And, to say truth, Verona brags of him
	To be a virtuous and well-govern'd youth:
	I would not for the wealth of all the town
	Here in my house do him disparagement:
	Therefore be patient, take no note of him:
	It is my will, the which if thou respect,
	Show a fair presence and put off these frowns,
	And ill-beseeming semblance for a feast.

Mix It Up

| TYBALT | It fits, when such a villain is a guest: |
| | I'll not endure him. |

CAPULET	He shall be endured:
	What, goodman boy! I say, he shall: go to;
	Am I the master here, or you? Go to.
	You'll not endure him! God shall mend my soul!
	You'll make a mutiny among my guests!
	You will set cock-a-hoop! You'll be the man!

| TYBALT | Why, uncle, 'tis a shame. |

CAPULET	Go to, go to;
	You are a saucy boy: is't so, indeed?
	This trick may chance to scathe you, I know what:
	You must contrary me! marry, 'tis time.
	Well said, my hearts! You are a princox; go:
	Be quiet, or – More light, more light! For shame!
	I'll make you quiet. What, cheerly, my hearts!

TYBALT	Patience perforce with wilful choler meeting
	Makes my flesh tremble in their different greeting.
	I will withdraw: but this intrusion shall
	Now seeming sweet convert to bitter gall.
	Exit

Act 3 scene 1, lines 55–92

Enter ROMEO

| TYBALT | Well, peace be with you, sir: here comes my man. |

MERCUTIO	But I'll be hanged, sir, if he wear your livery:
	Marry, go before to field, he'll be your follower;
	Your worship in that sense may call him 'man'.

| TYBALT | Romeo, the hate I bear thee can afford |
| | No better term than this, – thou art a villain. |

ROMEO	Tybalt, the reason that I have to love thee
	Doth much excuse the appertaining rage
	To such a greeting: villain am I none;
	Therefore farewell; I see thou know'st me not.

Mix It Up   121

Mixed Test-Style Questions

TYBALT	Boy, this shall not excuse the injuries That thou hast done me; therefore turn and draw.
ROMEO	I do protest, I never injured thee, But love thee better than thou canst devise, Till thou shalt know the reason of my love: And so, good Capulet, – which name I tender As dearly as my own, – be satisfied.
MERCUTIO	O calm, dishonourable, vile submission! Alla stoccata carries it away. *[Draws]* Tybalt, you rat-catcher, will you walk?
TYBALT	What wouldst thou have with me?
MERCUTIO	Good king of cats, nothing but one of your nine lives; that I mean to make bold withal, and as you shall use me hereafter, drybeat the rest of the eight. Will you pluck your sword out of his pitcher by the ears? Make haste, lest mine be about your ears ere it be out.
TYBALT	I am for you. *[Drawing]*
ROMEO	Gentle Mercutio, put thy rapier up.
MERCUTIO	Come, sir, your passado. *[They fight]*
ROMEO	Draw, Benvolio; beat down their weapons. Gentlemen, for shame, forbear this outrage! Tybalt, Mercutio, the prince expressly hath Forbidden bandying in Verona streets: Hold, Tybalt! good Mercutio! *[TYBALT under ROMEO's arm stabs MERCUTIO, and flies with his followers]*
MERCUTIO	I am hurt. A plague o' both your houses!

2 *As You Like It,* Act 1 scene 2, lines 1–48 and Act 3 scene 2, lines 186–246. In the first extract, Rosalind describes her feelings after her father's banishment.

In the second extract, Celia reveals to Rosalind that Orlando is also in the Forest of Arden with them.

In these extracts, how does Shakespeare present Rosalind's different characteristics?

Support your ideas by referring to both of the following extracts. **[18]**

Act 1 scene 2, lines 1–48

CELIA	I pray thee, Rosalind, sweet my coz, be merry.
ROSALIND	Dear Celia, I show more mirth than I am mistress of; and would you yet I were merrier? Unless you could teach me to forget a banished father, you must not learn me how to remember any extraordinary pleasure.
CELIA	Herein I see thou lovest me not with the full weight that I love thee. If my uncle, thy banished father, had banished thy uncle, the duke my father, so thou hadst been still with me, I could have taught my love to take thy father for mine: so wouldst thou, if the truth of thy love to me were so righteously tempered as mine is to thee.
ROSALIND	Well, I will forget the condition of my estate, to rejoice in yours.
CELIA	You know my father hath no child but I, nor none is like to have: and, truly, when he dies, thou shalt be his heir, for what he hath taken away from thy father perforce, I will render thee again in affection; by mine honour, I will; and when I break that oath, let me turn monster: therefore, my sweet Rose, my dear Rose, be merry.
ROSALIND	From henceforth I will, coz, and devise sports. Let me see; what think you of falling in love?
CELIA	Marry, I prithee, do, to make sport withal: but love no man in good earnest; nor no further in sport neither than with safety of a pure blush thou mayst in honour come off again.
ROSALIND	What shall be our sport, then?
CELIA	Let us sit and mock the good housewife Fortune from her wheel, that her gifts may henceforth be bestowed equally.
ROSALIND	I would we could do so, for her benefits are mightily misplaced, and the bountiful blind woman doth most mistake in her gifts to women.

Mixed Test-Style Questions

CELIA	'Tis true; for those that she makes fair she scarce makes honest, and those that she makes honest she makes very ill-favouredly.
ROSALIND	Nay, now thou goest from Fortune's office to Nature's: Fortune reigns in gifts of the world, not in the lineaments of Nature. *Enter TOUCHSTONE*
CELIA	No? When Nature hath made a fair creature, may she not by Fortune fall into the fire? Though Nature hath given us wit to flout at Fortune, hath not Fortune sent in this fool to cut off the argument?
ROSALIND	Indeed, there is Fortune too hard for Nature, when Fortune makes Nature's natural the cutter-off of Nature's wit.

Act 3 scene 2, lines 186–246

ROSALIND	Nay, I prithee now with most petitionary vehemence, tell me who it is.
CELIA	O wonderful, wonderful, and most wonderful, wonderful! And yet again wonderful, and after that, out of all whooping!
ROSALIND	Good my complexion! Dost thou think, though I am caparisoned like a man, I have a doublet and hose in my disposition? One inch of delay more is a South Sea of discovery; I prithee, tell me who is it quickly, and speak apace. I would thou couldst stammer, that thou mightst pour this concealed man out of thy mouth, as wine comes out of a narrow-mouthed bottle, either too much at once, or none at all. I prithee, take the cork out of thy mouth that I may drink thy tidings.
CELIA	So you may put a man in your belly.
ROSALIND	Is he of God's making? What manner of man? Is his head worth a hat, or his chin worth a beard?
CELIA	Nay, he hath but a little beard.
ROSALIND	Why, God will send more, if the man will be thankful: let me stay the growth of his beard, if thou delay me not the knowledge of his chin.
CELIA	It is young Orlando, that tripped up the wrestler's heels and your heart both in an instant.
ROSALIND	Nay, but the devil take mocking: speak, sad brow and true maid.
CELIA	I' faith, coz, 'tis he.

ROSALIND   Orlando?

CELIA   Orlando.

ROSALIND   Alas the day! What shall I do with my doublet and hose? What did he when thou sawest him? What said he? How looked he? Wherein went he? What makes him here? Did he ask for me? Where remains he? How parted he with thee? And when shalt thou see him again? Answer me in one word.

CELIA   You must borrow me Gargantua's mouth first: 'tis a word too great for any mouth of this age's size. To say ay and no to these particulars is more than to answer in a catechism.

ROSALIND   But doth he know that I am in this forest and in man's apparel? Looks he as freshly as he did the day he wrestled?

CELIA   It is as easy to count atomies as to resolve the propositions of a lover; but take a taste of my finding him, and relish it with good observance. I found him under a tree, like a dropped acorn.

ROSALIND   It may well be called Jove's tree, when it drops forth such fruit.

CELIA   Give me audience, good madam.

ROSALIND   Proceed.

CELIA   There lay he, stretched along, like a wounded knight.

ROSALIND   Though it be pity to see such a sight, it well becomes the ground.

CELIA   Cry 'holla' to thy tongue, I prithee; it curvets unseasonably. He was furnished like a hunter.

ROSALIND   O, ominous! He comes to kill my heart.

CELIA   I would sing my song without a burden: thou bringest me out of tune.

ROSALIND   Do you not know I am a woman? When I think, I must speak. Sweet, say on.

Mixed Test-Style Questions

3 *Macbeth*, Act 2 scene 2, lines 14–67 and Act 3 scene 2, lines 4–56

In the first extract, Macbeth has just killed King Duncan. In the second extract, Lady Macbeth tries to convince Macbeth to stop worrying about Banquo.

How should the actors playing Macbeth and Lady Macbeth show the relationship between the two characters in these extracts?

Support your ideas by referring to both of the following extracts.   [18]

Act 2 scene 2, lines 14–67

MACBETH	I have done the deed. Didst thou not hear a noise?
LADY MACBETH	I heard the owl scream and the crickets cry. Did not you speak?
MACBETH	When?
LADY MACBETH	Now.
MACBETH	As I descended?
LADY MACBETH	Ay.
MACBETH	Hark! Who lies i' the second chamber?
LADY MACBETH	Donalbain.
MACBETH	*[Looking at his hands]* This is a sorry sight.
LADY MACBETH	A foolish thought, to say a sorry sight.
MACBETH	There's one did laugh in's sleep, and one cried 'Murder!' That they did wake each other: I stood and heard them: But they did say their prayers, and address'd them Again to sleep.
LADY MACBETH	There are two lodged together.
MACBETH	One cried 'God bless us!' and 'Amen' the other; As they had seen me with these hangman's hands. Listening their fear, I could not say 'Amen,' When they did say 'God bless us!'
LADY MACBETH	Consider it not so deeply.

MACBETH	But wherefore could not I pronounce 'Amen'? I had most need of blessing, and 'Amen' Stuck in my throat.

LADY MACBETH	These deeds must not be thought After these ways; so, it will make us mad.

MACBETH	Methought I heard a voice cry 'Sleep no more! Macbeth does murder sleep', the innocent sleep, Sleep that knits up the ravell'd sleeve of care, The death of each day's life, sore labour's bath, Balm of hurt minds, great nature's second course, Chief nourisher in life's feast, –

LADY MACBETH	What do you mean?

MACBETH	Still it cried 'Sleep no more!' to all the house: 'Glamis hath murder'd sleep, and therefore Cawdor Shall sleep no more; Macbeth shall sleep no more.'

LADY MACBETH	Who was it that thus cried? Why, worthy thane, You do unbend your noble strength, to think So brainsickly of things. Go get some water, And wash this filthy witness from your hand. Why did you bring these daggers from the place? They must lie there: go carry them; and smear The sleepy grooms with blood.

MACBETH	I'll go no more: I am afraid to think what I have done; Look on't again I dare not.

LADY MACBETH	Infirm of purpose! Give me the daggers: the sleeping and the dead Are but as pictures: 'tis the eye of childhood That fears a painted devil. If he do bleed, I'll gild the faces of the grooms withal; For it must seem their guilt. *Exit. Knocking within*

MACBETH	Whence is that knocking? How is't with me, when every noise appals me? What hands are here? Ha! they pluck out mine eyes.

Will all great Neptune's ocean wash this blood
Clean from my hand? No, this my hand will rather
The multitudinous seas in incarnadine,
Making the green one red.
Re-enter LADY MACBETH

LADY MACBETH   My hands are of your colour; but I shame
To wear a heart so white.

[Knocking within]

I hear a knocking
At the south entry: retire we to our chamber;
A little water clears us of this deed:
How easy is it, then!

Act 3 scene 2, lines 4–56

LADY MACBETH   Nought's had, all's spent,
Where our desire is got without content:
'Tis safer to be that which we destroy
Than by destruction dwell in doubtful joy.
Enter MACBETH
How now, my lord! Why do you keep alone,
Of sorriest fancies your companions making,
Using those thoughts which should indeed have died
With them they think on? Things without all remedy
Should be without regard: what's done is done.

MACBETH   We have scotch'd the snake, not kill'd it:
She'll close and be herself, whilst our poor malice
Remains in danger of her former tooth.
But let the frame of things disjoint, both the
worlds suffer,
Ere we will eat our meal in fear and sleep
In the affliction of these terrible dreams
That shake us nightly: better be with the dead,
Whom we, to gain our peace, have sent to peace,
Than on the torture of the mind to lie
In restless ecstasy. Duncan is in his grave;
After life's fitful fever he sleeps well;
Treason has done his worst: nor steel, nor poison,
Malice domestic, foreign levy, nothing,
Can touch him further.

LADY MACBETH   Come on;
Gentle my lord, sleek o'er your rugged looks;
Be bright and jovial among your guests tonight.

MACBETH   So shall I, love; and so, I pray, be you:
Let your remembrance apply to Banquo;
Present him eminence, both with eye and tongue:
Unsafe the while, that we
Must lave our honours in these flattering streams,
And make our faces vizards to our hearts,
Disguising what they are.

LADY MACBETH   You must leave this.

MACBETH   O, full of scorpions is my mind, dear wife!
Thou know'st that Banquo, and his Fleance, lives.

LADY MACBETH   But in them nature's copy's not eterne.

MACBETH   There's comfort yet; they are assailable;
Then be thou jocund: ere the bat hath flown
His cloister'd flight, ere to black Hecate's summons
The shard-borne beetle with his drowsy hums
Hath rung night's yawning peal, there shall be done
A deed of dreadful note.

LADY MACBETH   What's to be done?

MACBETH   Be innocent of the knowledge, dearest chuck,
Till thou applaud the deed. Come, seeling night,
Scarf up the tender eye of pitiful day;
And with thy bloody and invisible hand
Cancel and tear to pieces that great bond
Which keeps me pale! Light thickens; and the crow
Makes wing to the rooky wood:
Good things of day begin to droop and drowse;
While night's black agents to their preys do rouse.
Thou marvell'st at my words: but hold thee still;
Things bad begun make strong themselves by ill.
So, prithee, go with me.
[*Exeunt*]

Spoken English

Typical Tasks

- Short speeches and presentations.
- Informal discussions, structured discussions and formal debates.
- Improvising, rehearsing and performing play scripts and poetry.

Key Speaking Skills

- Use Standard English, pronouncing your words clearly and avoiding slang.
- Make eye contact with your audience or the other speaker.
- Make use of your voice and vary tone, pace and volume.
- Match your facial expression and body language to your speech.
- Use pauses for dramatic or rhetorical effect.
- Keep focused on the topic, even if the situation is informal.

Speeches and Presentations

- Do plenty of preparation beforehand.
- Write your speech in full and practise it several times.
- Use your voice to emphasise key points and rhetorical techniques.
- Use visual aids, such as photographs or diagrams.

Formal Discussions and Debates

- In a debate, you may have to argue against what you actually believe.
- Organise your points beforehand, making sure you have evidence to back up your ideas.
- Listen carefully, so you can follow arguments and respond effectively.
- Challenge other people's points of view politely.
- If the discussion becomes heated, keep calm and controlled.

Scripts and Poetry

- Spend time working out the meaning of the writing, for example:
    - a character's personality, thoughts, feelings and motivation
    - the tone or atmosphere of a poem
    - the most important messages that need to be conveyed.
- Use your voice and body language and gestures to emphasise important points.
- Focus on the other actors (rather than the audience) in scripts.

Key Point

Keep calm, don't rush, and try to enjoy yourself!

Key Point

Using brief cue cards to help you, rehearse in front of a friend who can give you constructive criticism.

Answers

1. Which of them is the stronger. [1]
2. He is well-wrapped up / wearing warm clothes. [1]
3. Any two of 'icy', 'fierce' and 'rough'. [1]

> If you are asked for two details from the text and the answer carries one mark, you only get a mark if you give two correct answers. There are no half marks.

4. The journey – long
   The man's hat – woolly
   The shade – welcoming
   The sun – kind
   All four must be correct to get the mark. [1]
5. b [1]

> If you choose more than one answer in this sort of question, you will get no marks.

6. **Two of the following (or similar) answers:**
   There are a lot of short sentences, giving a fast pace / making you read more quickly.
   The wind makes three attempts, each one harder than the last.
   Because the wind is trying harder and harder, you keep thinking he will succeed but he fails.
   [2 marks – 1 for each correct answer]
7. **Answers similar to the following:**
   1 mark – The sun is stronger than the wind, so maybe it's like that for people.
   2 marks – You can achieve more by being gentle and warm than by being hard and rough.
   3 marks – By showing us that the warm and kind sun succeeds and the rough, fierce wind fails, the fable tells us that, if you want something, gentle persuasion works better than aggression. **[3]**

Page 7 Quick Test
1. Scanning the page quickly for key points.
2. No. **3.** No.

Page 9 Quick Test
1. Quotation and paraphrasing.
2. Putting information into your own words.
3. Words taken directly from the original text.
4. Point, Evidence, Explanation (or Point, Evidence, Exploration).

Page 11 Quick Test
1. The writer.
2. We make the meaning clearer / explain it / show our understanding of it. **3.** Yes.
4. By supporting it with close reference to the text.

Page 13 Quick Test
1. From the writer's description / from what the character says / from what the character does / from the reaction of other characters to them.
2. No. **3.** By using a quotation to support it.
   4. Yes.

1. Portugal [1]
2. The city had to be rebuilt, creating the smart/ elegant district of Baixa. [1]
3. 'Served by budget airlines'
   'Inexpensive'
   Both answers needed for mark [1]

> If the question asks you to 'pick out' words or phrases, you must quote the text exactly.

4. Referring to Cascais as Estoril's 'younger neighbour' implies that Caiscas appeals to the young, contrasting it with Estoril, which must, therefore, appeal to older people. [1]
5. **Your answers should be similar to these:**
   a) 'while you take in the sights and sounds of this lively, cosmopolitan city.' You can watch a lot of different things, from different cultures, going on around you.
   b) 'the haunting voices of the singers in the traditional Fado clubs.' At a Fado club you will experience something that is part of the local culture and history, and which will stay in your memory.
   c) 'full of stunning royal palaces and surrounded by beautiful countryside.' It is a place where you can enjoy history / art and nature.
   d) 'full of atmosphere and interest.' There is a lot to see and explore, and it has a special atmosphere.
   [2 marks – 1 for identifying four quotations; 1 for four reasonable explanations]
6. a) It says that you can do things like sitting outside a café, eating and drinking, going to the beach or the countryside. These are all activities that are quite gentle and relaxing.
   [2 marks – 1 for a less full answer]
   b) It also mentions 'lively' clubs you can go to and a lot of different places to go and things to do, which would keep you busy and active.
   [2 marks – 1 for a less full answer]

Page 17 Quick Test
1. To make the reader think about the subject.
2. To encourage the reader to act.
3. A significant/important point at which something happens to change the story.

Page 19 Quick Test
1. A blog or discussion forum.
2. A poem whose shape reflects its subject.
3. Because they stand out they can help readers find information quickly.
4. To express information clearly in a different form.

Page 21 Quick Test
1. Alliteration. **2.** Metaphor. **3.** Simile.
4. Onomatopoeia.

Page 23 Quick Test
1. Repetition. **2.** Hyperbole. **3.** Rhetorical question. **4.** Emotive language.

1. They beat their hands on their breasts.
   They stamp up and down on the pavement. [1]
2. So he can 'keep his eye upon his clerk.' [1]
3. We learn that he does not trust his clerk.
   Evidence – he keeps the door open so he can watch him.
   We learn that he is mean.
   Evidence – he will not let the clerk have more coal for the fire.
   [2 marks – 1 for two characteristics; 1 for two pieces of evidence]
4. The walk has warmed him up so he is 'all in a glow'; his face is 'ruddy'; 'his eyes sparkled, and his breath smoked'.
   [2 marks – 1 for saying he is warm/hot; 1 for evidence]
5. That it is a con or fake / that it is a waste of time / that he is not interested in it. [1]
6. **Answers similar to the following:**
   1 mark – He is handsome and friendly.
   2 marks – He is friendly and happy. His voice is described as 'cheerful' and he speaks 'gaily'. Scrooge says that he is 'poor'.
   3 marks – The nephew is completely different from Scrooge. He likes Christmas, although he is poor, wishing Scrooge a 'merry Christmas' and is 'cheerful', with his appearance reflecting his lively character: he is 'all in a glow'. Also, he is not afraid of Scrooge, answering him back and telling him not to be 'cross'. **[3]**

> Keep your quotations short and relevant.

1. b [1]
2. The boxes contain useful information / They give practical information / They tell you what to do rather than describing what happens at the hall. [1]
3. **Answers similar to:**
   1 mark – To avoid spoiling it for the visitors.
   2 marks – The writer is trying to get people to come to the hall, so tells enough of the story to get them interested. If they want to know what happens next they might visit the hall to find out. **[2]**
4. Because it is like going back in time, like the characters in the TV programme *Doctor Who*, who travel in a time machine called 'the Tardis'.
   [2 marks – 1 for a reference to time travel; 1 for mentioning *Doctor Who*]
5. Doing his bit means joining in / making a contribution / doing something useful in order to help the war effort / to win the war.
   [2 marks – 1 for an explanation of the phrase in general terms; 1 for a reference to the war]

> When you are asked to explain a word or phrase, relate your explanation to its use in the text.

6. **Two of the following answers:** Writing in the present tense can make something seem more vivid / come alive for the reader. They want the readers/visitors to feel as though they have travelled to the past and they are experiencing the events as they happen.
    When the actors perform it as if it is happening in the present / in front of you. [2]

Pages 28–35 Revise Questions

Page 29 Quick Test
1. To persuade. **2.** To instruct. **3.** To argue.
4. To advise.

Page 31 Quick Test
1. His or her feelings and opinions.
2. Their reaction / How it makes them feel and what it makes them think. **3.** Agree. **4.** No.

Page 33 Quick Test
1. All of them. 2. c 3. Yes.

Page 35 Quick Test
1. a, b and c are all correct.

Pages 36–37 Review Questions

1. A reader would think that Aunt Polly was shouting and was angry and/or frustrated. It also shows how important Tom is in the book and something about the kind of character he is. [2]

    > If a question attracts more than one mark, you will probably be expected to make more than one point.

2. It gives us an idea of how Aunt Polly would pronounce her words / imitates her regional accent. [1]
3. The metaphor means that it is hard to change your ways when you are older. Aunt Polly is comparing herself to an old dog because dogs cannot be trained/taught when they are older.
    [2 marks – 1 for each point similar to the above]
4. Up to this point it has been quite fast paced, exciting and amusing. Now it slows down and is more reflective. Before this Aunt Polly seems very angry and strict. Afterwards we realise that she is not really that angry and is very fond of Tom, perhaps spoiling him because of his situation.
    [2 marks – 2 for an answer that makes most of the above points; 1 for one or two of the points.]
5. Answers similar to the following:
    1 mark – It will be about Tom and his Aunt Polly and what happens to them.
    2 marks – It will probably be about Tom getting up to all sorts of 'tricks', like hiding in the cupboard. He might have adventures but they will mostly be childish or innocent. In the end things will turn out alright.
    3 marks – Because of the title I would expect Tom to have 'adventures'. However, they will probably be mostly funny rather than dangerous, like stealing the jam. He might get into more trouble with other people with his 'tricks'. Aunt Polly will try to do her 'duty' and control him but she may not manage it. We might see how things turn out when he is older. [3]

Pages 38–39 Practice Questions

1. The writer wants us to know that the kittens may have had no contact with humans or have been treated badly by them, and so do not trust them.
    The writer is explaining why they need to be fostered instead of being given away immediately. **[2 marks – 1 for each point]**
2. 'Our' gives the impression that the vet and the volunteer are both part of the organisation / It sounds affectionate, almost as if they're part of a family.
    'Volunteer' stresses that Meghan is working for nothing to help the cats.
    'Vet' tells us that Kanwal is a qualified professional, whose opinion can be trusted. First names suggest informality or friendliness
    [3 marks – 1 for each point]
3. Points to include:
    *   The leaflet gets the reader's sympathy straightaway by telling us it is for 'abandoned', 'unloved' and 'unwanted' cats. These are emotive words that make us feel sorry for the cats.
    *   It tells us some facts about what the charity does at the centre. This makes us feel that they know what they are doing and we can trust them: the cats are 'examined by qualified vets'.
    *   It is a professional organisation so we know the cats that come from there will be healthy. We also know they are well cared for because of what we are told about fostering.
    *   The story of Biffy makes it more personal because we can identify with one kitten and get a picture of what it is like for her.
    *   Emotive words like 'abandoned' and 'alone' are used to gain sympathy.
    *   The text talks about her 'mum' as if she were a human being, but implies that real humans might be to blame.
    *   The description of her ('a sad little bundle of fur and bones') is very emotive and makes you want to protect her.
    *   You admire Meghan and Kanwal and feel you would like to help too.
    *   The last part is more about practical matters.
    *   It gives you an idea about what you have to do and reassures you about any doubts you might have, saying they are 'happy to answer any queries'.
    *   It tells you how adopting a cat could make your life better; 'you'll be improving the quality of your own life'. This would make you think about how pets can be like friends and if you get one from the rescue centre you also have the satisfaction of doing something to help.
    [10 marks – 2 for one or two of these or similar points; 6 for about half of them; 10 for most of these points and some original points.]

    > In a test, answer a longer question in proper sentences and paragraphs. Do not use bullet points.

Pages 40–47 Revise Questions

Page 41 Quick Test
1. Persuade, argue, advise, inform, explain, describe.
2. More formal, respectful and sophisticated for head teacher.
3. Newspaper article, magazine column, email, letter, report, short story, speech.

Page 43 Quick Test
1. To make writing easier to understand.
2. When there is a change in time, place, focus.
3. To show how your account/argument is progressing or developing.
4. Time, place, sequence, compare/contrast.

Page 45 Quick Test
1. Simple, compound, complex.
2. Before, after, in the middle.
3. Past is used for events that have happened; present is used for something that is happening as you write.
4. Future is used for events that will definitely happen; conditional is for events that should, could, or might happen.

Page 47 Quick Test
1. To show ownership or abbreviation.
2. To separate the main clause from the subordinate clause.
3. A main clause will make sense on its own; the subordinate clause is extra information and will not make sense on its own.
4. To start a list or emphasise a point.

Pages 48–49 Review Questions

1. It is intended for children/young people and younger readers will be able to identify with him / sympathise with someone near their own age.
    He might not understand everything that is going on / he has an innocent viewpoint / he might be more open to new ideas and adventures.
    [2 marks – 1 for each point]
2. a, c, d
    [3 marks – 1 for each correct answer. No marks if more than 3 ticked.]
3. Points to include:
    *   The narrator says he remembers the stranger 'as if it were yesterday', which tells us that he made a big impression on him.
    *   He must have been travelling because he has his luggage with him.
    *   He is 'tall, strong, heavy and nut-brown'. All these adjectives make him sound impressive and maybe a bit intimidating. Together with the 'tarry pigtail' they paint a picture of an old sailor who might have been away for years.
    *   His clothes are described as being 'soiled' and his nails 'black', adding to the impression that he has been away from civilisation.
    *   The scarring on his hands and the sabre cut on his cheek show that he has been involved in fights and he might be a violent, dangerous man.
    *   When he talks he does not use Standard English ('sittyated', 'mought'). This might be the way sailors talked then.

- He is very familiar/friendly, calling people 'mate' and 'matey', which are also terms sailors would use.
- He gets straight to the point and says he is a 'plain man'.
- He does not say 'please' and 'thank you' but tells people what to do, suggesting he is used to giving orders, which is supported by the narrator saying he looked 'as fierce as a commander' and thinking he 'seemed like a mate or a skipper.'
- We know he has money because he throws down gold pieces and does not seem to be concerned about how much his stay will cost.
- The fact that he has come to the Admiral Benbow adds to his mystery, as he seems to want to be somewhere 'lonely'.
- He is described as a loner, going out on his own and not mixing.
- He is 'as silent as a mouse' if any other seamen arrive. This implies he is worried or frightened and he has a reason to hide from other sailors.
- When he asks the narrator to look out for 'the seafaring man with one leg', the mystery is deepened. The reader wonders about his past and what will happen if the one-legged man turns up.

[10 marks – 2 for one or two of these or similar points; 6 for about half of them; 10 for most of these points and some original points.]

In a test, answer a longer question in proper sentences and paragraphs. Do not use bullet points.

Pages 50–51 Practice Questions

1. a) To advise, a year 8 student, letter. **[3]**
   b) Paragraphs. **[1]**
   c) Connectives of sequence. **[1]**
   d) Simple, compound, complex. **[3]**
2. • **Paragraphing** **[2]**
   Secondly... / Once you have....
   • **Connectives** **[2]**
   Firstly, understand that... (or To begin with, First of all, Most importantly, etc.); As well as this, you could speak to... (or In addition, Furthermore, etc.)
   • **Punctuation** **[10]**
   ' / . / , / , / ' / ? / . / ' / ' / '
   • **Spelling** **[10]**
   there, accept, might, embarrassed, friends, you're, experience, sitting, to, for
   • **Grammar** **[5]**
   is/are; made/make; had/have; spent/spend; knew/knows

Dear Feeling Scared,

Firstly, understand that **it's** not your fault. **You are** not a bad person: the bully is. No one should be able to treat you like **this. You** are a victim and **there** are lots of people who can help you. Keep that in your mind, rather than worrying that you are to blame. // **Secondly,** do something about the bullying. Don't just **accept** it; you need to talk to someone. This **might** be your form **tutor,** the school counsellor, or your head of year. I know **you're** feeling scared and maybe **embarrassed,** but don't you think it's better to get this in the **open?** If you do, it will **make** you feel much better and show you that you're not alone. // Once you **have**

done this, you need to try to avoid the bully until the issue is dealt with. Try to get on with life rather than focusing on this **problem. It's** important that you **spend** time with your **friends,** as this will make you feel safe and remind you that **you're** not alone. It would also be a good idea to tell your best mates so they understand what you've been feeling and can look out for you while you get over this horrible **experience.**

As well as this, you could speak to the teacher **who's** been helping you about arranging a meeting with the bully. It can help to talk things over, so the bully **knows** how bad they've made you feel. This is also a chance to get over any misunderstanding, in case the bully has felt you've wronged them in some little way. **Sitting** down and talking like adults is always a good way **to** clear the air and move on.

You'll soon be enjoying life again and feeling safe around school.

Thanks **for** your letter,
Student Help

Pages 52–59 Revise Questions

Page 53 Quick Test
1. Purpose, audience, form. **2.** No.
3. So ideas flow sensibly and you can build up your writing.
4. Give lots of detail to make your ideas clear.

Page 55 Quick Test
1. What your audience is thinking/feeling.
2. FORESTRY.
3. Facts, Opinions, Rhetorical questions, Emotive/Empathetic, Statistics, Triplets, Repetition, You.
4. A high level of accuracy.

Page 57 Quick Test
1. You present both sides of the argument, not just one view. **2.** A conclusion.
3. Compare/Contrast and Cause/Effect.
4. To introduce the point of your paragraph.

Page 59 Quick Test
1. Because you need to sound both firm and friendly/supportive.
2. 'You are not on your own', 'Don't worry', etc...
3. So the reader feels you are talking directly to them.
4. Verbs of possibility or necessity, allowing you to give suggestions and orders.

Pages 60–61 Review Questions

1. a) Persuade, adults, article. **[3]**
   b) Paragraphs. **[1]**
   c) Sequence connectives. **[1]**
   d) Simple, Compound, Complex. **[3]**
2. • **Paragraphing** **[2]**
   As well as being famously... / Furthermore, the old town...
   • **Connectives** **[2]**
   However (or In addition, Moreover, etc.); At night time (or In the evening, etc.)
   • **Punctuation** **[10]**
   ? / , / , / ' / , / ' / , / , / , / ,
   • **Spelling** **[10]**
   no, beautiful, activities, stunning, colourful, disappear, beaches, lovely, friendly, forgetting

• **Grammar** **[5]**
relaxing/relax; was/is; is/are; english/ English; wanted/want

There's **Nowhere** Like Newquay!

Are you looking for an amazing beach resort in **England?** Then look **no** further than Newquay in Cornwall. This amazing town is home to **beautiful beaches,** lots of leisure **activities,** exciting entertainment, and friendly locals.

The main reason to come to Newquay is its nine amazing beaches. The warm, golden sands stretch for miles, providing the perfect place to **relax** and get a tan. **You'll** see clear blue waters lapping hypnotically against the shore and beckoning you to come in for a swim. // As well as being famously **stunning, Newquay's** coastline is also well-known for attracting surfers from all over the globe. You can join in, or just sit back and watch people tackling waves of up to six metres high. Watching the **colourful** boards ride the waves or **disappear** in the crashing foam can be almost as exhilarating as trying it yourself.

However, if you venture beyond the **beaches,** there's still plenty to do. You can visit the **zoo,** take a ride on the miniature railway, or play a round of mini-golf. There are also plenty of walks along the South West Coast Path (the longest in England) where you will be rewarded with picturesque views and lots of nature, from rare migrating birds to cute seals and sunbathing lizards. // **Furthermore,** the old town **is** a joy to walk around. The quaint streets are lined with pretty houses and gardens. There **are** also **lovely** arts and crafts shops, so you can buy something unique to remind you of your fantastic holiday. It's also a great opportunity to enjoy a traditional **English** cream tea, with home-baked **scones,** fresh strawberry jam, and lashings of Cornish cream.

In the evening, **there's** no reason to get bored. The town boasts lots of **friendly** pubs, tasty restaurants and lively clubs. There are also theatres, cinemas, bingo halls, and amusement arcades, not **forgetting** the chance to watch a match at Newquay FC's home ground.

Come to Newquay and you'll never **want** to leave!

Pages 62–63 Practice Questions

1. a) **Two ideas on why books are enjoyable, two ideas on why books are educational, at least two persuasive techniques** **[6]**
   Possible ideas: There are many genres of books – something to please everyone, whatever their interests; reading is relaxing.
   You learn from reading books – about history, other countries/cultures; reading broadens vocabulary and helps with grammar, punctuation and spelling. Rhetorical questions; Repetition; Second person, etc.
   b) An excellent answer will:
   • Display a full awareness of purpose, audience and form
   • Offer a variety of ideas using

vocabulary and features appropriate to writing to persuade, e.g. rhetorical questions, second person, facts and opinions, triplets (Remember the FORESTRY mnemonic)
- Use a range of sentence structures effectively
- Use paragraphs and a variety of connectives to effectively structure the leaflet
- Achieve a high level of technical accuracy: spelling, grammar, punctuation
- Engage the reader throughout and achieve a high level of effective persuasive techniques.

A good answer will:
- Display some awareness of purpose, audience and form
- Offer ideas using some vocabulary and features appropriate to writing to persuade, e.g. rhetorical questions, second person. (Remember the FORESTRY mnemonic)
- Use some different sentence structures.
- Use paragraphs and connectives to effectively structure the leaflet
- Achieve an acceptable level of technical accuracy: most familiar words spelled correctly, accurate grammar with only a few minor errors, a range of punctuation but some errors with complex constructions
- Engage the reader, but not always with highly effective persuasive techniques.

[30 marks – 14 for purpose, audience and form; 8 for sentence structure, punctuation and spelling; 8 for organisation.]

2. a) **Two ideas on supporting the ban; Two ideas against the ban; At least two effective techniques relevant to writing to argue and your own opinion given in a conclusion.** [6]
Possible ideas: The time could be better spent teaching – where students are able to interact with each other and the teacher to ask questions, discuss ideas, etc. Students are more likely to watch films in their own time than study, so films could be given as homework.
Watching an educational film can be just as useful and sometimes more effective than reading books; students learn in different ways so it's good to have variation in lessons.
Connectives of cause and effect/comparison and contrast; facts and opinions; empathy; triplets.
b) **An excellent answer will:**
- Display a full awareness of purpose, audience and form
- Use an appropriate tone (i.e. displaying empathy for both sides of the argument)
- Offer a variety of ideas using vocabulary and features appropriate to writing to argue, e.g. giving facts and opinions, using triplets, relevant connectives

- Use a range of sentence structures effectively
- Use paragraphs and a variety of connectives to effectively structure the article
- Achieve a high level of technical accuracy: spelling, grammar, punctuation
- Engage the reader throughout, offering interesting points for both sides of the argument
- Include a conclusion, in which you offer your own opinion.

A good answer will:
- Display some awareness of purpose, audience and form
- Display some use of appropriate tone (i.e. displaying empathy for both sides of the argument)
- Offer ideas using some vocabulary and features appropriate to writing to argue, e.g. giving facts and opinions, using relevant connectives
- Use some different sentence structures
- Use paragraphs and connectives to effectively structure the leaflet
- Achieve an acceptable level of technical accuracy: most familiar words spelled correctly, accurate grammar with only a few minor errors, a range of punctuation but some errors with complex constructions
- Engage the reader through most of the article
- Include a conclusion, in which you offer your own opinion.

[30 marks – 14 for purpose, audience and form; 8 for sentence structure, punctuation and spelling; 8 for organisation.]

3. a) **One idea on where to go, one idea on what to do; One idea on what to buy, one idea on how to make it memorable; Two effective advising techniques.** [6]
Possible ideas: A park; leisure centre; theme park. Eat out; meet up with friends. Engraved item of jewellery; gift experience voucher. Make a special cake; write and perform a song; use modal verbs; use imperatives.
b) **An excellent answer will:**
- Display a full awareness of purpose, audience and form
- Offer a variety of ideas using vocabulary and features appropriate to writing to advise, e.g. plenty of modal verbs and imperatives
- Use a range of sentence structures effectively
- Use paragraphs and a variety of connectives to effectively structure the response
- Achieve a high level of technical accuracy: spelling, grammar, punctuation
- Suggest a variety of useful, relevant pieces of advice.

A good answer will:
- Display some awareness of purpose, audience and form
- Offer ideas using some modal verbs and imperatives

- Use some different sentence structures
- Use paragraphs and connectives to effectively structure the response
- Achieve an acceptable level of technical accuracy: most familiar words spelled correctly, accurate grammar with only a few minor errors, a range of punctuation but some errors with complex constructions
- Suggest some useful, relevant pieces of advice.

[30 marks – 14 for purpose, audience and form; 8 for sentence structure, punctuation and spelling; 8 for organisation.]

Page 65 Quick Test
1. Go = creep, race, ran, etc. Get = buy, collect, gather, etc.
2. Pollution, greenhouse gases, carbon footprint, recycle, etc.
3. Emphasise a point or surprise the reader.
4. Statements, exclamations of emotion, questions, orders.

Page 67 Quick Test
1. Facts. 2. Time and place.
3. Chronologically or thematically.
4. Because the readers want the truth.

Page 69 Quick Test
1. The cause and effect of things.
2. Cause/Effect and Compare/Contrast.
3. For a current issue – present tense, for how something has happened – past tense.
4. To make your ideas clear and easy to follow.

Page 71 Quick Test
1. A vivid picture of something.
2. Chronologically or thematically.
3. Interesting verbs, adjectives, adverbs; simile, metaphor, personification; onomatopoeia, alliteration, sibilance; senses.
4. Maintain a high level of accuracy.

1. a) **Two reasons to support each idea** [6]
Possible ideas for your speech: different pitches or courts to encourage fitness and teamwork among young people; slides and swings for young people – it's better to be outside in the fresh air, and many families don't have a big garden; better lighting to keep people safe and allow longer play in autumn/winter; it will keep young people off the streets and out of trouble; will bring people in the community together – could even have matches with community leaders like the police; also a great area for charity days; a grand opening with a local sportsperson would also show people how hard the council have worked.
b) **An excellent answer will:**
- Display a full awareness of purpose, audience and form
- Include a full range of rhetorical techniques in order to persuade
- Present a variety of ideas, using a

- sophisticated range of vocabulary and sentence structures
- Use paragraphs and a variety of connectives to effectively structure the speech
- Achieve a high level of technical accuracy: spelling, grammar, punctuation
- Engage the reader throughout.

A good answer will:
- Display some awareness of purpose, audience and form
- Include some rhetorical techniques that are persuasive
- Present some variety of ideas, using effective vocabulary and different sentence structures
- Use paragraphs and connectives to introduce different parts of the speech
- Achieve an acceptable level of technical accuracy: most familiar words spelled correctly, accurate grammar with only a few minor errors, a range of punctuation but some errors with complex constructions
- Engage the reader, but not be fully convincing or effective throughout.

[30 marks – 14 for purpose, audience and form; 8 for sentence structure, punctuation and spelling; 8 for organisation.]

2. a) **Three ideas in each column** [6]
   Possible ideas for: allows you to communicate with people all over the world; allows you to find out lots of information; helps to keep people educated and informed, such as up-to-the-minute news; helps to fight crime through background checks and evidence, etc.
   Possible ideas against: people spend too much time online; criminals use the Internet to prey on people; online bullying; not everything is checked, so information can be inaccurate; encourages piracy of music and film, etc.

   b) **An excellent answer will:**
   - Display a full awareness of purpose, audience and form
   - Present a balanced argument, plus a conclusion
   - Include a range of rhetorical techniques to emphasise ideas
   - Present a variety of ideas, using a sophisticated range of vocabulary and sentence structures
   - Use paragraphs and a variety of connectives to effectively structure the argument
   - Achieve a high level of technical accuracy: spelling, grammar, punctuation
   - Engage the reader throughout.

   A good answer will:
   - Display some awareness of purpose, audience and form
   - Present an argument that is fairly balanced, plus a conclusion
   - Include some effective rhetorical techniques
   - Present some variety of ideas, using effective vocabulary and different sentence structures
   - Use paragraphs and connectives to introduce different parts of the argument

- Achieve an acceptable level of technical accuracy: most familiar words spelled correctly, accurate grammar with only a few minor errors, a range of punctuation but some errors with complex constructions
- Engage the reader, but not be fully convincing or effective throughout.

[30 marks – 14 for purpose, audience and form; 8 for sentence structure, punctuation and spelling; 8 for organisation.]

3. a) **Two ideas on coping with bullying, two ideas on telling people – how/who, four modal verbs** [8]
   Possible ideas: Try to stay strong, remember it's not your fault; avoid the bullies, make new friends; tell school/parents; find other interests.
   Tell school teachers/head teacher/school counsellor; tell your parents; tell friends/family; sit down with them and explain the issue, how it is making you feel. Should; could; must; might.

   b) **An excellent answer will:**
   - Display a full awareness of purpose, audience and form
   - Use an appropriate tone (i.e. helpful, understanding)
   - Offer a variety of ideas using vocabulary and features appropriate to writing to advise, e.g. plenty of modal verbs and imperatives
   - Use a range of sentence structures effectively
   - Use paragraphs and a variety of connectives to effectively structure the letter
   - Achieve a high level of technical accuracy: spelling, grammar, punctuation
   - Suggest a variety of useful, relevant pieces of advice.

   A good answer will:
   - Display some awareness of purpose, audience and form
   - Display some use of appropriate tone (i.e. helpful, understanding)
   - Offer ideas using some modal verbs and imperatives
   - Use some different sentence structures
   - Use paragraphs and connectives to effectively structure the letter
   - Achieve an acceptable level of technical accuracy: most familiar words spelled correctly, accurate grammar with only a few minor errors, a range of punctuation but some errors with complex constructions
   - Suggest some useful, relevant pieces of advice.

[30 marks – 14 for purpose, audience and form; 8 for sentence structure, punctuation and spelling; 8 for organisation.]

Pages 74–75 Practice Questions

1. a) **Information on what, when, where and how, three ideas for what the fire brigade have done, three opinions** [10]
   Possible ideas: Fire; nearby school (choose a name), cookery block then library;

daytime (choose a time); (decide how the fire started).
Evacuating people, putting out the fire, working out how it started.
Students may have been scared, parents may be relieved that their children are safe, and head teacher may be grateful to the fire brigade.

   b) **An excellent answer will:**
   - Display a full awareness of purpose, audience and form
   - Offer concise but extensive details (including facts, statistics, proper nouns, quotes, etc.) to make the article realistic
   - Offer a variety of information and ideas using sophisticated vocabulary and sentence structures
   - Use paragraphs and a variety of connectives to effectively structure the article
   - Achieve a high level of technical accuracy: spelling, grammar, punctuation
   - Engage the reader throughout and achieve a high level of relevant, useful information.

   A good answer will:
   - Display some awareness of purpose, audience and form
   - Offer plenty of detail but not always be fully concise or varied
   - Offer plenty of ideas, but not as varied as they could be, using effective vocabulary and different sentence structures
   - Use paragraphs and connectives to separate ideas
   - Achieve an acceptable level of technical accuracy: most familiar words spelled correctly, accurate grammar with only a few minor errors, a range of punctuation but some errors with complex constructions
   - Engage the reader, but not always with highly useful or relevant information.

[30 marks – 14 for purpose, audience and form; 8 for sentence structure, punctuation and spelling; 8 for organisation]

2. a) **Four ideas to explain – one in each column** [4]
   Possible ideas for your report: battery not lasting long enough, so replaced with a better version; camera not offering enough quality, so upgraded to higher definition; too heavy, so a lighter casing designed; ability to play games will appeal to young people and commuters; up-to-date sat-nav will appeal to all drivers, especially people in towns undergoing a lot of development; video camera could appeal to everyone from young people to parents; need to increase file storage, so people can keep more songs/videos than they can on our competitors' mobile phones.

   b) **An excellent answer will:**
   - Display a full awareness of purpose, audience and form
   - Offer full explanations for all of your ideas, linking to how they will help to sell the phone to the public
   - Present a variety of ideas, using a sophisticated range of vocabulary and sentence structures

- Use paragraphs and a variety of connectives to effectively structure the report
- Achieve a high level of technical accuracy: spelling, grammar, punctuation
- Engage the reader throughout and achieve a high level of clarity.

A good answer will:
- Display some awareness of purpose, audience and form
- Explain most ideas well, drawing some links to how they will help to sell the phone
- Present some variety of ideas, using effective vocabulary and different sentence structures
- Use paragraphs and connectives to separate ideas within the report
- Achieve an acceptable level of technical accuracy: most familiar words spelled correctly, accurate grammar with only a few minor errors, a range of punctuation but some errors with complex constructions
- Engage the reader, but not always explain ideas with full clarity.

[30 marks – 14 for purpose, audience and form; 8 for sentence structure, punctuation and spelling; 8 for the organisation]

3. a) Six ideas to describe in each column   [6]
   Possible ideas for your creative writing: a place during peace and during war; a shopping centre when open in the day and closed at night; a beach in the summer and winter; a jungle and a city; a wedding and a funeral; a desert and a flooded town.
   b) **An excellent answer will:**
   - Display a full awareness of purpose, audience and form
   - Include a full range of descriptive techniques: interesting verbs/adjectives/adverbs, simile, metaphor, personification, onomatopoeia, senses, etc.
   - Present a variety of ideas, using a sophisticated range of vocabulary and sentence structures
   - Use paragraphs and a variety of connectives to effectively structure the description and contrast
   - Achieve a high level of technical accuracy: spelling, grammar, punctuation
   - Engage the reader throughout with striking, and sometimes surprising, images.

   A good answer will:
   - Display some awareness of purpose, audience and form
   - Include some descriptive techniques to help the reader imagine
   - Present some variety of ideas, using effective vocabulary and different sentence structures
   - Use paragraphs and connectives to separate ideas within the creative writing
   - Achieve an acceptable level of technical accuracy: most familiar words spelled correctly, accurate grammar

with only a few minor errors, a range of punctuation but some errors with complex constructions
- Engage the reader, but not always create imaginative, interesting images.

[30 marks – 14 for purpose, audience and form; 8 for sentence structure, punctuation and spelling; 8 for the organisation]

Pages 76–83 Revise Questions

Page 77 Quick Test
1. Independent, strong-willed, clever.
2. Kind-hearted, loyal, romantic.
3. That he is a proper gentleman.
4. She teaches him to be a more attentive lover.

Page 79 Quick Test
1. Rosalind and Orlando, Celia and Oliver, Audrey and Touchstone.
2. Rosalind, Orlando, Duke Senior.
3. It is a contrast to the court, allowing freedom and healing the problems of the city.
4. Injustice, regret and reform.

Page 81 Quick Test
1. To make the audience think/feel; to show a character persuading or motivating others.
2. To help the audience imagine a scene, or understand how a character sees a situation.
3. To convey powerful emotions, getting the audience to understand how a character feels or helping them to share a character's feelings.
4. Rhetorical devices, such as repetition, triplets and emotive language; verbs, adjectives and adverbs; simile, metaphor and personification; short sentences, orders and exclamation; symbolism.

Page 83 Quick Test
1. Emphasise words and meaning by raising and lowering volume, altering the tone of voice; changing the pace, or introducing dramatic pauses.
2. Facial expressions and body language; movement around the stage, and interacting with other characters and props.
3. Specific words/lines of the play, and the meaning that Shakespeare is trying to convey.
4. The ideas and meaning that Shakespeare is trying to convey.

Pages 84–85 Review Questions

1. a) Two ideas for each section of information [8]
      Possible ideas for your tourist guide: the most important tourist sites near you, along with how to get there, prices, and contact details (some of this can be made up!); a range of places stay, and places to eat and drink – budget, mid-price and expensive, along with directions and prices; places to relax or have fun, with a range of places to appeal to different ages, along with directions and prices, etc.
   b) **An excellent answer will:**
      - Display a full awareness of purpose, audience and form
      - Offer concise but extensive details (including facts, statistics, proper nouns, directions, etc.) to make the

guide fully user-friendly
- Present a variety of ideas, using a sophisticated range of vocabulary and sentence structures
- Use paragraphs and a variety of connectives to effectively structure the guide
- Achieve a high level of technical accuracy: spelling, grammar, punctuation
- Engage the reader throughout and achieve a high level of useful, relevant detail.

A good answer will:
- Display some awareness of purpose, audience and form
- Offer plenty of detail, but not always be fully concise or complete
- Present some variety of ideas, using effective vocabulary and different sentence structures
- Use paragraphs and connectives to separate ideas within the guide
- Achieve an acceptable level of technical accuracy: most familiar words spelled correctly, accurate grammar with only a few minor errors, a range of punctuation but some errors with complex constructions
- Engage the reader, but not always include important details.

[30 marks – 14 for purpose, audience and form; 8 for sentence structure, punctuation and spelling; 8 for the organisation]

2. An idea for an introduction, an idea for an end statement and at least one idea for points 2–4   [10]
   a) **Possible ideas:** the amount of packaging we buy creates pollution, so try to buy products that cut down on this and reuse things like plastic bags; carelessly discarding of rubbish builds up, so always find a bin and try to recycle; getting driven to school pollutes the atmosphere, so use public transport or walk; cut down on energy use by turning off lights, computers, etc. when they're not in use; spend a minute less in the shower each day in order to reduce water and energy use.
   b) **An excellent answer will:**
      - Display a full awareness of purpose, audience and form
      - Offer full explanations for all of your ideas, linking to how they can reduce pollution
      - Present a variety of ideas, using a sophisticated range of vocabulary and sentence structures
      - Use paragraphs and a variety of connectives to effectively structure the speech
      - Achieve a high level of technical accuracy: spelling, grammar, punctuation
      - Engage the reader throughout and achieve a high level of clarity.

   A good answer will:
   - Display some awareness of purpose, audience and form
   - Explain most ideas well, drawing some links to how they will reduce pollution
   - Present some variety of ideas, using

- effective vocabulary and different sentence structures
- Use paragraphs and connectives to separate ideas within the speech
- Achieve an acceptable level of technical accuracy: most familiar words spelled correctly, accurate grammar with only a few minor errors, a range of punctuation but some errors with complex constructions
- Engage the reader, but not always explain ideas with full clarity.

[30 marks – 14 for purpose, audience and form; 8 for sentence structure, punctuation and spelling; 8 for the organisation]

3. a) **Three ideas for costumes, three ideas for feelings, four ideas for words/phrases describing atmosphere.** **[10]**
Possible ideas: a group of witches; people dressed up as famous pop stars; a gang of scarecrows; etc. felt a bit silly at first when getting into costume; happy because everyone was enjoying themselves; proud to have taken part and raised money; etc. exhilarating, chaotic, exuberant, energising.

   b) **An excellent answer will:**
   - Display a full awareness of purpose, audience and form
   - Offer a variety of ideas, using sophisticated vocabulary and sentence structures
   - Use paragraphs and a variety of connectives to effectively structure the article
   - Achieve a high level of technical accuracy: spelling, grammar, punctuation
   - Engage the reader throughout and achieve a high level of relevant, effective description.

   A good answer will:
   - Display some awareness of purpose, audience and form
   - Offer plenty of ideas, but not as varied as they could be, using effective vocabulary and different sentence structures
   - Use paragraphs and connectives to separate ideas
   - Achieve an acceptable level of technical accuracy: most familiar words spelled correctly, accurate grammar with only a few minor errors, a range of punctuation but some errors with complex constructions
   - Engage the reader, but not always with highly effective or relevant description.

   [30 marks – 14 for purpose, audience and form; 8 for sentence structure, punctuation and spelling; 8 for organisation]

Pages 86–87 Practice Questions

1. **1 mark for relevant quotation; 1 mark for explanation of how quotation answers the question**
   a) 'One out of suits with fortune' / 'My pride fell with my fortunes. ' These quotations indicate that Rosalind feels that her situation is not good since her father went into exile. **[2]**
   b) Orlando displays his loyalty to his father, and would not betray him for all Duke Frederick's favour, 'I am more proud to be Sir Rowland's son, / His youngest son; and would not change that calling, / To be adopted heir to Frederick.' **[2]**
   c) Orlando is so overcome by romantic feelings that he cannot speak: 'What passion hangs these weights upon my tongue?' **[2]**
   d) Celia's metaphor, 'My father's rough and envious disposition / Sticks me at my heart' shows she is upset by her father's behaviour. **[2]**

2. **1 mark for relevant quotation; 1 mark for explanation of how quotation answers the question**
   a) Rosalind gives Orlando a love token and says she would like to give him more: 'That could give more, but that her hand lacks means.' **[2]**
   b) Orlando describes himself as beaten by, and suffering for, love: 'O poor Orlando, thou art overthrown!' **[2]**
   c) When Rosalind offers her love token, Orlando does not speak (showing that he is overcome by love; he later says: 'Can I not say, I thank you?'). **[2]**
   d) When Rosalind says she is 'out of suits with fortune' we are reminded that her father has been exiled and she has lost her status. **[2]**

3. **a)-c) 1 mark for relevant quotation; 1 mark for explanation of how quotation answers the question**
   a) Orlando describes himself as 'proud' of his father; Rosalind says that she would have 'given him [Orlando] tears' if she had realised the family link to her own father. **[2]**
   b) Orlando uses emotive language, metaphor, rhetorical question and exclamation to show his shock at being in love, 'What passion hangs these weights upon my tongue/ O poor Orlando, thou art overthrown!' **[2]**
   c) Celia's descriptive speech shows her disappointment with her father ('Sticks me at heart') and her faith in love ('Your mistress shall be happy'). **[2]**
   d) The lack of pride she shows when making her feelings obvious to Orlando, and the loss of her father (and status) when he was exiled by Frederick. **[2]**

4. **2 marks for two relevant quotations; 2 marks for two explanations of how quotations answer the question**
   a) **For example,** when Rosalind mentions 'my father', she could clutch her hands to her heart to remind the audience how strong her love is for him. Her tone of voice should be melancholy to show her sadness at his exile, but also full of wonder to emphasise how highly she thinks of her father. When she refers to this 'young man' she could hold her hand out towards Orlando to suggest the bond that is growing between them, perhaps making a fist and emphasising the word 'tears' to emphasise her strength of feeling but also the highs and lows of love. **[4]**
   b) **For example,** Orlando should be speaking a little more loudly than is polite. This shows his strong love for his father, but also that he has not yet learned gentlemanly behaviour. His speech could speed up as he says 'his youngest son', but then pause to remind us of what he has lost by not being the eldest. His voice should go quieter, with a tone of disgust as he mentions Frederick (who has just criticised his father). He should then turn and walk away to emphasise his pride and his rejection of Frederick's world (as inhabited by Celia and Rosalind). **[4]**

Pages 88–95 Revise Questions

Page 89 Quick Test
1. Romeo is not interested in the feud between the Montagues and Capulets.
2. Love (and how painful it is).
3. She worries things are happening between her and Romeo too quickly, yet she is strong-minded and is willing to marry in secret.
4. At the start of the play, she is obedient and gets on well with her parents and they seem to care for her; by the middle of the play, they are angry at her defiance and turn their backs on her.

Page 91 Quick Test
1. Romeo and Juliet.
2. The feud between the Capulets and Montagues (shown at the start of the play, and between Tybalt, Romeo and Mercutio).
3. They rush into marriage; they only have a short amount of time together before Romeo's exile; the preparations for Juliet's marriage to Paris are rushed; the Friar's letter fails to reach Romeo in time; and Romeo kills himself just before Juliet wakes.
4. Romeo and Juliet are described as 'star-crossed', as if they were fated to be thwarted in their love; they are also said to be from the 'fatal loins' of enemy families, as if they are the only thing that can resolve the hatred but are doomed by the inherited conflict; their lives are full of coincidences that bring them together and tear them apart.

Page 93 Quick Test
1. To make the audience think/feel; to show a character persuading or motivating others.
2. To help the audience imagine a scene, or understand how a character sees a situation.
3. To convey powerful emotions, getting the audience to understand how a character feels or helping them to share a character's feelings.
4. Rhetorical devices, such as repetition, triplets and emotive language; verbs, adjectives and adverbs; simile, metaphor and personification; short sentences, orders and exclamation; symbolism.

Page 95 Quick Test
1. Emphasise words and meaning by raising and lowering volume, altering the tone of voice, changing the pace, or introducing dramatic pauses.
2. Facial expressions and body language; movement around the stage, and interacting with other characters and props.
3. Specific words/lines of the play.
4. The ideas and meaning that Shakespeare is trying to convey.

1. **Possible points on the first extract:** Orlando feels mistreated by Oliver (questions, similes, metaphors, comparisons to animals); they treat each other with mock politeness ('Sir') but then they fight; though Oliver is in a more powerful situation, Orlando is physically stronger; they insult each other ('villain'); Orlando wants their relationship to change (he demands to be heard and to be allowed to leave).

    Possible points on the second extract: Oliver is grateful to, and impressed by, Orlando for saving him from the lion (comparisons and adjectives); he now loves his brother (use of past/present tense, and 'shame'); he feels duty towards his brother (descriptions or actions).

    An excellent answer will:
    *   Focus on the how language shows the changes in Orlando and Oliver's relationship
    *   Present a variety of ideas, appreciating how the first extract shows their enmity, while the second shows their love
    *   Feature a balanced coverage of both extracts, with regular comparisons drawn between the two
    *   Offer concise analysis of the effects of Shakespeare's language, making use of a range of technical terms such as adjective and simile
    *   Successfully integrate regular, skilfully selected quotations into a well-developed discussion.

    A good answer will:
    *   Display a general focus on the changes in Orlando and Oliver's relationship
    *   Present a number of ideas, appreciating how the first extract shows their enmity, while the second shows their love
    *   Feature a balanced coverage of both texts, with some comparison
    *   Show awareness of the effects of Shakespeare's language, with some analysis and use of technical language
    *   Support all ideas with brief quotations. **[18]**

1. **a)–c) 1 mark for relevant quotation; 1 mark for explanation of how quotation answers the question**
    a) For example, Romeo asks for 'one kiss', and Juliet calls him, 'love, lord, ay, husband.' **[2]**
    b) She sounds desperate when she says 'I must hear from thee every day in the hour.' **[2]**
    c) He says 'I doubt it not,' and suggests that they will look back on these bad times in the future, 'sweet discourse in our time to come.' **[2]**
    d) She imagines she will be old before they see each other again; she questions how long it will be; then she has a vision of him dead. **[2]**
2. **1 mark for relevant quotation; 1 mark for explanation of how quotation answers the question**
    a) Romeo addresses her as 'love' several times, and uses romantic phrases like 'kiss' and 'sweet discourses' to show his feelings for her. **[2]**

b) Juliet's words 'for in a minute there are many days' shows that she feels time without Romeo will stretch and be almost unbearable. **[2]**
c) Romeo keeps repeating 'Farewell' but he does not leave. **[2]**
d) Juliet has a vision of the end of the play, seeing Romeo 'as one dead in the bottom of a tomb'. **[2]**

3. a) **1 mark for relevant quotation; 1 mark for explanation of how quotation answers the question** For example, her phrase 'let day in, and let life out' shows that now it is day Romeo must leave, but the contrasting phrase also emphasises her feelings that her life will be over when he goes. **[2]**
    b) Juliet uses rhetorical question, personification, alliteration and repetition to explore the idea that Fortune is toying with her and Romeo's relationship. **[2]**
    c) Juliet describes an image of Romeo dead and in a tomb to suggest that she thinks their relationship is being brought to an end. **[2]**
    d) The personification emphasises that they are both feeling miserable and hopeless at the idea of a life without the other. **[2]**
4. **2 marks for relevant quotation; 2 marks for explanation of how quotation answers the question**
    a) For example, when she says 'window, let day in, and let life out', she should speak slowly and mournfully, to convey her feeling that there is no life without Romeo. She could also stand in front of the window, barring it, to emphasise the idea in this scene that they both know he must go but they want to stay where they are. **[4]**
    b) For example, when Romeo repeats 'Farewell!' he could leap into the frame of the window, aware that he must go. However, he could then pause and turn, showing the audience that he doesn't want to leave. As he asks for 'one kiss', he could take Juliet's hand to emphasise the bond between them, then pull her hand to his lips before saying he must go. **[4]**

Page 101 Quick Test
1. Brave, respected, good-natured, and has a conscience.
2. He loses respect, becomes cruel and vicious, and begins to lose control of his mind.
3. She is more confident and manipulative, making plans and giving Macbeth orders.
4. She has lost her mind and is full of regret.

Page 103 Quick Test
1. Macbeth and Lady Macbeth.
2. Lady Macbeth and the witches.
3. She is full of regret and becomes mad, then dies. 4. Macbeth has killed the king chosen by God, and taken his place.

Page 105 Quick Test
1. To make the audience think/feel; to show a character persuading or motivating others.
2. To help the audience imagine a scene, or understand how a character sees a situation.
3. To convey powerful emotions, getting the

audience to understand how a character feels or helping them to share a character's feelings.
4. Rhetorical devices, such as repetition, triplets and emotive language; verbs, adjectives and adverbs; simile, metaphor and personification; short sentences, orders and exclamation; symbolism.

Page 107 Quick Test
1. Emphasise words and meaning by raising and lowering volume, altering the tone of voice, changing the pace, or introducing dramatic pauses.
2. Facial expressions and body language; movement around the stage, and interacting with other characters and props. **3.** Specific words/lines of the play. **4.** The ideas and meaning that Shakespeare is trying to convey.

1. **Possible points on the first extract:** Capulet loves his daughter and thinks she is too young to marry (comparison); we find she is his only child (metaphor); he values her opinions and wants her to fall in love with Paris; he wants to be sure Paris really loves Juliet (metaphor and imperatives).

    Possible points on the second extract: angry with Juliet, he shouts at her, insults her, and gives her orders; he calls her a curse; he thinks she is ungrateful (list, mimicry); he threatens her (short sentences, exclamations, verbs)

    An excellent answer will:
    *   Focus on the how language shows the changes in Lord Capulet's feelings towards Juliet
    *   Present a variety of ideas, appreciating how the first extract shows his love and consideration, while the second shows anger and lack of love
    *   Feature a balanced coverage of both extracts, with regular comparisons drawn between the two
    *   Offer concise analysis of the effects of Shakespeare's language, making use of a range of technical terms such as adjective and simile
    *   Successfully integrate regular, skilfully-selected quotations into a well-developed discussion.

    A good answer will:
    *   Display a general focus on the changes in Lord Capulet's feelings towards Juliet
    *   Present a number of ideas, appreciating how the first extract shows his love, while the second shows his hostility
    *   Feature a balanced coverage of both texts, with some comparison
    *   Awareness of the effects of Shakespeare's language, with some analysis and use of technical language
    *   Support all ideas with brief quotations. **[18]**

1. **1 mark for relevant quotation; 1 mark for explanation of how quotation answers the question**
    a) She is dominant over Macbeth and mocks him: 'O proper stuff! This is the very painting of your fear.' **[2]**

b) He seems less brave and more cunning (pretending he does not know Banquo is dead); 'Thou canst not say I did it'. **[2]**

c) 'Were the graced person of our Banquo present' shows he is dishonest, because he does not consider Banquo as 'graced', and he knows Banquo is dead. 'Thou canst not say I did it: never shake / Thy gory locks at me,' shows he feels guilty for what he has done and is frightened by the appearance of Banquo's ghost. **[2]**

d) Fear and guilt; 'If thou canst nod, speak too'. **[2]**

2. **1 mark for relevant quotation; 1 mark for explanation of how quotation answers the question**

a) Only Macbeth can see the ghost of Banquo, so he seems mad: 'When all's done you look but on a stool'. Perhaps it is not really there and he is mad. **[2]**

b) Lady Macbeth manipulates Macbeth by belittling him: 'O, these flaws and starts, / Impostors to true fear, would well become / A woman's story at a winter's fire.' **[2]**

c) Macbeth talks about people returning from the dead, 'our graves must send / Those that we bury back'. **[2]**

d) Macbeth speaks like a King, using the plural pronouns 'we' and 'our' and referring to 'our country'. **[2]**

3. **1 mark for relevant quotation; 1 mark for explanation of how quotation answers the question**

a) 'never shake / Thy gory locks at me' sounds as if Macbeth is desperate for the ghost to stop, with the phrase 'gory locks' creating a particularly horrible image. **[2]**

b) She uses repeated exclamations to show her anger, repeats 'This...' to suggest that Macbeth is just imagining Banquo, and uses the rhetorical question 'Why do you make such faces?' to try to get him to behave more normally. **[2]**

c) When Macbeth describes people coming back from the dead, we can tell that he is terrified, but also that his mind is disturbed. **[2]**

d) They repeatedly call him 'Sir', and say that they would be honoured to have him sit with them. **[2]**

4. **2 marks for two relevant quotations; 2 marks for two explanations of how quotations answer the question**

a) For example, when Lady Macbeth tries to calm the guests down after Macbeth's outburst, she should sound friendly but also pleading in order to remind us that she is pretending all is well. As she says, 'Sit worthy friends' she could put her arms out to indicate their places but, in doing so, also shield Macbeth from them a little. When she explains away Macbeth's behaviour, 'my lord is often thus', she could stumble a little at first to indicate that she is making it up, with her voice going up a pitch and her speech being quite fast to betray her nervousness. **[4]**

b) For example, at the start of this extract, Macbeth should seem calm and confident. He should circle the room as he talks to suggest his power over them all, linking with his repeated use of the possessive

pronoun 'our'. When he comes to Banquo's name, he could arrive at his empty seat and grasp it as he comments on his absence. This will highlight to the audience how easily Macbeth now lies to his people. **[4]**

Pages 112–113 Review Questions

1. **Possible points on the first extract:** Ross reports how impressed the King is (lots of positive nouns); he also reports that the lords have been praising Macbeth (simile and metaphor); Macbeth has been awarded Thane of Cawdor (exclamation and repetition).

Possible points on the second extract: Macduff describes how bad Scotland has become (repetition, exclamations and verbs); Malcolm calls Macbeth a tyrant and treacherous, and comments on how he has changed (metaphor); Malcolm compares Scotland to an injured woman (personification) and says he wants to kill Macbeth.

An excellent answer will:
- Focus on the how language shows how people's opinions of Macbeth change
- Present a variety of ideas, appreciating how the first extract shows people's respect for Macbeth, while the second shows anger and hatred towards him
- Feature a balanced coverage of both extracts, with regular comparisons drawn between the two
- Offer concise analysis of the effects of Shakespeare's language, making use of a range of technical terms such as adjective and simile
- Successfully integrate regular, skilfully-selected quotations into a well-developed discussion.

A good answer will:
- Display a general focus on how people's opinions of Macbeth change
- Present a number of ideas, appreciating how the first extract shows people's respect for Macbeth, while the second shows hatred towards him
- Feature a balanced coverage of both texts, with some comparison
- Show awareness of the effects of Shakespeare's language, with some analysis and use of technical language
- Support all ideas with brief quotations. **[18]**

Pages 114–117 Reading Mixed Test-Style Questions

1. a) i) They are easy to grow and colourful. **[1]**
   ii) Children will enjoy eating them. **[1]**

b) So that children cannot get hold of them and possibly injure themselves. **[2]**

c) i) To enjoy/get satisfaction from the results of hard work. **[2]**
   ii) One of the results of gardening is getting fruit to eat, so here it is not just a metaphor but really what happens. Brackets show it is an 'aside', an extra remark. The exclamation mark shows that it is a joke/pun.

[2 marks – 1 for explanation; 1 for comment on punctuation]

d) i) Safety First; Parents need to do this to stop children falling in the water, so it is a matter of safety.
   ii) Fun and Educational Too; If you are learning something, like responsibility, you are being educated.
   iii) Getting Kids Involved; Showing them these things might make them want to learn gardening. **[3]**

e) **Suggested content:**
- The leaflet is aimed at parents who are already thinking about gardening with their children.
- It starts with 'If your children are showing an interest in gardening', so it is not saying they should try to make children interested in something new, but giving ways of encouraging their interest.
- The advice is simple and sensible. It makes it sound quite easy and cheap: 'a few plant pots or a window box will do'.
- It focuses on things that might appeal to children, like colourful plants or playing in the mud and it explains why they might like these things.
- There is a section about safety because parents would worry about children getting hurt. This would reassure parents their children could garden without much risk if they followed the advice, such as locking away tools and using sunscreen.
- The last section is about it being 'educational' because parents often like to think children are learning from things. This shows it is more for adults than children.
- There are lots of imperatives, e.g. 'Get the right equipment'. It is an advice leaflet and the people who read it want to be told what to do.
- It also tries to be friendly and informal. 'Let them get dirty!' has an exclamation mark to show it is fun.
- Contractions like 'they'll' and 'you're' are used (instead of 'they will' and 'you are'), which makes it sound like someone talking.
- The leaflet is clearly divided into three sections, with sub-headings that make it easy to find information.
- Bullet points are used to break up the text and make the instructions clear.
- The picture helps give the idea that gardening is fun because the children look so happy in them.

[10 marks – 2 for one or two of these or similar points; 6 for about half of them; 10 for most of these points and some original points]

> Longer answers often come at the end of a test. Make sure you leave enough time to answer them properly.

2. a) She is happy/ enjoying herself/content ('a little laugh of pleasure'/'she laughed again'). No mark for 'a good mood'. **[3 marks – 1 for identifying mood plus 2 for a quotation]**

b) i) He follows her and he greets her. [2]
   ii) Animals, like dogs and cats, follow people they know / following her could show he trusts her and/or wants to be near her.
   'Greeting' means saying 'hello'. You do this if you see someone you know/ recognise. [2]
c) i) It has been hidden by the ivy. [2]
   ii) A gust of wind blows the ivy away so she can see the door knob. [2]
d) **Suggested content:**
   * At the beginning of the extract Mary is very happy, skipping in the gardens, and there is no sense of mystery.
   * When she sees the robin, she feels 'something heavy in her pocket.' This makes her remember how the robin 'helped' her find the key and she still does not know where the door is that the key fits.
   * She says to the robin, 'You ought to show me the door', but she laughs, suggesting that she does not really think he could actually do this.
   * Then the writer builds up the sense of mystery by referring to magic. She says that Mary 'always said that what happened ... was Magic.' Therefore, we expect something mysterious to happen and wonder what it will be.
   * The writer describes the wind rushing down the walk, as if it had a will of its own and wanted to reveal what the ivy is hiding. It is as if the robin and the wind are part of the 'Magic'.
   * The word 'suddenly' is used twice and Mary 'jumped' towards the ivy, giving a sense of speed and excitement.
   * The second paragraph ends with a very short sentence: 'It was the knob of a door.' This is important information and it helps build excitement and mystery because we now need to know whether the key fits.
   * Hodgson Burnett then describes how Mary feels. Her 'heart began to thump and her hands to shake'.
   * Her mood of 'delight and excitement' makes the reader excited too. The fact that the robin also appears to be excited adds to this.
   * This paragraph ends with a rhetorical question (What was this...?'), which makes the reader wonder if it is the lock to the door.
   * Making the door difficult to open ('it took two hands') adds to the tension, because it would have been disappointing if Mary had not been able to open the door.
   * Mary pauses to take a breath, adding to the excitement and mystery by delaying the opening of the door.
   * She looks around, making us think that if anyone came she would not open the door.
   * At last she opens the door, 'breathing quite fast with... wonder and delight.'
   * The writer ends with a paragraph that contains only one sentence. This

emphasises the importance of the moment Mary stands in the garden for the first time and makes the reader look forward to finding out more.
[10 marks – 2 for one or two of these or similar points; 6 for about half of them; 10 for most of these points and some original points]

> Refer to the author by his or her surname or as 'the writer'.

Pages 118–119 Writing Mixed Test-Style Questions

1. **Possible ideas for your letter:** check your timetable every night so you pack the right equipment for the next day; keep a diary of your homework so you have plenty of time to complete work and get it in on time; wear your school uniform neatly; try to share your ideas in class with confidence, without being domineering; follow the school rules and be well behaved; introduce yourself to people; suggest things to others, like going to the canteen together or joining a club.
   An excellent answer will:
   * Display a full awareness of purpose, audience and form
   * Include a full range of techniques in order to convey advice effectively, such as second person, statements and imperatives, rhetorical question, alternatives, etc.
   * Present a variety of ideas, using a sophisticated range of vocabulary and sentence structures
   * Use paragraphs and a variety of connectives to effectively structure the letter
   * Achieve a high level of technical accuracy: spelling, grammar, punctuation
   * Engage the reader throughout and offer convincing advice.
   A good answer will:
   * Display some awareness of purpose, audience and form
   * Include some techniques to emphasise the advice being offered
   * Present some variety of ideas, using effective vocabulary and different sentence structures
   * Use paragraphs and connectives to introduce different parts of the letter
   * Achieve an acceptable level of technical accuracy: most familiar words spelled correctly, accurate grammar with only a few minor errors, a range of punctuation but some errors with complex constructions
   * Engage the reader, but not be fully convincing throughout.
   [30 marks – 14 for purpose, audience and form; 8 for sentence structure, punctuation and spelling; 8 for organisation.]
2. **Possible ideas for your creative writing:** include detailed descriptions of settings, people, events, thoughts and feelings; build up a sense of the atmosphere at the time; try to capture small details that the reader will be able to imagine in order to add realism and interest.

An excellent answer will:
* Display a full awareness of purpose, audience and form
* Include a full range of descriptive techniques: interesting verbs/adjectives/ adverbs, simile, metaphor, personification, onomatopoeia, senses, etc.
* Present a variety of ideas, using a sophisticated range of vocabulary and sentence structures
* Use paragraphs and a variety of connectives to effectively structure the description
* Achieve a high level of technical accuracy: spelling, grammar, punctuation
* Engage the reader throughout with striking, sometimes surprising, images, and an effective narrative voice.
A good answer will:
* Display some awareness of purpose, audience and form
* Include some descriptive techniques to help the reader imagine
* Present some variety of ideas, using effective vocabulary and different sentence structures
* Use paragraphs and connectives to separate ideas within the creative writing
* Achieve an acceptable level of technical accuracy: most familiar words spelled correctly, accurate grammar with only a few minor errors, a range of punctuation but some errors with complex constructions
* Engage the reader, but not always create imaginative, interesting images.
[30 marks – 14 for purpose, audience and form; 8 for sentence structure, punctuation and spelling; 8 for organisation]

Pages 120–129 Shakespeare Mixed Test-Style Questions

1. **Possible points on the first extract:** young Tybalt wants to keep the family feud going, but the older family members want to stop the conflict; conflict caused by a sense of personal slight; conflict is about having power (Capulet doesn't like Tybalt disobeying him); conflict shown through insulting language and exclamations.

   Possible points on the second extract: Tybalt tries to continue the conflict through insults and threats, while Romeo tries to calm it down; Mercutio gets caught up in the conflict, in order to protect Romeo's honour; conflict results in death.

   An excellent answer will:
   * Focus on the how characters, events and language are used to show the theme of conflict
   * Present a variety of ideas, appreciating how similar and different aspects of conflict appear in the two extracts
   * Feature a balanced coverage of both extracts, with regular comparisons drawn between the two
   * Offer concise analysis of the effects of Shakespeare's language and stagecraft, making use of a range of technical terms such as adjective and simile
   * Successfully integrate regular, skilfully-selected quotations into a well-developed discussion.

A good answer will:
- Display a general focus on the theme of conflict
- Present a number of ideas, appreciating how the two extracts show different aspects of conflict
- Feature a balanced coverage of both texts, with some comparison
- Show awareness of the effects of Shakespeare's language and stagecraft, with some analysis and use of technical language
- Support all ideas with brief quotations. **[18]**

2. **Possible points on the first extract:** Rosalind is loyal to her father and unhappy about his banishment; despite this she can be quite jolly; she is witty and quite wise; she is realistic and a bit cynical about love.

   Possible points on the second extract: Rosalind can be impatient, but is still witty; she is strong-willed and resourceful, having entered the forest and dressed as a man; she is in love with Orlando and nervous about seeing him; she doubts Orlando's love.

   An excellent answer will:
   - Focus on the how language shows Rosalind's different characteristics
   - Present a variety of ideas, appreciating how the two extracts show similar and different aspects of her personality
   - Feature a balanced coverage of both extracts, with regular comparisons drawn between the two
   - Offer concise analysis of the effects of Shakespeare's language and stagecraft, making use of a range of technical terms such as adjective and simile
   - Successfully integrate regular, skilfully-selected quotations into a well-developed discussion.

   A good answer will:
   - Display a general focus on Rosalind's characteristics
   - Present a number of ideas, appreciating how the extracts show different sides of her personality
   - Feature a balanced coverage of both texts, with some comparison
   - Show awareness of the effects of Shakespeare's language and stagecraft, with some analysis and use of technical language
   - Support all ideas with brief quotations. **[18]**

3. **Possible points on the first extract:** Macbeth needs to appear nervous, with Lady Macbeth being annoyed by his reflective behaviour; she should be more confident, ordering him around; Macbeth should seem increasingly frightened and disturbed by what he has done, in contrast with Lady Macbeth's matter-of-fact calmness; he should appear to want her support, but she finds this weak.

   Possible points on the second extract: Lady Macbeth appears worried about Macbeth rather than annoyed; he seems less panicked but still concerned about their future, and he takes her advice; they show more love towards each other; she looks to him to take control of their future, and he wants to shield her from any more dark deeds.

   An excellent answer will:
   - Focus on the relationship between Macbeth and Lady Macbeth, and how this can be conveyed through the performance of specific lines
   - Present a variety of ideas, appreciating how the extracts show differing amounts of love, dominance and problems
   - Feature a balanced coverage of both extracts, with regular comparisons drawn between the two
   - Offer concise analysis of the effects of Shakespeare's language, making use of a range of technical terms such as adjective and simile
   - Successfully integrate regular, skilfully-selected quotations into a well-developed discussion.

   A good answer will:
   - Display a general focus on how the relationship between Macbeth and Lady Macbeth can be performed
   - Present a number of ideas, appreciating how Lady Macbeth seems more domineering in the first and more loving in the second, and Macbeth more reliant then more in control
   - Feature a balanced coverage of both texts, with some comparison
   - Show awareness of the effects of Shakespeare's language, with some analysis and use of technical language
   - Support all ideas with brief quotations. **[18]**

Glossary

a

abbreviation   a shortened form of a word or phrase

adjective   a describing word

adverb   word that describes a verb

advise   offer suggestions about the best course of action

alliteration   repetition of a sound at the beginning of two or more words

alphabetical   in the order of the letters of the alphabet

ambition   the wish to achieve success

apostrophe   a punctuation mark used to indicate either possession or the omission of letters or numbers

assonance   repetition of a *vowel sound* within words

argue   give reasons or cite evidence in support of an idea, action, or theory

attitude   someone's feelings or opinions

audience   the people addressed by a writer or speaker

b

balanced argument   presenting both sides of an issue

bullet point   each of several items in a list, typically the ideas or arguments in an article or presentation

c

cause   why something happens

character   a person in a text or what a person is like

choice   selecting or making a decision when faced with two or more possibilities

chronological order   the order in which things happen

clause   a unit of grammatical organisation within a sentence

colon   a punctuation mark (:)

comma   a punctuation mark (,)

comment   a remark expressing an opinion or reaction

complex sentence   a sentence comprising a main clause and a subordinate clause

compound sentence   a sentence combining two main clauses, joined by a conjunction

conclusion   a final summary, making any necessary judgements about a topic

conditional   something that is dependent on something else happening

conjunction   a joining word, such as 'and', 'but', 'if'

connective   a word or phrase that links ideas, such as 'however', 'in contrast'

connotation   a meaning that is suggested by the use of a word or phrase

conscience   a moral sense of right or wrong

content   subject matter; what something contains

context   parts of the text before and after a passage, influencing its meaning

corruption   a loss of morals

d

deduction   a conclusion, something worked out by the reader but not overtly stated by the writer

describe   create images to help a reader imagine something

develop   to clarify an idea, build upon it, or take it in a new direction

dialect   a form of language particular to a region

Divine Right   the belief that a position of power is given to someone by God

e

effect   the result or consequence of something

ellipsis   punctuation (three dots:...) indicating that something has been omitted

emotive language   words or phrases that convey or create powerful feelings

empathy   sympathising with someone else's emotions

emphasis   stressing, or attaching importance to, something

entertain   provide amusement or enjoyment

euphemism   replacing a harsh, blunt phrase with something that sounds kinder or more polite

evidence   information provided to support what the writer is saying

exclamation   something exclaimed, as if in shock

exclamation mark   a punctuation mark (!)

experience   practical contact with and observation of facts or events

explain   make clear to by describing in more detail

extended metaphor   a series of similar metaphors combining to create one image

f

fact   something that is real or true

fate   the future, as if controlled by some higher power or god

fiction   any text that is made up (not real)

focus   the central point

font   the style and size of type used

form   a type of writing or the way it is presented for a particular purpose, e.g. a leaflet or newspaper

formal   following rules or convention, not relaxed

future tense   describing events that will happen

h

headline   heading at the top of a newspaper or magazine article

hyperbole   exaggeration

i

illustration   a picture that complements the text

imagery   words and phrases that build up pictures in the reader's mind

imperative   an order, instruction or command

imply   suggest the truth or existence of something not expressly stated

inference   a deduction from the text about something that is implied but not openly stated by the writer

inform   provide facts or information

instruct   direct to do something

interpret   to explain or make clearer

introductory   starting

irony   getting across your point while appearing to state the opposite of what you mean

l

language   the method of human communication, either spoken or written

list   a series of words, items or small ideas

literal   taking words in their most basic sense, without metaphor or allegory

m

main clause   the main part of a sentence (it should make sense on its own)

manipulate/manipulation   to get people to do what you want in an indirect or dishonest way

melancholy   sadness

metaphor   a way of describing something by referring to it as something else

mime   an acting performance without words

mimicry   to imitate someone else's words, behaviour or way of talking

modal verb   a verb that shows the mood or state of another verb

n

non-fiction   any text that is mainly based on facts and not made up

o

onomatopoeia   words that sound like the sound they describe

opinion   what someone thinks

oppression   treating someone harshly and keeping them down

order   telling someone what to do

ownership   possession

oxymoron   a phrase consisting of contradictory words

p

pace   the speed of a speech or how rapidly events are described in a piece of writing

paragraph   a distinct section of a piece of writing, usually dealing with a single theme

paraphrase   to put into your own words

parody   imitating something in a humorous way

past tense   describing events that have happened

pause   a break in speech or writing

PEE   point, evidence, explanation

personification   describing an object as if it has human qualities

persuade   cause to do or believe something through reasoning or argument

plan   the method by which someone intends to do something

plural   denoting more than one

point   a single item or detail in an extended discussion, list, or text

present tense   describes events that are currently happening

presentation   how something looks on the page

pronoun   a word used instead of, and to indicate, a noun, such as 'he', 'it'

purpose   the reason for writing or saying something

q

quotation   words or phrases taken directly from the text

r

reaction   experience in response to a situation or event

reference   mentioning or alluding to something

repartee   making witty retorts or quick replies

repetition   saying or writing something more than once

rhetorical device   use of words in a certain way to convey meaning or persuade

rhetorical question   a question to get someone to think, rather than to get an answer

rhyme   correspondence of sound between words or the endings of words

s

second person   addressing your audience, using 'you'

select   choose

senses   sight, smell, sound, taste, touch

sentence   words conveying a statement, question, command or exclamation

sibilance   repetition of 's' sounds

simile   a way of describing something by comparing it to something else using 'like' or 'as'

simple sentence   a sentence that only contains a main clause

skim reading   reading quickly to find something in the text

slang   informal language, often local and changing quickly

speech mark   each of a set of punctuation marks, single (' ') or double (" ")

Standard English   the variety of English generally accepted as the correct form for formal writing and speaking

stanza   a section of a poem, often called a verse

statistic   numerical data

structure   the way in which a text is organised

sub-heading   a word or phrase, in bold or underlined, which breaks up and organises text

subordinate clause   extra information that is added to a main clause

symbolism   the use of symbols (things that represent other things or ideas)

t

tense   form of a verb, indicating time (past, present, future)

text   a book or other written or printed work, regarded in terms of its content rather than its physical form

text box   a box containing text

the second person   you

thematic   linking to subjects or topics

tone   the general feeling or mood of the text

topic sentence   a sentence that expresses the main idea of the paragraph in which it occurs

triplet   three similar ideas arranged together for effect

turning point   a point in the text when things change.

u

unrequited   not returned

usurp   take the place of

v

verb   a doing or being word

w

wit   quick intelligence and humour

Index

Collins

KS3
English
Workbook

Paul Burns and Ian Kirby

Revision Tips

Rethink Revision

Have you ever taken part in a quiz and thought '*I know this*!', but no matter how hard you scrabbled around in your brain you just couldn't come up with the answer?

It's very frustrating when this happens, but in a fun situation it doesn't really matter. However, in tests and assessments, it is essential that you can recall the relevant information when you need to.

Most students think that revision is about making sure you **know** *stuff*, but it is also about being confident that you can **retain** that *stuff* over time and **recall** it when needed.

Revision that Really Works

Experts have found that there are two techniques that help with *all* of these things and consistently produce better results in tests and exams compared to other revision techniques.

Applying these techniques to your KS3 revision will ensure you get better results in tests and assessments and will have all the relevant knowledge at your fingertips when you start studying for your GCSEs.

It really isn't rocket science either – you simply need to:

* **test yourself** on each topic as many times as possible
* **leave a gap** between the test sessions.

It is most effective if you leave a good period of time between the test sessions, e.g. between a week and a month. The idea is that just as you start to forget the information, you force yourself to recall it again, keeping it fresh in your mind.

Three Essential Revision Tips

1 Use Your Time Wisely
* Allow yourself plenty of time
* Try to start revising six months before tests and assessments – it's more effective and less stressful
* Your revision time is precious so use it wisely – using the techniques described on this page will ensure you revise effectively and efficiently and get the best results
* Don't waste time re-reading the same information over and over again – it's time-consuming and not effective!

2 Make a Plan
* Identify all the topics you need to revise (this Complete Revision & Practice book will help you)
* Plan at least five sessions for each topic
* A one-hour session should be ample to test yourself on the key ideas for a topic
* Spread out the practice sessions for each topic – the optimum time to leave between each session is about one month but, if this isn't possible, just make the gaps as big as realistically possible.

3 Test Yourself
* Methods for testing yourself include: quizzes, practice questions, flashcards, past-papers, explaining a topic to someone else, etc.
* This Complete Revision & Practice book gives you seven practice test opportunities per topic
* Don't worry if you get an answer wrong – provided you check what the right answer is, you are more likely to get the same or similar questions right in future!

Visit **collins.co.uk/collinsks3revision** to download your free flashcards, for more information about the benefits of these revision techniques and for further guidance on how to plan ahead and make them work for you.

Contents

Reading 1

Selecting Key Words and Ideas

Read the passage below and answer the questions that follow.

The Railways of Victorian Britain

Prince Albert, the husband of Queen Victoria, organised a 'Great Exhibition' of industry and culture from around the world, which opened in Crystal Palace, London, in 1851. Most of the working people who went to the Great Exhibition arrived by rail, often from the north of England. King's Cross Station had opened in 1850 and there were nearly 7,000 miles of track linking London with the towns of the Midlands and the North.

The most popular way of getting to the Great Exhibition was by buying a ticket that included a return rail journey and entry to the exhibition. Hundreds of thousands of people took advantage of these day trips, which were the idea of Thomas Cook. He booked trains from all over Britain to accommodate the visitors and charged them 4, 5 or 6 shillings each. He had invented the 'day out'.

As Cook's business grew, he began to offer excursions to more and more places, including trips to other European countries. Soon the railway companies began to run their own excursions.

At first, railway companies tried to avoid dealing with poorer people and ran trains that only offered first and second class carriages. They also left out many stations on their routes. However, in 1844 the Railways Act stated that at least one train per day must stop at every station and all trains must include third class carriages. Now many more Victorians could afford to travel by train.

The railways made a huge difference to the leisure activities of the Victorians. Not only were opportunities for day trips and holidays increased, but sporting events also grew in popularity. Special trains were run to take people to the races, cricket matches and the FA Cup Final, which was held for the first time in 1872. It was not only spectators who benefitted: the football clubs that were starting up in Britain's towns and cities could now travel away from home to play against each other.

In 1888 the Football League was founded. It was made up of professional teams. It would have been impossible for the first teams to travel to away matches without regular trains, so the railways were very important in the development of professional football.

For most people, the most significant development was probably the introduction of cheap day-return tickets. In 1871, Bank Holidays – days when working people in the country had a day off work – were introduced. This was the start of the great British tradition of the day at the seaside, where people from all social classes enjoyed walks along the pier, funfairs and treats such as sticks of rock, candy-floss, and, of course, fish and chips.

1 Who was Price Albert married to?.. [1]

2 According to the text, who invented the 'day out'?.. [1]

3 According to the writer, which two of these statements are true? Tick the correct answers.

   a) People travelled by train to get to the Great Exhibition. ☐

   b) Only rich people used the railways. ☐

   c) The Great Exhibition took place in London. ☐

   d) Before 1844, all trains had third-class carriages. ☐ [2]

4 Give two ways in which the Railways Act made sure more people (especially poorer people) could use the railways.

   ....

   .... [2]

5 Put the following events in chronological order by putting the numbers 1–5 in the boxes (1 being the earliest event, 5 being the latest).

   a) The Football League was founded. ☐

   b) The Railways Act was passed. ☐

   c) The first FA Cup Final was held. ☐

   d) Bank holidays were introduced. ☐

   e) King's Cross Station was opened. ☐ [5]

6 List four things that the Victorians enjoyed at the seaside, according to the text.

   ....

   ....

   .... [4]

Total Marks .... / 15

Reading 2

Inference, Deduction and Interpretation

Read the passage below and answer the questions that follow.

The Wind in the Willows describes the adventures of animals who live near the Wild Wood. One day, Mole, who has never been into the Wild Wood before, leaves Ratty's house to explore the woods, ignoring Ratty's warnings.

'The Wild Wood' from *The Wind in the Willows* by Kenneth Grahame

It was a cold still afternoon with a hard steely sky overhead, when he slipped out of the warm parlour into the open air. […] He was glad that he liked the country undecorated, hard, and stripped of its finery. He had got down to the bare bones of it, and they were fine and strong and simple. He did not want the warm clover and the play of seeding grasses; the screens of quickset, the billowy drapery of beech and elm seemed best away; and with great cheerfulness of spirit he pushed on towards the Wild Wood, which lay before him low and threatening, like a black reef in some still southern sea.

There was nothing to alarm him at first entry. Twigs crackled under his feet, logs tripped him, funguses on stumps resembled caricatures, and startled him for the moment by their likeness to something familiar and far away; but that was all fun, and exciting. It led him on, and he penetrated to where the light was less, and trees crouched nearer and nearer, and holes made ugly mouths at him on either side.

Everything was very still now. The dusk advanced on him steadily, rapidly, gathering in behind and before; and the light seemed to be draining away like flood-water.

Then the faces began.

It was over his shoulder, and indistinctly, that he first thought he saw a face; a little evil wedge-shaped face, looking out at him from a hole. When he turned and confronted it, the thing had vanished.

He quickened his pace, telling himself cheerfully not to begin imagining things, or there would be simply no end to it. He passed another hole, and another, and another; and then—yes!—no!—yes! certainly a little narrow face, with hard eyes, had flashed up for an instant from a hole, and was gone. He hesitated—braced himself up for an effort and strode on. Then suddenly, and as if it had been so all the time, every hole, far and near, and there were hundreds of them, seemed to possess its face, coming and going rapidly, all fixing on him glances of malice and hatred: all hard-eyed and evil and sharp.

If he could only get away from the holes in the banks, he thought, there would be no more faces. He swung off the path and plunged into the untrodden places of the wood.

Then the whistling began.

Very faint and shrill it was, and far behind him, when first he heard it; but somehow it made him hurry forward. Then, still very faint and shrill, it sounded far ahead of him, and made him hesitate and want to go back. As he halted in indecision it broke out on either side, and seemed to be caught up and passed on throughout the whole length of the wood to its farthest limit. They were up and alert and ready, evidently, whoever they were! And he—he was alone, and unarmed, and far from any help; and the night was closing in.

Then the pattering began.

He thought it was only falling leaves at first, so slight and delicate was the sound of it. Then as it grew it took a regular rhythm, and he knew it for nothing else but the pat-pat-pat of little feet still a very long way off. Was it in front or behind? It seemed to be first one, and then the other, then both. It grew and it multiplied, till from every quarter as he listened anxiously, leaning this way and that, it seemed to be closing in on him. As he stood still to hearken, a rabbit came running hard towards him through the trees. He waited, expecting it to slacken pace, or to swerve from him into a different course. Instead, the animal almost brushed him as it dashed past, his face set and hard, his eyes staring. "Get out of this, you fool, get out!" the Mole heard him mutter as he swung round a stump and disappeared down a friendly burrow.

1 Write a phrase from the first paragraph which shows that Mole is happy and optimistic.

.... [1]

2 Pick out two phrases from the second paragraph which 'personify' the woods, giving the impression that the woods are alive.

....

.... [2]

3 What do the following quotations tell us about Mole's attitude to the faces in the woods? Complete the table below. The first one has been done for you.

Quotation	What it tells us
He quickened his pace, telling himself not to begin imagining things...	Mole thinks that the 'faces' are not real and that, if he is confident, they will go away.
certainly a little narrow face, with hard eyes, had flashed up...	
...all fixing on him glances of malice and hatred: all hard-eyed and evil and sharp.	

[2]

4 Which of the following statements about the text are true and which are false? Write 'True' or 'False' in the table.

Mole knows the Wild Wood very well.	
Mole imagines the faces.	
At the end of the extract, we do not know whose faces they are.	
At the end of the extract, Mole is safe.	

[4]

Total Marks .... / 9

Reading 3

How Ideas are Organised

Read the passage below and answer the questions that follow.

This is the opening of a short story, the first in a collection called Lady Molly of Scotland Yard, *in which a female detective, working for the fictional 'Female Department' of the police, solves a series of crimes.*

Extract from 'The Ninescore Mystery' by Baroness Orczy

WELL, you know, some say she is the daughter of a duke, others that she was born in the gutter, and that the handle has been soldered on to her name in order to give her style and influence.

I could say a lot, of course, but "my lips are sealed," as the poets say. All through her successful career at the Yard she honoured me with her friendship and confidence, but when she took me in
5 partnership, as it were, she made me promise that I would never breathe a word of her private life, and this I swore on my Bible oath–"wish I may die," and all the rest of it.

Yes, we always called her "my lady," from the moment that she was put at the head of our section; and the chief called her "Lady Molly" in our presence. We of the Female Department are dreadfully snubbed by the men, though don't tell me that women have not ten times as much
10 intuition as the blundering and sterner sex; my firm belief is that we shouldn't have half so many undetected crimes if some of the so-called mysteries were put to the test of feminine investigation.

Do you suppose for a moment, for instance, that the truth about that extraordinary case at Ninescore would ever have come to light if the men alone had had the handling of it? Would any man have taken so bold a risk as Lady Molly did when–But I am anticipating.
15 Let me go back to that memorable morning when she came into my room in a wild state of agitation.

"The chief says I may go down to Ninescore if I like, Mary," she said in a voice all a-quiver with excitement.

"You!" I ejaculated. "What for?"
20 "What for–what for?" she repeated eagerly. "Mary, don't you understand? It is the chance I have been waiting for–the chance of a lifetime? They are all desperate about the case up at the Yard; the public is furious, and columns of sarcastic letters appear in the daily press. None of our men know what to do; they are at their wits' end, and so this morning I went to the chief–"

"Yes?" I queried eagerly, for she had suddenly ceased speaking.
25 "Well, never mind now how I did it–I will tell you all about it on the way, for we have just got time to catch the 11 a.m. down to Canterbury. The chief says I may go, and that I may take whom I like with me. He suggested one of the men, but somehow I feel that this is woman's work, and I'd rather have you, Mary, than anyone. We will go over the preliminaries of the case together in the train, as I don't suppose that you have got them at your fingers' ends yet, and you have only just got
30 time to put a few things together and meet me at Charing Cross booking-office in time for that 11.0 sharp."

She was off before I could ask her any more questions, and anyhow I was too flabbergasted to say much. A murder case in the hands of the Female Department! Such a thing had been unheard of until now. But I was all excitement, too, and you
35 may be sure I was at the station in good time.

Fortunately Lady Molly and I had a carriage to ourselves. It was a non-stop run to Canterbury, so we had plenty of time before us, and I was longing to know all about this case, you bet, since I was to have the honour of helping Lady Molly in it.

The murder of Mary Nicholls had actually been committed at Ash Court, a fine old mansion
40 which stands in the village of Ninescore. The Court is surrounded by magnificently timbered grounds, the most fascinating portion of which is an island in the midst of a small pond, which is spanned by a tiny rustic bridge. The island is called "The Wilderness," and is at the furthermost end of the grounds, out of sight and earshot of the mansion itself. It was in this charming spot, on the edge of the pond, that the body of a girl was found on the
45 5th of February last.

1 The first paragraph establishes the style of narration used in the story. Which of the following best describes it?

A third person narrative written in formal English. ☐

A first person narrative written in formal English. ☐

A first person narrative written in a colloquial style. ☐ [1]

2 Look again at the first four paragraphs. What do we learn about each of the following?

a) Lady Molly ....

.... [1]

b) The narrator ....

.... [1]

c) The treatment of the Female Department by the rest of Scotland Yard ....

.... [1]

d) The narrator's opinion of male detectives ....

.... [1]

3 How does the writer use dialogue in lines 17 to 31 to interest the reader in the 'case'?

....

....

....

.... [3]

Total Marks .... / 8

Reading 4

Exploring Language Choices

Read the poem below and answer the questions that follow.

After the Winter

By Claude McKay

Some day, when trees have shed their leaves

And against the morning's white

The shivering birds beneath the eaves

Have sheltered for the night,

We'll turn our faces southward, love,

Toward the summer isle

Where bamboos spire to shafted grove

And wide-mouthed orchids smile.

And we will seek the quiet hill

Where towers the cotton tree,

And leaps the laughing crystal rill,

And works the droning bee.

And we will build a cottage there

Beside an open glade,

With black-ribbed blue-bells blowing near,

And ferns that never fade.

1 a) In which tense (past, present or future) is the poem written? _____ [1]

b) Why do you think the poet uses that tense?

_____

_____ [2]

2 What does the poet mean by 'the morning's white'?

_____ [1]

3 a) Of what literary technique is 'wide-mouthed orchids smile' an example?

_____ [1]

b) Explain how this phrase helps to convey the poet's feelings about the 'summer isle'.

_____

_____ [2]

4 What effect does the repetition of 'and' at the beginning of lines have?

_____

_____ [2]

5 a) Which of these literary techniques does the poet use in the last two lines? Tick one answer.

Alliteration ☐

Assonance ☐

Onomatopoeia ☐

Oxymoron ☐ [1]

b) How does the use of this technique in the final line give a sense of the poet's feelings?

_____

_____ [2]

Total Marks _____ / 12

Read the article below and answer the questions that follow.

Adopt a Granny or Grandpa!

A new scheme connecting generations

Traditionally, in Britain and all over the world, grandparents have played a hugely important role in their grandchildren's lives: looking after them when their parents are busy; playing with them; teaching them useful skills; or just lending a sympathetic ear. But recent studies show that more and more children are growing up not even knowing their grandparents.

Sometimes, sadly, this is because their grandparents have died. More often it is because they simply live too far away. The days of spending your life in the same village or town, living down the road from, or even next door to, members of your extended family, are long gone for most of us. Grandparents are more likely to be on the other side of the country or even the other side of the world.

This means all generations are missing out. We're often told about the difficulties young parents have bringing up their children with little or no support – perhaps some of their problems could be solved by a little bit of timely advice from Nan, Gran or Grandpa. Young children, too, miss out on a lot when they don't get the chance to interact with older people. Grandparents often have more time to play with them and listen to them than their parents do. The benefits of the company of youngsters to older folk, too, are many. Lots of senior citizens will tell you that being with their grandchildren 'keeps them young'.

That's why a group of community volunteers set up an 'Adopt a Granny or Grandpa!' scheme here in Puddington.

The idea is simple. If you're a senior citizen – whether or not you have grandchildren of your own – and you have something to offer to the young, or if you're a parent who thinks your children would benefit from contact with the older generation, get in touch with us now. We'll try to match you with someone who lives close to you. You can meet, see how you get along – and take it from there!

Stan and Vera have been part of the scheme for two years now and, according to Stan, they've had 'a smashing time' getting to know Alfie and Rhianna, who live just round the corner from them.

'Our own grandchildren live in Australia,' says Vera. 'We're lucky if we get to see them once a year and Skype just isn't the same. Frankly, we were beginning to find life a bit boring until we joined 'Adopt a Granny or Grandpa!'. It's as if a little bit of sunshine has come into our lives. We always look forward to seeing Rhianna and Alfie and we feel part of village life again. It's like a new lease of life.'

Of course, there are certain rules we have to keep to for everyone's safety and comfort, and certain checks that have to be made. We're a registered charity, working closely with the District Council, and we make sure everything's properly organised and supervised.

So what can you do once you've been matched with someone? There are countless activities you can do together: going on days out; baking cakes (Vera's speciality); playing football in the park; helping with homework; whatever you enjoy doing. In addition, we organise fun days from time to time so you can meet other people who are taking part in the scheme, swap notes and just have fun together.

So, why not give it a go? Pop into your local library or village hall to pick up a leaflet and application form or contact us now on 0779 687 9.

1 What is the purpose of 'Adopt a Granny or Grandpa!'? Tick two of the following.

To inform people about the scheme. ☐

To argue that children do not need grandparents. ☐

To persuade people to get involved with people from a different generation. ☐

To advise old people about their health. ☐ [2]

2 From the second paragraph, give two reasons that, according to the writer, children might not see their own grandparents.

_____

_____ [2]

3 How, according to the writer, would each of the following groups benefit from the scheme?

a) Older people

_____

b) Parents

_____

c) Children

_____ [3]

4 What two reasons do Stan and Vera give for joining the scheme?

_____

_____ [2]

5 How does the writer reassure readers that the 'Adopt a Granny or Grandpa!' scheme is safe and genuine?

_____

_____

_____

_____ [3]

Total Marks _____ / 12

Reading 6

Structuring a Longer Response

Read the extract and answer the questions that follow.

In this extract from Great Expectations *by Charles Dickens, Pip, who lives with his older sister, has been sent for by the mysterious Miss Havisham. He has been left at the door by his uncle, Mr Pumblechook, and a young girl, Estella, is taking him into the house.*

We went into the house by a side door, the great front entrance had two chains across it outside,— and the first thing I noticed was, that the passages were all dark, and that she had left a candle burning there. She took it up, and we went through more passages and up a staircase, and still it was all dark, and only the candle lighted us.

At last we came to the door of a room, and she said, 'Go in.'

I answered, more in shyness than politeness, 'After you, miss.'

To this she returned: 'Don't be ridiculous, boy; I am not going in.' And scornfully walked away, and—what was worse—took the candle with her.

This was very uncomfortable, and I was half afraid. However, the only thing to be done being to knock at the door, I knocked, and was told from within to enter. I entered, therefore, and found myself in a pretty large room, well lighted with wax candles. No glimpse of daylight was to be seen in it. It was a dressing-room, as I supposed from the furniture, though much of it was of forms and uses then quite unknown to me. But prominent in it was a draped table with a gilded looking-glass, and that I made out at first sight to be a fine lady's dressing-table.

Whether I should have made out this object so soon if there had been no fine lady sitting at it, I cannot say. In an arm-chair, with an elbow resting on the table and her head leaning on that hand, sat the strangest lady I have ever seen, or shall ever see.

She was dressed in rich materials,—satins, and lace, and silks,—all of white. Her shoes were white. And she had a long white veil dependent from her hair, and she had bridal flowers in her hair, but her hair was white. Some bright jewels sparkled on her neck and on her hands, and some other jewels lay sparkling on the table. Dresses, less splendid than the dress she wore, and half-packed trunks, were scattered about. She had not quite finished dressing, for she had but one shoe on,—the other was on the table near her hand,— her veil was but half arranged, her watch and chain were not put on, and some lace for her bosom lay with those trinkets, and with her handkerchief, and gloves, and some flowers, and a Prayer-Book all confusedly heaped about the looking-glass.

It was not in the first few moments that I saw all these things, though I saw more of them in the first moments than might be supposed. But I saw that everything within my view which ought to be white, had been white long ago, and had lost its lustre and was faded and yellow. I saw that the bride within the bridal dress had withered like the dress, and like the flowers, and had no brightness left but the brightness of her sunken eyes. I saw that the dress had been put upon the rounded figure of a young woman, and that the figure upon which it now hung loose had shrunk to skin and bone. Once, I had been taken to see some ghastly waxwork at the Fair, representing I know not what impossible personage lying in state. Once, I had been taken to one of our old marsh churches to see a skeleton in the ashes of a rich dress that had been dug out of a vault under the church pavement. Now, waxwork and skeleton seemed to have dark eyes that moved and looked at me. I should have cried out, if I could.

'Who is it?' said the lady at the table.

'Pip, ma'am.'

'Pip?'

'Mr. Pumblechook's boy, ma'am. Come—to play.'

'Come nearer; let me look at you. Come close.'

It was when I stood before her, avoiding her eyes, that I took note of the surrounding objects in detail, and saw that her watch had stopped at twenty minutes to nine, and that a clock in the room had stopped at twenty minutes to nine.

'Look at me,' said Miss Havisham. 'You are not afraid of a woman who has never seen the sun since you were born?'

I regret to state that I was not afraid of telling the enormous lie comprehended in the answer 'No.'

'Do you know what I touch here?' she said, laying her hands, one upon the other, on her left side.

'Yes, ma'am.' (It made me think of the young man.)

'What do I touch?'

'Your heart.'

'Broken!'

She uttered the word with an eager look, and with strong emphasis, and with a weird smile that had a kind of boast in it. Afterwards she kept her hands there for a little while, and slowly took them away as if they were heavy.

'I am tired," said Miss Havisham. "I want diversion, and I have done with men and women. Play.'

I think it will be conceded by my most disputatious reader, that she could hardly have directed an unfortunate boy to do anything in the wide world more difficult to be done under the circumstances.

'I sometimes have sick fancies,' she went on, 'and I have a sick fancy that I want to see some play. There, there!' with an impatient movement of the fingers of her right hand; 'play, play, play!'

1 After reading this extract, a student said, 'Dickens creates an eerie atmosphere and an air of mystery surrounding Miss Havisham.'

To what extent do you agree?

In your response you could:

- give your own impressions of Miss Havisham and her home
- evaluate how Dickens tells us about them and Pip's reaction to them
- support your response with references to the text.

Write your answer on a separate piece of paper.   [20]

Writing 1

Purpose, Audience and Form

What would be the purpose, audience and form of the following tasks?

1 You have been asked to submit an article to your school newspaper, arguing whether students are set too much homework. Your title is 'Too Much Homework?' Remember to include both sides of the argument.

Purpose: ....

Audience: ....

Form: .... [3]

2 You work for the advice section of a teen magazine. You have received a letter from a teenager who isn't getting along with her best friend and would like some ideas about how to save their friendship. Write your letter of reply.

Purpose: ....

Audience: ....

Form: .... [3]

3 You have just been employed by your local leisure centre. Your first job is to write the text for a leaflet that can be given to new visitors. It should inform them of the centre's different facilities, classes and rules, plus any other vital details.

Purpose: ....

Audience: ....

Form: .... [3]

4 Wasting time and resources has become a problem at your company. As the boss, you need to send out a polite letter to all staff persuading them to work more efficiently and look after company resources such as printer paper.

Purpose: ....

Audience: ....

Form: .... [3]

Total Marks .... / 12

Writing 2

Paragraphs and Connectives

1 You should start a new paragraph to show changes in what three things?

.... [3]

2 Where could you start three new paragraphs in the following piece of writing?
Mark each with //.

> It was midnight and the darkness seemed to envelop the boy as he walked through the forest. He felt as if the night was pressing against his eyes. It was a blackness so absolute that he could barely see. After a few minutes, he began to see glimmers of light in the distance. The break from the darkness lifted his spirits and he made his way forward. The lights felt like hope after his trudge through the woods. Suddenly, he heard footsteps behind him. He turned but there was no-one there. His eyes scanned the empty road, the gate leading back into the woods, and the thick blackness. No more footsteps broke through the eerie silence. Seconds later, music burst from his pocket as his mobile began to ring. Surprise led quickly to relief as he saw his friend's name flashing back at him from the screen. The familiarity calmed him down and he felt safe once more.

[3]

3 Circle the connectives used at the start of the paragraphs in the writing above. What do they have in common?

....

.... [4]

4 Write the following connectives in the correct column in the table.

Because of this,	Conversely,	Due to,	Finally,
Firstly,	Further down the street,	However,	In the next room,
Next,	On the other hand,	Thus,	Twenty miles away,

Place	Sequence	Compare and Contrast	Cause and Effect

[12]

Total Marks .... / 22

Writing 3

Grammar

1 Identify these three different sentence structures.

   a) The chocolate was very tasty. ....

   b) The chocolate was very tasty and it made her want more. ....

   c) Encasing a thick pool of caramel, the chocolate was very tasty. .... [3]

2 What are the two uses of a comma in a sentence?

   ....

   .... [2]

3 How can you vary the position of a subordinate clause in a complex sentence?

   ....

   ....

   .... [3]

4 In what tense have each of the following verbs been written?

   a) I would have eaten more. ....

   b) I am tired. ....

   c) I went to the shop yesterday. ....

   d) I will meet you tomorrow. ....

   e) They are waiting for their friends. ....

   f) She will need a rest after the match. ....

   g) He could have stayed at the park longer. ....

   h) They finished watching the film. .... [8]

5 Rewrite the sentences so they are grammatically correct. Use the past tense and the first person.

   I went to the cinema yesterday and I watch a comedy. It is really funny and I couldn't stop laughing. I buying loads of popcorn and sweets. It will be quite difficult not making lots of rustling noises but I just about managing it. Everyone is laughing, though, so it wouldn't of mattered. I have a great time.

   ....

   ....

   ....

   ....

   ....

   .... [8]

   Total Marks .... / 24

Punctuation and Spelling

1 Add the correct apostrophes to these sentences to show abbreviation (omission).

a) I didnt want any more dinner as it wasnt very nice.

b) We werent supposed to go alone and we shouldve listened.

c) I couldnt understand the maths question and my friend wouldnt help me.   [6]

2 Add the correct apostrophes to these sentences to show ownership (possession).

a) Sharons dad was making the familys dinner.

b) Zains hamster was in its cage, tearing up a page of yesterdays newspaper.

c) The cats meals were ready but they were busy playing with my youngest daughters football.   [6]

3 Put the commas in the correct places in these four sentences.

a) Coming in from the garden she began to wash her hands.

b) He looked around wondering if he was really alone.

c) The bird beating its wings frantically tried to reach the next branch of the tree.

d) The fireworks bursting with noise and colour were a lovely end to the celebration.   [6]

4 Circle the fifteen incorrect spellings in the paragraph below and write your corrections.

There were three babys at the party that keeped on screamming. If it hadn't been four the fact that their was plenty of cake, I wood have left early. Everyone seemed to ignore the hideouse noise they were makeing but I found it intolerabley irritatting. At one point, they quietend down onley to start howlling once again when someone bursted a baloon.

_____

_____

_____

_____

    [15]

Writing 5

Plan, Structure and Develop your Response

1 Read through the sample writing task and complete the plan that has been started for you.

> You have been asked to write a speech about a school issue. It is to be presented to the school governors. You have chosen to argue the pros and cons of extending your school lunchtime. Remember to offer a balanced debate, but to make your view clear at the end.

Pros	Cons
More time for lunchtime clubs and activities.	Overall, it will make the school day longer.

[6]

2 Imagine you are completing this task in a test. The first paragraph has been started for you; try to complete it by arguing that this is a good reason for extending the school's lunchtime.

The first reason why it may be a good idea to extend the school lunch break is that it will allow more time for lunch clubs and activities. Currently... ....

....

....

....

....

[4]

3 Now choose one of your own points from the 'cons' column in Question 1 and develop it into a paragraph, arguing why this is a good reason for not extending the school's lunchtime.

....

....

....

....

....

....

[5]

Total Marks .... / 15

Writing 6

Writing to Persuade

1 Complete the FORESTRY mnemonic of persuasive techniques.

F ....

O ....

R ....

E ....

S ....

T ....

R ....

Y ....   [8]

2 Underline and label the persuasive techniques from the FORESTRY mnemonic in this paragraph.

'Treat' is the tastiest chocolate bar you haven't yet tried. It's available in shops now. You've worked hard all day and must be feeling tired and hungry. Why don't you take a 'Treat'? You deserve its thick, sweet, luxurious layers of 70% cocoa dark chocolate. Sit back, relax and 'Treat' yourself.

[8]

3 Imagine you are creating an advertising campaign encouraging families to exercise more. Write four persuasive statements, each using a different technique from the FORESTRY mnemonic.

- ....

   ....

- ....

   ....

- ....

   ....

- ....

   ....   [8]

Total Marks .... / 24

Writing 7

> **Writing to Argue**

1 Complete the notes in this table to provide a balanced argument for each of the four topics.

Pros	Cons
Topic A: We shouldn't have to wear school uniform	
Own clothes = expression of individuality.	
Topic B: People should be able to vote when they're 16	
	Young people not all mature enough?
Topic C: Cigarettes should be completely banned	
No smokers = healthier society.	
Topic D: Mobile phones should be banned in schools	
	Educational apps = useful in lessons.

[12]

2 Which two types of connectives are useful when writing to argue, and what would you use each of them for?

....

....

.... [4]

3 What key features of writing to persuade can you also make use of in writing to argue?

....

....

.... [5]

4 Choose one of the topics from Question 1. Turn your notes into four topic sentences that would clearly establish each of your main points.

....

....

....

.... [4]

Total Marks .... / 25

Writing 8

Writing to Advise

1 Circle three words from below that describe the tone needed when writing to advise.

aggressive   conciliatory   enthusiastic   firm   friendly

funny   pessimistic   sarcastic   supportive   [3]

2 What word do you need to use in order to make the reader feel personally involved?

_____ [1]

3 What is the role of imperative sentences in writing to advise?

_____ [1]

4 **a)** Circle the five modal verbs in the list below.

could   eat   not   must   need

offer   ought   perhaps   should   try   [5]

b) Why are modal verbs important in writing to advise?

_____

_____ [2]

5 Rewrite the four sentences below by introducing modality to each one.

Try to avoid these stressful situations. Speak to your family about how you're feeling. If this doesn't help, talk to a friend or a teacher at school. Put yourself first and get on with your life.

_____

_____

_____

_____

_____

_____ [4]

Total Marks _____ / 16

Writing 9

Vocabulary and Sentences

1 Find two synonyms for each of these verbs.

Begin	Eat	Say	Think	Walk

[10]

2 Come up with five synonyms for each of these adjectives.

Good	Bad

[10]

3 Match the sentence structure to its effect.

Sentence structure	Effect
Simple	Join two ideas or create a contrast
Compound	Emphasise a point or build up a powerful image
Complex	Emphasise an idea or surprise the reader
List	Build up a point or add extra detail

[4]

4 Write an exciting, five-sentence description of a trip to the fairground. Use each of the four sentence structures, including two different complex sentence structures. Use one of your synonyms for each of the words from Questions 1 and 2.

....

....

....

....

....

....

[12]

Total Marks .... / 36

Writing 10

> ## Writing to Inform

1 What is the difference between writing an article chronologically and writing it thematically?

....

.... [2]

2 Would the task below be best approached thematically or chronologically? Why?

You write for an online music magazine. You have been asked to produce an article informing readers about a particular genre of music.

.... [2]

3 Which of the following statements are facts and which are opinions?

   a) Science fiction books are really exciting. ....

   b) They filmed scenes for the new movie in Newcastle. ....

   c) The house was struck by lightning at 3pm. ....

   d) Her new song is better than the previous one. ....

   e) That dress is too expensive. ....

   f) These shoes are a size 6. .... [6]

4 Fill in the table below with four connectives of time and four connectives of place.

Time	Place

[8]

5 Imagine you have been asked to turn an event in your life into a third-person newspaper article. For example, a birthday party, winning a competition, competing in a sports or music event.

Plan your response on a separate piece of paper. Think of at least three key moments and at least three different pieces of factual information that you could include for each moment. [9]

Total Marks .... / 27

Writing 11

Writing to Explain

1 What is the difference between writing to inform and writing to explain?

....

.... [1]

2 Note down four connectives of cause and effect.

....

.... [4]

3 Think of two causes and effects for the topics below.

Causes	Effects
Topic A: Explain the dangers of extreme dieting amongst young people	
Topic B: Explain how lack of recycling is affecting the environment	

[8]

4 When writing to explain, when would you use the past tense and when would you use the present tense?

....

.... [2]

5 You work for a lifestyle magazine. You have been asked to write an article, explaining how changes in evening habits can improve your readers' sleep. On a separate piece of paper, plan a possible response to this task.

You might start with:

Don't eat for at least an hour before bed...
Higher blood sugar levels lead to spikes in energy rather than rest...
Not allowing enough time to digest food could create indigestion which will disrupt sleep... [6]

Total Marks .... / 21

Writing 12

Writing to Describe

1 Rewrite the sentences below, replacing the underlined words with more interesting verbs, adjectives and adverbs.

Glen <u>ran</u> <u>quickly</u> up the <u>busy</u> road. His cheeks were <u>red</u> and sweat <u>ran</u> down his face. By the time he <u>got to</u> the shop, he was <u>breathing</u> <u>heavily</u>. He was <u>surprised</u> by how <u>tired</u> he felt.

[10]

2 Describe your favourite meal in fewer than 50 words, referring to all five senses.

[5]

3 Match the technique to the example.

Technique	Example
Simile	Freezing gusts of wind bit into his skin.
Metaphor	The clock ticked loudly in the empty house.
Personification	The old car shuddered like a dying animal.
Onomatopoeia	Turning to my friend, I was met with a wall of silence.

[4]

4 Think of an everyday object, such as a kettle, and describe it using a simile and a metaphor.

[2]

5 On a separate piece of paper, write a description of an alien world in no more than 100 words. Try to use as many different descriptive techniques as you can. Once you have finished, highlight the different techniques that you have used. [9]

Total Marks ___ / 30

Shakespeare 1

As You Like It

1 Circle three adjectives from the list below that describe Rosalind.

rude   disorganised   independent   cold-hearted   unimaginative

strong-willed   generous   excitable   clever   [3]

2 Circle three adjectives from the list below that describe Orlando.

aggressive   disloyal   perceptive   kind-hearted   sarcastic

treacherous   uneducated   romantic   weak   [3]

3 In what way do Orlando and Rosalind have different outlooks on love?

....

.... [2]

4 What role do Aubrey and Touchstone play in how the theme of love is explored?

.... [1]

5 How have Orlando and Rosalind been mistreated, and by whom, during their lives?

....

....

.... [4]

6 In what ways is the Forest of Arden linked to freedom?

....

....

.... [3]

7 In what ways does the play have a happy ending?

....

....

.... [3]

8 What are the effects of rhetorical language in this extract from Act 1 scene 1, in which Orlando is talking to Oliver?

Orlando: Shall I keep your hogs and eat husks with them?
             What prodigal portion have I spent that I should come to such penury?

....

....

.... [2]

9 How is descriptive language used to convey character in this extract from Act 1 scene 2, where Celia is discussing her father, Duke Frederick, with Rosalind?

Celia: My father's rough and envious disposition
             Sticks me at my heart.

....

....

.... [2]

10 How is emotive language used in this extract from Act 1 scene 3, in which Celia begs her father not to banish her best friend, Rosalind?

Celia: If she be a traitor,
             Why so am I. We still have slept together,
             Rose at an instant, learn'd, play'd, eat together,
             And wheresoe'er we went, like Juno's swans,
             Still we went coupled and inseparable.

....

....

.... [2]

11 How could an actor perform these lines from Act 1 scene 3, in which Rosalind discovers that she faces banishment or execution?

Rosalind: I do beseech your Grace,
             Let me the knowledge of my fault bear with me.

....

....

.... [2]

Total Marks .... / 27

Shakespeare 2

Romeo and Juliet

1 Circle a positive adjective and underline a negative adjective from the list below to describe Romeo. Explain your choices.

devoted	cheerful	romantic	peaceful	clever
headstrong	aggressive	fickle	cruel	arrogant

....

.... [4]

2 Circle a positive adjective and underline a negative adjective from the list below to describe Juliet. Explain your choices.

romantic	faithful	creative	strong-minded	obedient
headstrong	unreliable	distrusting	uncaring	spoilt

....

.... [4]

3 How does Romeo appear to be different to the other Montague and Capulet men?

.... [1]

4 How and why does Juliet's relationship with her parents change during the play?

....

....

.... [3]

5 Circle the phrase that best describes the love Romeo and Juliet experience when they meet.

unrequited love   love at first sight   forbidden love   familial love   [1]

6 Give three consequences of the feud between the Capulets and Montagues.

....

....

.... [3]

7 How is the theme of fate linked to the characters of Romeo and Juliet from the very start of the play?

.... [1]

8 What are the effects of emotive language in this extract from Act 1 scene 1, in which Romeo is talking to Benvolio?

Romeo:
> O me! What fray was here?
> Yet tell me not, for I have heard it all.
> Here's much to do with hate, but more with love.
> Why then, O brawling love, O loving hate,
> O anything of nothing first create!

[2]

9 How is descriptive language used to convey character in this extract from Act 1 scene 2, where Lord Capulet is discussing Juliet with Paris?

Capulet:
> My child is yet a stranger in the world,
> She hath not seen the change of fourteen years.
> Let two more summers wither in their pride
> Ere we may think her ripe to be a bride.

[2]

10 How is rhetorical language used in this extract from Act 1 scene 3, in which Lady Capulet talks to Juliet about love?

Lady Capulet:
> Read o'er the volume of young Paris' face
> And find delight writ there with beauty's pen.

[2]

11 How could an actor perform these lines from Act 1 scene 4, in which Mercutio tries to convince Romeo to attend the Capulet party?

Mercutio: Nay, gentle Romeo, we must have you dance.
Romeo: Not I, believe me. You have dancing shoes
> With nimble soles, I have a soul of lead

[2]

Total Marks _____ / 25

Shakespeare 3

Macbeth

1 Think of two positive adjectives to describe Macbeth at the start of the play. Explain your choices.

_____

_____ [4]

2 Think of two negative adjectives to describe Macbeth later in the play. Explain your choices.

_____

_____ [4]

3 How does Lady Macbeth change during the play?

_____

_____

_____ [4]

4 Who seems more ambitious, Macbeth or Lady Macbeth? Explain your answer.

_____

_____

_____

_____ [3]

5 What does Macbeth upset, or over-turn, by killing the King and taking his place?

_____ [1]

6 Identify two points in the play that link to the theme of madness.

_____ [2]

7 Which characters appear to be manipulating all the events of the play and know what will happen?

_____ [1]

8 What are the effects of descriptive language in this extract from Act 1 scene 2, in which the Captain describes Macbeth and Banquo's acts of valour to the King?

Captain: If I say sooth, I must report they were
                  As cannons overcharg'd with double cracks.

_____

_____

_____ [2]

9 How is rhetorical language used in this extract from Act 1 scene 3, where Macbeth thinks about being made Thane of Cawdor, and what does it suggest about the witches' prophecies?

Macbeth: *[Aside]* This supernatural soliciting
Cannot be ill; cannot be good:
If ill, why hath it given me earnest of success,
Commencing in a truth?

[2]

10 How is emotive language used in this extract from Act 1 scene 4, in which the King greets Macbeth after the battle?

King Duncan: O worthiest cousin!
The sin of my ingratitude even now
Was heavy on me.

[2]

11 How could the actors playing Duncan, Malcolm, Macbeth and Banquo perform these lines from Act 1 scene 3, in which the King announces that his eldest son Malcolm will succeed him?

King Duncan: We will establish our estate upon
Our eldest, Malcolm; whom we name hereafter
The Prince of Cumberland.

[2]

Total Marks _____ / 27

Mixed Test-Style Questions

Reading Task 1

Read the text below and answer the questions that follow.

Aim to complete the test in 30 minutes.

In this poem the writer describes a place where a road used to run through some woods.
The road has now disappeared under trees and undergrowth.

'The Way through the Woods'
by Rudyard Kipling

They shut the road through the woods
    Seventy years ago.
Weather and rain have undone it again,
    And now you would never know
5   There was once a road through the woods
    Before they planted the trees.
It is underneath the coppice and heath,
    And the thin anemones.
    Only the keeper sees
10   That, where the ring-dove broods,
    And the badgers roll at ease,
There was once a road through the woods.

    Yet, if you enter the woods
    Of a summer evening late,
15   When the night-air cools on the trout-ringed pools
    Where the otter whistles his mate,
(They fear not men in the woods,
    Because they see so few.)
You will hear the beat of a horse's feet,
20   And the swish of a skirt in the dew,
    Steadily cantering through
The misty solitudes,
    As though they perfectly knew
    The old lost road through the woods.
25   But there is no road through the woods.

1 The way through the woods has disappeared partly because of nature and partly because of people. Give two ways in which people are responsible.

2 marks

2 The phrase 'only the keeper sees' (line 9) suggests the keeper is different from other people. How do you think he is different?

☐ 2 marks

....

....

3 The poem is in two stanzas. Explain how the focus of the poem changes between the first and second stanzas.

☐ 4 marks

....

....

....

....

4 How does the poet use language to give an impression of mystery and the supernatural?

You should comment on:

☐ 8 marks

- words and phrases he uses to describe the woods in the first stanza
- what he says you will hear in the woods
- the effect of his language on the reader.

....

....

....

....

....

....

....

....

....

....

....

TOTAL

☐

16

Reading Task 2

Read the text below and answer the questions that follow.

Aim to complete the test in 30 minutes.

Writing in 1871, Thomas Goodman remembers his school days at Oundle. The head teacher, Mr Bullen, is referred to as 'the master' and the other teachers as 'ushers'.

The cane was very generally used in the school. Indeed, the ushers (of whom there were four) allowed to use it; but the birch was reserved for special occasions only. I remember once, when Mr Bullen was caning a boy who seemed terribly frightened at the punishment, he exclaimed, 'Oh pray, Sir, don't because you are in a passion,' to which he replied by an interrogation, 'Am I in a passion?' When the boy immediately answered, 'Oh no, Sir, you are not in a passion.' The master then rejoined, with a sharper cut of the cane than ever, 'but I am in a passion.'

Oundle has a very convenient river for bathing and occasionally, I believe more to save the trouble of feet-washing than anything else, we were taken down to the river, in one part of which those who were unable to swim might venture to bathe with safety. But when the art had been acquired, they were then allowed to go into deeper water, and the elder Mr Dix sometimes for fun's sake, used to take hold of a boy with one hand at the wrist, and another at the ankle, and throw him several yards into deep water – a feat which seemed to gratify the swimmer as an evidence of his skill and courage. I remember a boy once coming behind me when I was swimming and seizing me by the neck, sent me down several feet under the water, and I believe I am right in the assumption that my eyes were open and able to see the fish as they swam along.

We had no other playground than the churchyard. There were many walnut trees planted in the churchyard: two of which, in the north-west corner, a retired spot, served capitally for a swing, which was also a favourite pastime with the boys, and many became skilled at either swinging themselves standing upon the rope, or, putting one leg above the rope and the other under it, turning themselves over repeatedly while they were at full swing […] There was considerable danger in boys jumping from one gravestone to another and sometimes in jumping over the tombstones. I was once attempting to go over one which was very easy on the one side, but difficult on the other, as the slab at the top was far from being level […] I caught my toe against the edge of the stone and my body went upon the ground with such violence that I began to think I should never get my breath again and I naturally abstained from making a second effort.

We were very irregular in our walks. Indeed. According to my recollections, we scarcely ever took them except on Sunday evenings, but I think we have done so occasionally on other days, as I know it was a great treat to hear Mr Dix tell a story as we clustered round him at the river side, which he composed as he walked along with a pipe or cigar in his mouth – the smoking of which gave him time to recollect himself.

The punishments at Oundle school were very badly and unjustly regulated, in consequence of which the ushers were much more severe than the master, especially in their tasks. The latter would occasionally order a boy to write a sheet of paper, which […] would of course, if properly filled, take up a considerable time, but the ushers would more frequently set half a dozen sheets. Again the amount depended upon what they were to write, the usual custom being to state the offence which had been committed as, for example,

'I must not jump over the desks' or 'I must get up when the bell rings.' It often happened that a boy would get his companions to help him in writing these tasks, and it was thought to be done more expeditiously[1] if one boy wrote the letter 'I' from top to bottom of the sheet and another undertook to write the next word 'must' in the same way, and so on to the end, until the whole of the sheets were filled. This practice, of course, was discovered and in its place a boy was desired to fill his paper by copying from some book, which would take him twice as long, if not more.

The classical usher[2], named Hinde, while a boy was repeating his lesson, if he found him defective, was accustomed to make him stand by his side and, taking hold of one of his ears, used to give it a pull for every mistake he made. Thus, I think, was always done in the absence of the master, for I don't believe Mr Bullen would have allowed such a cruel mode of torturing a boy, as with all the master's gusts of passion, he had his periods of patience and forbearance, and I do not think that upon the whole he was disliked by the pupils.

[1] *quickly*
[2] *the teacher of Latin and Greek*

---

1 What does the boy mean by Mr Bullen being 'in a passion'?

☐ 1 mark

....

2 Name two games played by the boys in the churchyard.

☐ 2 marks

....

3 Give two reasons why the writer remembers Mr Dix with affection.

☐ 2 marks

....

....

4 Which of the following statements accurately reflect Thomas Goodman's feelings about his school days? Tick three.

☐ 3 marks

He hated everything about Oundle. ☐

He thinks the punishments were inconsistent and sometimes cruel. ☐

On the whole, he respected Mr Bullen. ☐

He had some enjoyable times at Oundle. ☐

He thinks all the ushers were very caring. ☐

He never thinks about his school days. ☐

Mixed Test-Style Questions

5 In the text, Goodman describes discipline at Oundle school. How do you think modern readers would react to this? Explain as fully as you can.

8 marks

Reading Task 3

Spend about 15 minutes reading the text below and then spend 45 minutes answering the questions.

In this extract from The Railway Children *by E. Nesbit, Peter, his older sister Bobbie and younger sister Phyllis are going to pick cherries near the railway line when they notice that something strange and potentially very dangerous is happening.*

They were almost at the gate when Bobbie said:—

"Hush. Stop! What's that?"

"That" was a very odd noise indeed—a soft noise, but quite plainly to be heard through the sound of the wind in tree branches, and the hum and whir of the telegraph wires. It was a sort of
5 rustling, whispering sound. As they listened it stopped, and then it began again.

And this time it did not stop, but it grew louder and more rustling and rumbling.

"Look"—cried Peter, suddenly—"the tree over there!"

The tree he pointed at was one of those that have rough grey leaves and white flowers. The berries, when they come, are bright scarlet, but if you pick them, they disappoint you by turning
10 black before you get them home. And, as Peter pointed, the tree was moving—not just the way trees ought to move when the wind blows through them, but all in one piece, as though it were a live creature and were walking down the side of the cutting.

"It's moving!" cried Bobbie. "Oh, look! and so are the others. It's like the woods in Macbeth."

"It's magic," said Phyllis, breathlessly. "I always knew this railway was enchanted."
15 It really did seem a little like magic. For all the trees for about twenty yards of the opposite bank seemed to be slowly walking down towards the railway line, the tree with the grey leaves bringing up the rear like some old shepherd driving a flock of green sheep.

"What is it? Oh, what is it?" said Phyllis; "it's much too magic for me. I don't like it. Let's go home."
20 But Bobbie and Peter clung fast to the rail and watched breathlessly. And Phyllis made no movement towards going home by herself.

The trees moved on and on. Some stones and loose earth fell down and rattled on the railway metals far below.

"It's ALL coming down," Peter tried to say, but he found there was hardly any voice to say
25 it with. And, indeed, just as he spoke, the great rock, on the top of which the walking trees were, leaned slowly forward. The trees, ceasing to walk, stood still and shivered. Leaning with the rock, they seemed to hesitate a moment, and then rock and trees and grass and bushes, with a rushing sound, slipped right away from the face of the cutting and fell on the line with a blundering crash that could have been heard half a mile off. A cloud of dust rose up.
30 "Oh," said Peter, in awestruck tones, "isn't it exactly like when coals come in?—if there wasn't any roof to the cellar and you could see down."

"Look what a great mound it's made!" said Bobbie.

"Yes," said Peter, slowly. He was still leaning on the fence. "Yes," he said again, still more slowly.

35   Then he stood upright.

"The 11.29 down hasn't gone by yet. We must let them know at the station, or there'll be a most frightful accident."

"Let's run," said Bobbie, and began.

But Peter cried, "Come back!" and looked at Mother's watch. He was very prompt and
40 businesslike, and his face looked whiter than they had ever seen it.

"No time," he said; "it's two miles away, and it's past eleven."

"Couldn't we," suggested Phyllis, breathlessly, "couldn't we climb up a telegraph post and do something to the wires?"

"We don't know how," said Peter.

45   "They do it in war," said Phyllis; "I know I've heard of it."

"They only CUT them, silly," said Peter, "and that doesn't do any good. And we couldn't cut them even if we got up, and we couldn't get up. If we had anything red, we could get down on the line and wave it."

"But the train wouldn't see us till it got round the corner, and then it could see the mound just
50 as well as us," said Phyllis; "better, because it's much bigger than us."

"If we only had something red," Peter repeated, "we could go round the corner and wave to the train."

"We might wave, anyway."

"They'd only think it was just US, as usual. We've waved so often before. Anyway, let's get
55 down."

They got down the steep stairs. Bobbie was pale and shivering. Peter's face looked thinner than usual. Phyllis was red-faced and damp with anxiety.

"Oh, how hot I am!" she said; "and I thought it was going to be cold; I wish we hadn't put on our—" she stopped short, and then ended in quite a different tone—"our
60 flannel petticoats."

Bobbie turned at the bottom of the stairs.

"Oh, yes," she cried; "THEY'RE red! Let's take them off."

1 Look again at lines 1–6. Pick out four words that describe the new, strange sound that the children hear.

4 marks

2 Look in detail at lines 10-17, from 'And, as Peter pointed...' to '...green sheep.'

How does the writer use language to create an atmosphere of mystery and danger?

You could include the writer's choice of:

8 marks

- words and phrases
- language features and techniques
- sentence forms.

Mixed Test-Style Questions

3 You now need to think about the whole of the text. The chapter from which the extract is taken is an important turning point in the novel.

8 marks

How has the writer structured the text to interest you as a reader?

You could write about:

- what the writer focuses your attention on at the beginning of the extract
- how and why she changes the focus during the extract
- any other structural features that interest you.

4 Focus your answer on the second part of the extract, from 'The trees moved on and on' (line 22) to the end.

20 marks

After reading this, a student said, 'In this extract, the writer conveys both the danger that the train is in and the very practical way in which the children go about saving the train.'

To what extent do you agree? Write your answer on a separate piece of paper.

In your response you could:

- consider your own impressions of the danger and the children's response to it
- evaluate how the writer tells us about the situation and how the children deal with it
- support your response with references to the text.

TOTAL

40

Mixed Test-Style Questions

Writing Task 1: Writing to Persuade

Spend 45 minutes on this task (including 10 minutes planning time).

Write your answer on a separate piece of paper.

Young people should spend more time with pensioners.

A national organisation is encouraging young people to spend more time with older people in society. You have been asked to give a speech in assembly, persuading your peers to take part in the campaign.

Make some notes to prepare for your speech. (These will not be marked.)

Different ways in which young people could interact with pensioners.	Why some pensioners will benefit from interaction with young people.	How young people will benefit from being part of the campaign.

Write your speech, persuading young people to spend more time with pensioners.

30 marks

TOTAL

30

Writing Task 2: Writing to Argue

Spend 45 minutes on this task (including 10 minutes planning time).

Write your answer on a separate piece of paper.

Young People and Community Service

The government is considering making all young people, as part of their schooling, take part in a community service project. You have been asked to write a report to be handed to the Prime Minister.

Below is a brief from the government:

> Should young people complete a community service project as part of their schooling?
>
> Some ministers are suggesting this would be excellent for young people's development and the impression that society has of young people. However, others are suggesting that young people are too lazy to take community projects seriously and their time is better spent studying for exams.
>
> Present the argument for both sides, but give your decision at the end.

Using two columns, make a plan that notes down different sides of the argument. (This will not be marked.)

Community project: pros   Community project: cons

Write your report, arguing whether young people should complete community service as part of their schooling.

30 marks

TOTAL

30

Writing Task 3: Writing to Advise

Spend 45 minutes on this task (including 10 minutes planning time).

Write your answer on a separate piece of paper.

Advise young people how to get more fit and healthy.

You work for the advice page of a local magazine for young people and have received the following letter:

Dear Advice Page,

I'm feeling unfit and unhealthy. I'm 13 and I seem to spend all my time either sitting at a desk in school or in my bedroom on my phone. What can I do to make a change and sort myself out?

Thanks,

Tristan

Using the spidergram below, make a plan of ideas for improving health and fitness. (This will not be marked.)

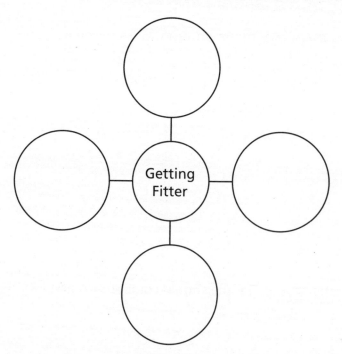

Getting Fitter

Write your letter, giving advice on how young people can improve their health and fitness.

30 marks

TOTAL

30

Writing Task 4: Writing to Inform

Spend 45 minutes on this task (including 10 minutes planning time).

Write your answer on a separate piece of paper.

You work for a social media company. You have been asked to write an information leaflet, to be made available to all over 60s, about social media.

Below is an email from your boss, suggesting the kind of information to include:

> This leaflet's really important! I want all over 60s to know what social media is (its benefits as well as the problems) and how they can access it on a phone or tablet. Make sure you get across the range of things they can do on social media and don't forget they're over 60, not teenagers.

Make some notes for your leaflet. (These will not be marked.)

Different social media apps and sites, and how to access them	Advantages of social media	Negative aspects to be aware of	Aspects of social media that might particularly interest the over 60s

Write your information leaflet about social media.

30 marks

TOTAL

30

Mixed Test-Style Questions

Writing Task 5: Writing to Explain

Spend 45 minutes on this task (including 10 minutes planning time).

Write your answer on a separate piece of paper.

Improvements to your school site.

You have been asked by the school governors to lead a group of students in inspecting the school site and considering ways in which it could be improved. The governors are keen to make the school a place where students and teachers feel happy, and where the learning environment is positive and welcoming.

Now you need to write a letter to the governors, explaining your suggestions for improvement.

Make notes for your letter. (These will not be marked.)

Part of the school	How it could be improved	Explanation of why this would be a beneficial improvement

Write your letter, explaining your ideas.

30 marks

TOTAL

30

Writing Task 6: Writing to Describe

Spend 45 minutes on this task (including 10 minutes planning time).

Write your answer on a separate piece of paper.

The Seasons

A creative writing website is running a competition. They are asking for powerful descriptions of a specific season of the year.

Below are the competition details:

> The seasons of the year change our environment in interesting ways. Can you describe a season in a way that allows the reader to imagine they are there? If so, you could win this month's prize. You might be writing about spring in the countryside, summer at the beach, autumn in your street, or winter in the city. Your description might include the joys of the season or some of its negative sides.
>
> Our readers will want to be able to picture the season from your description.

Use the spidergram below to make notes for your description. (This will not be marked.)

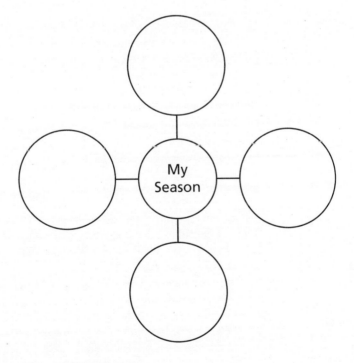

Write your description for the competition.

30 marks

TOTAL

30

Shakespeare: *As You Like It*

Spend 45 minutes on this task.

Write your answer on a separate piece of paper.

As You Like It: Act 1 scene 3, lines 35–85 and Act 3 scene 1, lines 1–18

In the first extract, Duke Frederick banishes Rosalind upon threat of death. In the second extract, convinced that Orlando has run away with Celia and Rosalind, Duke Frederick threatens Oliver: he must bring Orlando back or be financially ruined.

In these extracts, how does Shakespeare present the theme of injustice?

Support your answer by referring to the following extracts.

18 marks

Act 1 scene 3, lines 35–85

ROSALIND	Look, here comes the duke.
CELIA	With his eyes full of anger.
Enter DUKE FREDERICK, with Lords	
DUKE FREDERICK	Mistress, dispatch you with your safest haste
	And get you from our court.
ROSALIND	Me, uncle?
DUKE FREDERICK	You, cousin
	Within these ten days if that thou be'st found
	So near our public court as twenty miles,
	Thou diest for it.
ROSALIND	I do beseech your grace,
	Let me the knowledge of my fault bear with me:
	If with myself I hold intelligence
	Or have acquaintance with mine own desires,
	If that I do not dream or be not frantic,--
	As I do trust I am not--then, dear uncle,
	Never so much as in a thought unborn
	Did I offend your highness.
DUKE FREDERICK	Thus do all traitors:
	If their purgation did consist in words,
	They are as innocent as grace itself:
	Let it suffice thee that I trust thee not.
ROSALIND	Yet your mistrust cannot make me a traitor:
	Tell me whereon the likelihood depends.
DUKE FREDERICK	Thou art thy father's daughter; there's enough.
ROSALIND	So was I when your highness took his dukedom;
	So was I when your highness banish'd him:
	Treason is not inherited, my lord;
	Or, if we did derive it from our friends,
	What's that to me? my father was no traitor:
	Then, good my liege, mistake me not so much
	To think my poverty is treacherous.

CELIA	Dear sovereign, hear me speak.
DUKE FREDERICK	Ay, Celia; we stay'd her for your sake,
	Else had she with her father ranged along.
CELIA	I did not then entreat to have her stay;
	It was your pleasure and your own remorse:
	I was too young that time to value her;
	But now I know her: if she be a traitor,
	Why so am I; we still have slept together,
	Rose at an instant, learn'd, play'd, eat together,
	And wheresoever we went, like Juno's swans,
	Still we went coupled and inseparable.
DUKE FREDERICK	She is too subtle for thee; and her smoothness,
	Her very silence and her patience
	Speak to the people, and they pity her.
	Thou art a fool: she robs thee of thy name;
	And thou wilt show more bright and seem more virtuous
	When she is gone. Then open not thy lips:
	Firm and irrevocable is my doom
	Which I have pass'd upon her; she is banish'd.
CELIA	Pronounce that sentence then on me, my liege:
	I cannot live out of her company.
DUKE FREDERICK	You are a fool. You, niece, provide yourself:
	If you outstay the time, upon mine honour,
	And in the greatness of my word, you die.

Exeunt DUKE FREDERICK and Lords

Act 3 scene 1, lines 1–18
Enter DUKE FREDERICK, Lords, and OLIVER

DUKE FREDERICK	Not see him since? Sir, sir, that cannot be:
	But were I not the better part made mercy,
	I should not seek an absent argument
	Of my revenge, thou present. But look to it:
	Find out thy brother, wheresoe'er he is;
	Seek him with candle; bring him dead or living
	Within this twelvemonth, or turn thou no more
	To seek a living in our territory.
	Thy lands and all things that thou dost call thine
	Worth seizure do we seize into our hands,
	Till thou canst quit thee by thy brothers mouth
	Of what we think against thee.
OLIVER	O that your highness knew my heart in this!
	I never loved my brother in my life.
DUKE FREDERICK	More villain thou. Well, push him out of doors;
	And let my officers of such a nature
	Make an extent upon his house and lands:
	Do this expediently and turn him going.

Exeunt

TOTAL

18

Shakespeare: *Romeo and Juliet*

Spend 45 minutes on this task.

Write your answer on a separate piece of paper.

Romeo and Juliet: Act 2 scene 2, lines 2–32 and Act 5 scene 3, lines 91–120

In the first extract, Romeo waits below Juliet's bedroom, hoping to see her again after their brief encounter at the Capulet party. In the second extract, Romeo enters the Capulet tomb and sees Juliet's apparently dead body.

In these extracts, how does the language used show Romeo's feelings for Juliet?

Support your ideas by referring to both of the following extracts.

18 marks

Act 2 scene 2, lines 2–32
JULIET appears above at a window
ROMEO

But, soft! what light through yonder window breaks?
It is the east, and Juliet is the sun.
Arise, fair sun, and kill the envious moon,
Who is already sick and pale with grief,
That thou her maid art far more fair than she:
Be not her maid, since she is envious;
Her vestal livery is but sick and green
And none but fools do wear it; cast it off.
It is my lady, O, it is my love!
O, that she knew she were!
She speaks yet she says nothing: what of that?
Her eye discourses; I will answer it.
I am too bold, 'tis not to me she speaks:
Two of the fairest stars in all the heaven,
Having some business, do entreat her eyes
To twinkle in their spheres till they return.
What if her eyes were there, they in her head?
The brightness of her cheek would shame those stars,
As daylight doth a lamp; her eyes in heaven
Would through the airy region stream so bright
That birds would sing and think it were not night.
See, how she leans her cheek upon her hand!
O, that I were a glove upon that hand,
That I might touch that cheek!

JULIET
ROMEO

Ay me!
She speaks:
O, speak again, bright angel! for thou art
As glorious to this night, being o'er my head
As is a winged messenger of heaven
Unto the white-upturned wondering eyes
Of mortals that fall back to gaze on him
When he bestrides the lazy-pacing clouds
And sails upon the bosom of the air.

Act 5 scene 3, lines 91–120
ROMEO

O my love! my wife!
Death, that hath suck'd the honey of thy breath,
Hath had no power yet upon thy beauty:
Thou art not conquer'd; beauty's ensign yet
Is crimson in thy lips and in thy cheeks,
And death's pale flag is not advanced there.
Tybalt, liest thou there in thy bloody sheet?
O, what more favour can I do to thee,
Than with that hand that cut thy youth in twain
To sunder his that was thine enemy?
Forgive me, cousin! Ah, dear Juliet,
Why art thou yet so fair? shall I believe
That unsubstantial death is amorous,
And that the lean abhorred monster keeps
Thee here in dark to be his paramour?
For fear of that, I still will stay with thee;
And never from this palace of dim night
Depart again: here, here will I remain
With worms that are thy chamber-maids; O, here
Will I set up my everlasting rest,
And shake the yoke of inauspicious stars
From this world-wearied flesh. Eyes, look your last!
Arms, take your last embrace! and, lips, O you
The doors of breath, seal with a righteous kiss
A dateless bargain to engrossing death!
Come, bitter conduct, come, unsavoury guide!
Thou desperate pilot, now at once run on
The dashing rocks thy sea-sick weary bark!
Here's to my love! [*He drinks*] O true apothecary!
Thy drugs are quick. Thus with a kiss I die.

[*He falls*]

TOTAL

18

Shakespeare: *Macbeth*

Spend 45 minutes on this task.

Write your answer on a separate piece of paper.

Macbeth: Act 1 scene 7, lines 1–35 and Act 4 scene 1, lines 95–154

In the first extract, Macbeth thinks about how wrong it is to kill King Duncan and decides not to continue with his wife's plan. In the second extract, the witches' apparitions create both confidence and worry in Macbeth; he is then brought news that Macduff has joined the rebels in England.

In these extracts, how does the language used present the character of Macbeth?

Support your ideas by referring to both of the following extracts.

18 marks

Act 1 scene 7, lines 1–35
MACBETH

If it were done when 'tis done, then 'twere well
It were done quickly: if the assassination
Could trammel up the consequence, and catch
With his surcease success; that but this blow
Might be the be-all and the end-all here,
But here, upon this bank and shoal of time,
We'd jump the life to come. But in these cases
We still have judgment here; that we but teach
Bloody instructions, which, being taught, return
To plague the inventor: this even-handed justice
Commends the ingredients of our poison'd chalice
To our own lips. He's here in double trust;
First, as I am his kinsman and his subject,
Strong both against the deed; then, as his host,
Who should against his murderer shut the door,
Not bear the knife myself. Besides, this Duncan
Hath borne his faculties so meek, hath been
So clear in his great office, that his virtues
Will plead like angels, trumpet-tongued, against
The deep damnation of his taking-off;
And pity, like a naked new-born babe,
Striding the blast, or heaven's cherubim, horsed
Upon the sightless couriers of the air,
Shall blow the horrid deed in every eye,
That tears shall drown the wind. I have no spur
To prick the sides of my intent, but only
Vaulting ambition, which o'erleaps itself
And falls on the other.

Enter LADY MACBETH

How now! what news?

LADY MACBETH   He has almost supp'd: why have you left the chamber?

MACBETH   Hath he ask'd for me?

LADY MACBETH   Know you not he has?

MACBETH   We will proceed no further in this business:

He hath honour'd me of late; and I have bought

Golden opinions from all sorts of people,

Which would be worn now in their newest gloss,

Not cast aside so soon.

Act 4 scene 1, lines 95–154

MACBETH   Who can impress the forest, bid the tree

Unfix his earth-bound root? Sweet bodements! good!

Rebellion's head, rise never till the wood

Of Birnam rise, and our high-placed Macbeth

Shall live the lease of nature, pay his breath

To time and mortal custom. Yet my heart

Throbs to know one thing: tell me, if your art

Can tell so much: shall Banquo's issue ever

Reign in this kingdom?

ALL WITCHES   Seek to know no more.

MACBETH   I will be satisfied: deny me this,

And an eternal curse fall on you! Let me know.

Why sinks that cauldron? and what noise is this?

FIRST WITCH   Show!

SECOND WITCH   Show!

THIRD WITCH   Show!

ALL WITCHES   Show his eyes, and grieve his heart;

Come like shadows, so depart!

A show of Eight Kings, the last with a glass in his hand; GHOST OF BANQUO following

MACBETH   Thou art too like the spirit of Banquo: down!

Thy crown does sear mine eye-balls. And thy hair,

Thou other gold-bound brow, is like the first.

A third is like the former. Filthy hags!

Why do you show me this? A fourth! Start, eyes!

What, will the line stretch out to the crack of doom?

Another yet! A seventh! I'll see no more:

And yet the eighth appears, who bears a glass

Which shows me many more; and some I see

That two-fold balls and treble sceptres carry:

Horrible sight! Now, I see, 'tis true;

For the blood-bolter'd Banquo smiles upon me,

And points at them for his.

The Apparitions vanish

	What, is this so?
FIRST WITCH	Ay, sir, all this is so: but why
	Stands Macbeth thus amazedly?
	Come, sisters, cheer we up his sprites,
	And show the best of our delights:
	I'll charm the air to give a sound,
	While you perform your antic round:
	That this great king may kindly say,
	Our duties did his welcome pay.

Music. The witches dance and then vanish.

MACBETH	Where are they? Gone? Let this pernicious hour
	Stand aye accursed in the calendar!
	Come in, without there!

Enter LENNOX

LENNOX	What's your grace's will?
MACBETH	Saw you the weird sisters?
LENNOX	No, my lord.
MACBETH	Came they not by you?
LENNOX	No, indeed, my lord.
MACBETH	Infected be the air whereon they ride;
	And damn'd all those that trust them! I did hear
	The galloping of horse: who was't came by?
LENNOX	'Tis two or three, my lord, that bring you word
	Macduff is fled to England.
MACBETH	Fled to England!
LENNOX	Ay, my good lord.
MACBETH	Time, thou anticipatest my dread exploits:
	The flighty purpose never is o'ertook
	Unless the deed go with it; from this moment
	The very firstlings of my heart shall be
	The firstlings of my hand. And even now,
	To crown my thoughts with acts, be it thought and done:
	The castle of Macduff I will surprise;
	Seize upon Fife; give to the edge o' the sword
	His wife, his babes, and all unfortunate souls
	That trace him in his line. No boasting like a fool;
	This deed I'll do before this purpose cool.

TOTAL

18

Answers

Pages 148–149 Reading 1: Selecting Key Words and Ideas

1. Queen Victoria [1]
2. Thomas Cook [1]
3. a) ✔ and   c) ✔ **[1] for each correct answer up to [2]**
4. Some trains had to stop at every station. All trains had to have third-class carriages. **[1] for each correct answer up to [2]**
5. a) 5   b) 1   c) 4   d) 3   e) 2 **[1] for each correct answer up to [5]**
6. **Any four from:** Walks along the pier; Funfairs; (Sticks of) rock; Candy-floss; Fish and chips. **[1] for each correct answer up to [4]**

Pages 150–151 Reading 2: Inference, Deduction and Interpretation

1. 'with great cheerfulness (of spirit)'. [1]
2. **Any two of the following:** 'logs tripped him'; 'trees crouched (nearer and nearer)'; 'holes made ugly mouths'. **[1] for each correct answer up to [2]**
3.

Quotation	What it tells us
certainly a little narrow face, with hard eyes, had flashed up…	He is sure that he has seen something and it is not pleasant.
…all fixing on him glances of malice and hatred: all hard-eyed and evil and sharp.	He sees so many of them that he knows he cannot be mistaken. He is also sure that they are dangerous/evil.

[2]

4.

Mole knows the Wild Wood very well.	False
Mole imagines the faces.	False
At the end of the extract we do not know whose faces they are.	True
At the end of the extract Mole is safe.	False

[1] for each correct answer up to [4]

Pages 152–153 Reading 3: How Ideas are Organised

1. c) ✔ [1]
2. a) Her background is mysterious/She is secretive/She is a successful detective. [1]
   b) She is a friend and colleague of Lady Molly. She works for the police. [1]
   c) The female detectives are 'snubbed' by the men. [1]
   d) She thinks that they are inferior to women detectives. [1]
3. **[1] for any of the following points up to [3]**
   - The dialogue conveys Lady Molly and Mary's excitement and enthusiasm by the way they speak.
   - The subject of the mystery they have to solve is introduced.
   - The reader is not given all the information that Lady Molly has.

Pages 154–155 Reading 4: Exploring Language Choices

1. a) Future [1]
   b) **[1] for any of the following points up to [2]**
   He is contrasting the present with what the future might hold/The poem is about his hopes or dreams/He is expressing optimism or confidence about what might happen.
2. Snow or Ice. [1]
3. a) Metaphor/Personification. **Either answer valid for [1]**
   b) **Up to [2] for an answer that includes points similar to these:**
   - It gives the impression that the island is alive and colourful.
   - Even the flowers are happy and optimistic.
4. **Up to [2] for an answer that includes points similar to these:**
   - It creates a sense of abundance and variety.

- It conveys an excited, almost child-like, enthusiasm.
5. a) Alliteration ✔ [1]
   b) **Up to [2] for points similar to these:**
   - The softness of the 'f' and 'v' sounds conveys a gentle atmosphere.
   - The poem ends in a quiet, content way, reflecting the poet's mood.

Pages 156–157 Reading 5: Explaining Purposes and Viewpoints

1. To inform people about the scheme. ✔ [1]
   To persuade people to get involved with people from a different generation.✔ [1]
2. • They may no longer be alive.
   • They might be living in a different place.
   [1] for each correct answer up to [2]
3. a) Contact with young people makes them feel younger and keeps them busy.
   b) They could get help with, or advice about, bringing up children.
   c) Older people often have more time to play with them and listen to them.
   [1] for each answer similar to these up to [3]
4. • They were bored/finding life a bit boring.
   • They were missing their own grandchildren.
   [1] for each answer similar to these up to [2]
5. The writer mentions that:
   • It is a registered charity.
   • They work closely with the local authority/district council.
   • Checks are made before people can join.
   • Everything they do is properly organised and supervised.
   [1] for any answer similar to these up to [3]

Pages 158–159 Reading 6: Structuring a Longer Response

1. **An excellent answer (16–20 marks) will:**
   • Evaluate the text and its effect on the reader critically.

- Show perceptive understanding of the writer's methods.
- Select a range of judicious detail from the text.
- Develop a convincing and critical response to the focus of the question.
- Include the following content:
  - Comment on the language used to describe the room and Miss Havisham and what it makes the reader think of.
  - The way different characters speak.
  - The comparisons Pip makes, e.g. 'waxwork'.
  - Pip's naivety and the differences of age and class between him and Miss Havisham.
  - The 'Gothic', almost supernatural, atmosphere.

A good answer (11–15 marks) will:
- Clearly evaluate the text and its effect on the reader.
- Show clear understanding of the writer's methods.
- Select a range of relevant detail from the text.
- Make a clear and relevant response to the focus of the question.
- Include the following content:
  - Comments on the language used to describe the room and Miss Havisham.
  - The way different characters speak.
  - Pip describes the room almost like in a horror story.
  - Nothing is explained to Pip before he meets Miss Havisham.

Writing pages 160–171

Page 160 Writing 1: Purpose, Audience and Form

1. Argue; Students; Article [3]
2. Advise; Teenager; Letter [3]
3. Inform; Adults and young people; Text for a leaflet [3]
4. Persuade; Adults; Letter [3]

Page 161 Writing 2: Paragraphs and Connectives

1. Time, place, focus. [3]
2. It was midnight and the darkness seemed to envelop the boy as he walked through the forest. He felt as if the night was pressing against his eyes. It was a blackness so absolute that he could barely see.//

    After a few minutes, he began to see glimmers of light in the distance. The break from the darkness lifted his spirits and he made his way forward. The lights felt like hope after his trudge through the woods.//

    Suddenly, he heard footsteps behind him. He turned but there was no-one there. His eyes scanned the empty road, the gate leading back into the woods, and the thick blackness. No more footsteps broke through the eerie silence.//

    Seconds later, music burst from his pocket as his mobile began to ring. Surprise led quickly to relief as he saw his friend's name flashing back at him from the screen. The familiarity calmed him and he felt safe once more.
    [1] for each correct paragraph marker up to [3]

3. **The following words circled**: After a few minutes; Suddenly; Seconds later. They are all connectives of time.
    [3] for three connective circled, [1] for what they have in common

4.

Place	Sequence	Compare and Contrast	Cause and Effect
In the next room, Twenty miles away, Further down the street,	Firstly, Next, Finally,	However, On the other hand, Conversely,	Due to, Because of this, Thus,

[1] for each correctly grouped connective up to [12]

Page 162 Writing 3: Grammar

1. **[1] for each correct sentence structure up to [3]**
    a) Simple
    b) Compound
    c) Complex

2. To separate clauses and separate items in a list. **[1] for each correct use up to [2]**

3. It can go before, after, or within the main clause. **[1] for each correct position up to [3]**

4. a) Conditional [1]
    b) Present [1]
    c) Past [1]
    d) Future [1]
    e) Present [1]
    f) Future [1]
    g) Conditional [1]
    h) Past [1]

5. I went to the cinema yesterday and I **watched** a comedy. It **was** really funny and I couldn't stop laughing. I **bought** loads of popcorn and sweets. It **was** quite difficult not making lots of rustling noises but I just about **managed** it. Everyone **was** laughing, though, so it wouldn't **have** mattered. I **had** a great time.
    [1] for each correction up to [8]

Page 163 Writing 4: Punctuation and Spelling

1. a) I didn't want any more dinner as it wasn't very nice. [2]
    b) We weren't supposed to go alone and we should've listened. [2]
    c) I couldn't understand the maths question and my friend wouldn't help me. [2]

2. a) Sharon's dad was making the family's dinner. [2]
    b) Zain's hamster was in its cage, tearing up a page of yesterday's newspaper. [2]
    c) The cats' meals were ready but they were busy playing with my youngest daughter's football. [2]

3. **[1] for each correct comma**
    a) Coming in from the garden, she began to wash her hands. [1]

b) He looked around, wondering if he was really alone. **[1]**

c) The bird, beating its wings frantically, tried to reach the next branch of the tree. **[2]**

d) The fireworks, bursting with noise and colour, were a lovely end to the celebration. **[2]**

4. There were three **babies** at the party that **kept** on **screaming**. If it hadn't been **for** the fact that **there** was plenty of cake, I **would** have left early. Everyone seemed to ignore the **hideous** noise they were **making** but I found it **intolerably irritating**. At one point, they **quietened** down **only** to start **howling** once again when someone **burst** a **balloon**. **[1] for each corrected spelling up to [15]**

Page 164 Writing 5: Plan, Structure and Develop your Response

1. **Possible Pros:**
   - Everyone will have plenty of time to eat their lunch instead of rushing.
   - There will be fewer arguments about queues and pushing in.
   - More time to relax at lunch is better for students' mental health.
   - It will also give the teachers more of a break.
   - Students will work harder in the afternoon because they won't be as stressed.

   Possible Cons:
   - Students may get bored.
   - More unstructured time could mean students misbehaving.
   - Students may relax too much and then not work hard enough in the afternoon.
   - Lunch monitors will need to be employed for longer.
   - The school may need to provide more lunchtime clubs and activities.

   [1] for any of these points up to a maximum of [6]

2. **[1] for explaining your reason; [1] for developing it with an example; [1] for using a rhetorical device; [1] for accurate writing.**

3. **[1] for introducing your idea and using a connective; [1] for explaining your reason; [1] for developing it with an example; [1] for using a rhetorical device; [1] for accurate writing.**

Page 165 Writing 6: Writing to Persuade

1. **[1] for each correct element of the mnemonic up to [8]**
   Facts
   Opinions
   Rhetorical questions
   Empathy and emotive language
   Statistics
   Triplets
   Repetition
   You

2. **[1] for each element of the mnemonic that is identified up to [8]**
   Fact – it's available in shops now
   Opinion – tastiest
   Rhetorical question – why don't you take a 'Treat'?
   Empathy and emotive language – you've worked hard all day and must be feeling tired and hungry
   Statistics – 70%
   Triplets – thick, sweet, luxurious; sit back, relax and 'Treat' yourself
   Repetition – 'Treat'; you; chocolate
   You – you, you've, yourself

3. **[1] for each statement encouraging exercise and [1] for each use of a persuasive technique up to [8]**

Page 166 Writing 7: Writing to Argue

1. **[1] for each idea up to maximum of [12]**
   Possible ideas:
   A: (pros) being more comfortable will mean students work harder; choice of clothing will help mental health; (cons)

uniform helps good behaviour; uniform creates equality; school should be focussed on learning not fashion.

B: (pros) lots of government decisions affect young people so they should have their say; it will encourage young people to take an interest in the world; it will improve maturity and intelligence; (cons) politics is too complex for many young people; people aren't considered adult until 18.

C: (pros) it will stop young people being pressured to smoke; just banning advertising hasn't done enough; it will save the NHS lots of money; (cons) people have a right to choose; cigarette trade employs lots of people; cigarette companies contribute to tax, etc.

D: (pros) students will focus more in class; it will help to end cyber bullying; no competition for having the newest phone; (cons) students feel safer with their phone; students can relax to music, etc. during breaks which is good for mental health.

2. **[1] for each of the two types of connective, and [1] for why each would be used up to [4].**
    Compare/contrast to show different sides of the argument; cause/effect to show why you think what you do.

3. **[1] for each feature:** Facts, opinions, empathy, statistics, triplets.

4. **[1] for each topic sentence up to [4]**

Page 167 Writing 8: Writing to Advise

1. firm, friendly, supportive [3]
2. You [1]
3. To urge people to follow your advice. [1]
4. a) could, must, need, ought, should [5]
    b) To make the reader act while also creating some sense of choice. [2]
5. **[1] for each sentence that has been given modality up to [4]**

Possible ideas: You should try to avoid these stressful situations. You could speak to your family about how you're feeling. If this doesn't help, you might talk to a friend or a teacher at school. You must put yourself first and get on with your life.

Page 168 Writing 9: Vocabulary and Sentences

1. **[1] for each synonym up to [10]**
    Possible alternatives: (begin) start, commence, initiate; (eat) devour, dine, stuff; (say) whisper, reply, shout; (think) wonder, consider, debate; (walk) wander, stroll, trudge.

2. **[1] for each synonym, up to [5] for 'good and [5] for 'bad'**
    Possible alternatives: (good) amazing, brilliant, wonderful, terrific, positive; (bad) awful, terrible, horrendous, poor, rubbish.

3. **[1] for each correctly identified effect up to [4]**

Sentence structure	Effect
Simple	Join two ideas or create a contrast
Compound	Emphasise a point or build up a powerful image
Complex	Emphasise an idea or surprise the reader
List	Build up a point or add extra detail

4. **[1] for each use of a simple, compound, and complex sentence, and a list; [1] for an additional complex sentence with the subordinate clause in a different position; [1] for using a synonym for begin, eat, say, think, walk, good and bad. Up to a maximum of [12]**

Page 169 Writing 10: Writing to Inform

1. Chronologically means writing the sequence of events as they happened [1]; Thematically means grouping information into sub-topics [1]

2. **[1] for identifying 'thematically' and [1] for a correct explanation:**
Thematically as it isn't focussed on an event and key information needs to be grouped together.

3. **a)** Opinion [1]
b) Fact [1]
c) Fact [1]
d) Opinion [1]
e) Opinion [1]
f) Fact [1]

4. **[1] for each connective, up to [4] for time and [4] for place:**
Possible ideas: (time) yesterday, later, at 3pm, next month; (place) in the city centre, down the road, in the next room, ten miles away.

5. **[1] for each of the three key moments, and [1] for each of the three facts for each of those three moments up to a maximum of [9]**

Page 170 Writing 11: Writing to Explain

1. Writing to explain goes into more detail about cause and effect. [1]

2. **[1] for each connective up to [4]**
Possible ideas: as a result, because of this, consequently, therefore

3. **[1] for each cause or effect up to [8]**
Possible ideas:
(A): peer or media pressure = unrealistic body ideals leads to continual unhappiness; not consuming enough vitamins, etc. = unhealthy organs, blood, and bones.
(B): need more landfill = fewer rural areas; dumping of plastics = more greenhouse gases and global warming.

4. Past tense to explain something that has happened [1]; present tense to explain a current issue [1]

5. **Up to [2] for each idea about improving sleep; Up to [2] for each cause of poor sleep; Up to [2] for each specific effect that this cause has on sleep**

Page 171 Writing 12: Writing to Describe

1. **[1] for each correctly altered word up to [10]**
Possible ideas: Glen <u>raced</u> <u>urgently</u> up the <u>bustling</u> road. His cheeks were <u>scarlet</u> and sweat <u>poured</u> down his face. By the time he <u>reached</u> the shop, he was <u>panting</u> <u>hoarsely</u>. He was <u>shocked</u> by how <u>exhausted</u> he felt.

2. **[1] for each description of food using a different sense up to [5]**

3. **[1] for each correctly matched example up to [4]**

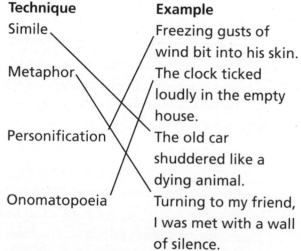

Technique	Example
Simile	Freezing gusts of wind bit into his skin.
Metaphor	The clock ticked loudly in the empty house.
Personification	The old car shuddered like a dying animal.
Onomatopoeia	Turning to my friend, I was met with a wall of silence.

4. **[1] for a simile and [1] for a metaphor**
Possible ideas: the chrome of the kettle shone like daylight and its spout was a steaming volcano.

5. **[1–3] for** writing about the alien planet with some adjectives; **[4–6] for** consistently using descriptions to depict an alien world, including adjectives, verbs, a sense other than sight, and a simile or metaphor; **[7–9] for** a range of descriptive techniques (metaphor, simile, personification, the senses) and varied vocabulary to create an interesting depiction of the alien world.

Shakespeare pages 172–177

Pages 172–173 Shakespeare 1: *As You Like it*

1. independent, strong-willed, clever **[3]**
2. kind-hearted, uneducated, romantic **[3]**
3. Orlando is idealistic (believing in love at first sight) **[1]** while Rosalind is realistic. **[1]**

4. They parody romantic love. [1]
5. **[1] for each explanation up to [4]**
   Rosalind is banished (after her father was usurped); by Frederick; while Orlando has been kept uneducated and unrefined; by Oliver.
6. **[1] for each link to freedom up to [3]**
   Characters escape the oppression and injustice of the court; characters fall in love; characters can transform their identities.
7. **[1] for each link to a happy ending up to [3]**
   Four marriages; Duke Senior's position is restored; Oliver regrets his treatment of Orlando.
8. **[1] for identifying a feature of rhetorical language and [1] for explaining its effect:**
   Possible ideas: Orlando raises the unfairness of his treatment through rhetorical question; exaggeration (the animal imagery) is used to emphasise his lowly existence.
9. **[1] for identifying a feature of descriptive language and [1] for explaining its effect:**
   Possible ideas: Celia's adjectives depict Frederick's negative qualities (he is harsh and distrusting); the metaphor shows that Celia is upset by her father's behaviour which suggests she has a gentler nature.
10. **[1] for identifying a feature of emotive language and [1] for explaining its effect:**
    Possible ideas: use of hyperbole (calling herself a 'traitor') to emphasise her belief in Rosalind's innocence; the list of verbs to convey the strength and closeness of their friendship; the simile (and classical allusion), images of pairs, or the two synonyms for being connected to convey her feelings for Rosalind and her grief at the idea of Rosalind's banishment.
11. **[1] for a suggestion about performance and [1] for a clear reason, linked to the text:**
    Possible ideas: tone of voice could be surprised as she does not know why she is suddenly banished ('Let me the knowledge of my fault'); tone of voice could be upset or desperate as she is begging for survival ('I do beseech'); to show her desperation

and suggest respect ('I do beseech your Grace'), she could fall to her knees or hold her arms out towards Frederick.

Pages 174–175 Shakespeare 2: *Romeo and Juliet*

1. **[1] for each suitable adjective, and [1] for each clear explanation up to [4]**
   Possible ideas: devoted – the strength of his love for Juliet; romantic – how he woos Juliet; peaceful – not wanting to fight with Tybalt; headstrong – killing Tybalt; fickle – quickly falling in love with Juliet after Rosaline.
2. **[1] for each suitable adjective, and [1] for each clear explanation up to [4]**
   Possible ideas: romantic – her feelings about Romeo as she waits for their wedding night; faithful – her willingness to do anything to be with Romeo; strong-minded – she stands up to her father when he wants her to marry Paris; headstrong – marrying in secret; spoilt – she gets the Nurse to help arrange the marriage despite the dangers.
3. He is more interested in falling in love than feuding with the other family. [1]
4. **[1] for commenting that the relationship is generally good at the start, [1] for commenting that her parents mistreat her later on by forcing her into a future marriage, and [1] for linking the change to her love for Romeo, her parents' feelings after Tybalt's death, or her refusal to marry Paris.**
5. Love at first sight [1]
6. **[1] for each consequence, up to [3]**
   Possible ideas: Romeo and Juliet's secret marriage; Mercutio's death; Tybalt's death; Romeo's banishment; Romeo and Juliet's suicides.
7. The Prologue tells the audience that Romeo and Juliet are fated to fall in love and die. [1]
8. **[1] for identifying a feature of emotive language and [1] for explaining its effect:**

Possible ideas: Romeo's use of the rhetorical question to show his despair at the family feud; the use of contrasts, oxymorons, or a triplet to convey both his inner turmoil about love and conflict; the repetition of 'O' to emphasise his despair.

9. **[1] for identifying a feature of descriptive language and [1] for explaining its effect:**
   Possible ideas: Capulet's metaphors depict Juliet's innocence; his metaphors also convey his love for his daughter; the natural image of ripeness could also suggest Capulet and Paris's attitudes to women as a type of commodity to be traded.

10. **[1] for identifying a feature of rhetorical language and [1] for explaining its effect:**
    Possible ideas: use of imperatives ('read'/'find') to urge Juliet to fall in love with Paris; use of metaphors to persuade Juliet of Paris's great qualities; use of emotive language (such as the adjective 'delight') to make romance and marriage sound appealing.

11. **[1] for a suggestion about performance and [1] for a clear reason linked to the text:**
    Possible ideas: the actors could use contrasting tones of voice to show Mercutio's lively happiness ('dance') and Romeo's melancholy ('soul of lead'); actions and facial expression could also show their difference, with Mercutio smiling and perhaps even dancing ('dancing shoes') while Romeo trudges and looks unhappy ('soul of lead'); Mercutio could try to engage Romeo in dancing to cheer him up ('we must have you dance') but be denied ('Not I').

Pages 176–177 Shakespeare 3: *Macbeth*

1. **[1] for each suitable adjective, and [1] for each clear explanation, up to [4]**
   Possible ideas: brave or loyal (fought well in battle for the King); good or kind or honourable (Lady Macbeth talks of his kind nature); respected (is praised by others and made Thane of Cawdor).

2. **[1] for each suitable adjective, and [1] for each clear explanation, up to [4]**
   Possible ideas: over-ambitious (his wish to be King); treacherous or dishonourable (the killing of the King); paranoid (his fears about Banquo and Fleance); unstable (his loss of mental control); cruel and vicious (the killing of Macduff's family).

3. **[2] for each change, up to [4]**
   Possible ideas: at the start she is confident and manipulative but by the end she has lost control of her mind; at the start she is ambitious but by the end she regrets her actions; at the start she lacks a conscience and seems evil but by the end she is tortured by the idea that she is going to Hell.

4. **[1] for identifying Lady Macbeth, [1] for a clear explanation, and [1] for making a link to Macbeth:**
   Possible ideas: Macbeth wants to be King but will not do anything evil to achieve it, while Lady Macbeth will do anything to achieve her ambitions; Lady Macbeth manipulates Macbeth into killing the King; Lady Macbeth comes up with the plan to kill the King and teaches Macbeth how to deceive others.

5. The natural order or the Divine Right of Kings. **[1]**

6. **[1] for identifying a relevant point in the play, up to [2]**
   Macbeth's disturbed mind on the night of the murder; Macbeth seeing Banquo's ghost at the banquet; Lady Macbeth being mad with guilt towards the end of the play.

7. The witches. **[1]**

8. **[1] for identifying a feature of descriptive language and [1] for explaining its effect:**
   Possible ideas: The Captain's simile shows how well Macbeth and Banquo fought; the plural pronoun or the image of doubles emphasises the strength of Macbeth and Banquo's friendship; the adjective 'overcharg'd' conveys their determination and implies they fought better than would seem possible.

9. **[1] for identifying a feature of rhetorical language and [1] for explaining its effect: Possible ideas:** Macbeth's use of contrasts to show him debating whether he trusts the witches; the contrasts also show his doubts and hopes about the witches' prophecies, and the treacherous idea of becoming the King; the rhetorical question shows him contemplating the prophecies and the idea that he could become King; the use of the aside also increases the secretive, treacherous nature of his rhetorical language.

10. **[1] for identifying a feature of emotive language and [1] for explaining its effect: Possible ideas:** the adjective 'worthiest' shows the King's great respect for Macbeth, and this is highlighted by the exclamation mark (suggesting the line should be performed with zeal); the metaphor conveys his feeling that he cannot thank Macbeth enough for what he has done in battle.

11. **[1] for a suggestion about performance and [1] for a clear reason, linked to the text: Possible ideas:** the actor playing the King should speak grandly and have similarly regal gestures as this is an important moment in terms of family and the monarchy ('We will establish our estate'); most of the characters should look pleased as this is a happy occasion ('whom we name'); Malcolm should look pleased but also humbled as he is being confirmed as next in line to the throne ('Prince of Cumberland'); the actor playing Macbeth could try to show that he is jealous that Malcolm has been named the next King while pretending to be as pleased as everyone else ('our estate upon our eldest').

Reading

Pages 178–179: Reading Task 1

1. **[1] for each of the following up to a maximum of [2]**
   - They have closed the road through the woods.
   - They have planted trees.

2. **[1] for any of the following up to a maximum of [2]**
   - He is the only person who still goes into the woods.
   - He knows the woods better than anyone else does.
   - Because of his job he knows a lot about nature/the woods.

3. **[1] for any of the following up to a maximum of [4]**
   - The first stanza describes what the woods are like now.
   - The tone of the first stanza is gentle and peaceful.
   - The first stanza is about the daytime.
   - The second stanza is about what the woods are like at night.
   - In the second stanza, the tone becomes disturbing/eerie/frightening.
   - The second stanza introduces the idea of the past and/or the woods being haunted.

4. **An excellent answer (7–8 marks) will:**
   - Show perceptive understanding of the writer's use of language.
   - Select a range of judicious detail from the text.
   - Use subject terminology in a sophisticated and accurate way.
   - Include the following content:
     - The poet uses literal images throughout, the lists of sights and sounds building a vivid picture for the reader.
     - The repetition of 'through the woods' give an insistent, almost threatening, quality.

- Onomatopoeia ('whistles'/'swish'), alliteration and repetition combine to build a mysterious, supernatural atmosphere in the second stanza.

A good answer (5–6 marks) will:

- Explain clearly the effects of the writer's choice of language.
- Select a range of relevant details from the text.
- Make clear and relevant use of subject terminology.
- Include the following content:
  - In the first stanza, the poet lists what can be seen in the woods but in the second he focuses on sounds.
  - He uses the second person 'you' to get the reader involved and imagine what it is like.
  - Alliteration is used to create an eerie atmosphere: 'the swish of a skirt'.

Pages 180–182: Reading Task 2

1. He was angry/in a bad temper. **[1]**
2. **[1] for each correct answer up to a maximum of [2]**
   - Swinging on a rope.
   - Jumping over graves/tombstones.
3. **[1] for each point similar to the following, up to a maximum of [2]**
   - The boys enjoyed being thrown into the river by him.
   - He would take them on walks.
   - He told them stories.
4. **[1] for each correct answer up to a maximum of [3]**
   He thinks the punishments were inconsistent and sometimes cruel. ✔
   On the whole he respected Mr Bullen. ✔
   He had some enjoyable times at Oundle. ✔
5. **An excellent answer (7–8 marks) will:**
   - Select a range of judicious detail from the text.
   - Develop a convincing and critical response to the focus of the question.

- Include the following content:
  - Some might find the use of corporal punishment shocking and cruel while others might think there is an argument for bringing it back.
  - They might notice that the writer's attitude to the formal punishment of the 'birch' and 'cane' differs from his reaction to the pulling of a boy's ears, which he compares to torture.
  - Most would agree with the writer that, on his evidence, discipline would suffer when punishments were 'badly and unjustly regulated'.
  - Some would recognise the boys' practice of sharing their punishments and think it shows resourcefulness and friendship.

A good answer (5–6 marks) will:

- Select a range of relevant detail from the text.
- Make a clear and relevant response to the focus of the question.
- Include the following content:
  - They would probably agree punishments were 'badly and unjustly regulated'.
  - They would probably find corporal punishment cruel and be surprised that it was allowed.
  - They might be surprised that the writer seems to accept the birch and the cane.

Pages 183–187: Reading Task 3

1. **[1] for each of the following words up to a maximum of [4]**
   - odd
   - soft
   - whispering
   - rustling
2. **An excellent answer (7–8 marks) will:**
   - Show perceptive understanding of the writer's use of language.

- Select a range of judicious detail from the text.
- Use subject terminology in a sophisticated and accurate way.
- Include the following content:
  - The writer uses an extended simile, describing the tree as a 'creature... walking'. 'Creature' implies something not human and threatening.
  - Bobbie refers to a well-known scene in Shakespeare when soldiers covered with branches attack Macbeth's castle, implying that the trees are aggressive and war-like.
  - Phyllis's references to 'magic' and 'enchanted' reflect her age, contrasting with Bobbie's literary reference while helping to create a sense of wonder in the reader.
  - A second extended simile personifies the woods, this time in a more homely and less threatening way as the last tree is compared to 'some old shepherd'.

A good answer (5–6 marks) will:

- Explain clearly the effects of the writer's choice of language.
- Select a range of relevant details from the text.
- Make clear and relevant use of subject terminology.
- Include the following content:
  - The writer uses a simile of a 'creature' to make the woods seem threatening.
  - Reference to 'Macbeth' might make the reader think of war and tragedy.
  - The words 'magic' and 'enchanted' convey a sense of mystery and excitement.
  - The woods are personified – a tree is compared to a shepherd.

3. **An excellent answer (7–8 marks) will:**
- Show perceptive understanding of the writer's use of structure.

- Select a range of judicious detail from the text.
- Use subject terminology in a sophisticated and accurate way.
- Include the following content:
  - At the beginning, we are drawn into the children's experience by the urgency of Bobbie's 'Hush. Stop! What's that?' The two imperatives and the question create a sense of urgency bringing our attention to the noises.
  - The next part of the extract focuses on descriptions of the sounds and sights, with dialogue conveying the children's sense of wonder.
  - The short simple sentence, 'Then he stood upright' marks a turning point in the extract as the children realise that the train is in danger.
  - The focus changes to what they might do to help, their dialogue conveying a rising sense of excitement as well as their thought processes as they try to work out what to do.
  - Things change again when Phyllis mentions 'petticoats' and the children realise that they have a way of saving the train. At this stage, readers might not be able to follow their thinking and will be intrigued about what exactly they plan to do and whether it will work.

A good answer (5–6 marks) will:

- Explain clearly the effects of the writer's choice of structure.
- Select a range of relevant details from the text.
- Make clear and relevant use of subject terminology.
- Include the following content:
  - At the beginning, when Bobbie says 'stop', the children realise that something strange is happening.

- After a while, there is a change shown by the short sentence, 'Then he stood upright'. Then they try to work out the best thing to do as they go towards the railway line.
- Their mood changes when Phyllis mentions 'petticoats' and it strikes the children that they have a way of saving the train.
- The writer uses a lot of dialogue to show the children's reactions and how they form their plan.

4. **An excellent answer (16–20 marks) will:**
- Evaluate the text and its effect on the reader critically.
- Show perceptive understanding of the writer's methods.
- Select a range of judicious detail from the text.
- Develop a convincing and critical response to the focus of the question.
- Include the following content:
  - This part of the extract begins with the children watching the trees, aware that something strange and perhaps even supernatural is happening. The trees are personified and appear unstoppable.
  - As the trees fall on the railway line, the children are still awestruck and unaware of the danger, comparing it to the mundane sight of 'the coals coming 'down'.
  - The mood shifts as Peter realises the seriousness of the event and, in contrast with Bobbie's instinct to 'run', is described as 'businesslike', reacting calmly and in a practical way.
  - Their actions and speech bring out the children's different characters, but they all cooperate and play a part in coming up with a plan.
  - Ideas are thought of and rejected as time passes, increasing the tension, until one of the ideas they have rejected – waving something red –

returns because of a chance reference to the girls' petticoats.

A good answer (11–15 marks) will:
- Clearly evaluate the text and its effect on the reader.
- Show clear understanding of the writer's methods.
- Select a range of relevant detail from the text.
- Make a clear and relevant response to the focus of the question.
- Include the following content:
  - The writer continues to personify the trees and the description of how they stop and fall on the track gives a sense of the danger and the children's weakness.
  - At first they react by comparing it to something every day – 'the coals coming 'down' – but then Peter realises the seriousness of the event.
  - Bobbie's instinct is to 'run' but Peter stops her. He is described as 'businesslike' and reacts calmly and in a practical way.
  - The dialogue shows the children's plan developing.
  - Ideas are thought of and rejected as time passes, increasing the tension.
  - The solution is found in something everyday and even comic – the girls' petticoats.

Writing

Writing tasks 1–6 have a maximum of [30]:
- **[14] for how successfully you write for your purpose, audience and form**
- **[8] for sentence structure, punctuation and spelling**
- **[8] for the organisation of your writing.**

An excellent answer (24–30 marks) will:
- Display a full awareness of purpose, audience and form.

- Include a full range of techniques to effectively convey purpose.
- Present a range of ideas, using a sophisticated range of vocabulary and sentence structures.
- Use paragraphs and a variety of connectives to effectively structure the writing.
- Achieve a high level of technical accuracy: spelling, grammar, punctuation.
- Engage the reader throughout and be convincing.

A good answer (16–23 marks) will:
- Display some awareness of purpose, audience and form.
- Include some techniques to emphasise purpose.
- Present some variety of ideas, using effective vocabulary and different sentence structures.
- Use paragraphs and connectives to introduce different parts of the writing.
- Achieve an acceptable level of technical accuracy: most familiar words spelled correctly, accurate grammar with only a few minor errors, a range of punctuation but some errors with complex constructions.
- Engage the reader, but not be fully convincing throughout.

Page 188 – Writing Task 1: Writing to Persuade

Possible ideas:
- Young people could spend more time with grandparents, contact neighbours who are pensioners, or visit old people's homes.
- This could benefit pensioners who are lonely or isolated: they will have someone to talk to or even do odd jobs.
- Pensioners might also feel safer in their area, knowing more of the young people; they may get a better impression of what young people are really like.
- Young people could gain a sense of achievement through helping; it might also provide good work experience.
- Young people could learn from older people's experiences, as well as gaining empathy for others.

Page 189 – Writing Task 2: Writing to Argue

Possible ideas:
- Pros: give young people a sense of achievement; help young people feel more of a part of the community, as well as giving communities a better impression of young people; develop skills beyond the classroom, such as leadership, teamwork, initiative, etc; it could save local councils money through free volunteering.
- Cons: students need to be focussed on their studies; young people might resent working for free; all young people might not be committed, which could create conflict among peers and within the community; organisation would be complex as all students from a year group would have to be off school at the same time otherwise learning would be disrupted.

Page 190 – Writing Task 3: Writing to Advise

Possible ideas:
- Aim for a more rounded diet, ensuring the correct suggested amounts of calories, fat, protein, salt, etc.
- Make sure you eat at least five portions of fruit and vegetables a day, while avoiding unhealthy snacks and fast food.
- Drink more water rather than carbonated drinks.
- Walk or cycle to school rather than travelling by car or bus.
- Complete at least ten minutes of rigorous physical exercise a day, such as jogging, press-ups, cycling, etc.
- Join a school or local gym and find an exercise class that you enjoy, such as aerobics, spin, or cross-training, etc.

Page 191 – Writing Task 4: Writing to Inform

Possible ideas:
- Social media apps and sites such as Whatsapp, Twitter, Instagram, Facebook, TikTok; where/how to download them; how to create a memorable password.

- Benefits include connecting with friends and family (especially those who live a long way away), sharing interests, getting likes and feeling valued, discovering new things, taking part in discussions and knowing what is happening locally, nationally and globally.
- Disadvantages include trolling, the risk of having more virtual than real communication, other people using social media as a way to make money illegally, information can be inaccurate and biased.
- Older people may be especially interested in sharing photos of holidays, connecting with family, developing hobbies (such as travel, gardening, eating out, etc).

Page 192 – Writing Task 5: Writing to Explain

Possible ideas:

- Change colour scheme and displays in classrooms; this could create a happier environment that pupils respect more.
- Ensure more open spaces; this would allow more sporting activities as well as giving students areas to spread out, thereby reducing conflicts, etc.
- Create a staffroom that has a private garden; this would allow staff to relax more, giving them a break from students and ensuring fresh air.
- More outdoor sports/games facilities, such as table tennis, all-weather pitches, giant chess boards, etc; this would help students relax outside of lessons, as well as developing new skills and competitiveness; teachers might even join in, creating better pupil-staff relationships.

Page 193 – Writing Task 6: Writing to Describe

Possible ideas:

- Include detailed descriptions of settings, weather, and people; build up a sense of the atmosphere at the time, considering light, temperature, people's mood, etc; try to capture small details that the reader will be able to imagine in order to add realism and interest (such as a bird looking for food in springtime, a child eating an ice cream in the summer, a leaf falling in autumn, or icicles dripping in the winter); try to use all the senses.

Shakespeare

Pages 194–195 – Shakespeare: *As You Like It*

An excellent answer (16–18 marks) will:

- Focus on the how language shows different ideas about injustice.
- Present a range of ideas, appreciating how the two extracts show similar and different aspects of injustice.
- Feature a balanced coverage of both extracts, with regular comparisons drawn between the two.
- Offer concise analysis of the effects of Shakespeare's language and stagecraft, making use of a range of technical terms such as adjective and simile.
- Successfully integrate regular, skilfully selected quotations into a well-developed discussion.

A good answer (16–18 marks) will:

- Display a general focus on the theme of injustice.
- Present a number of ideas, appreciating how the extracts show different things about injustice.
- Feature a balanced coverage of both texts, with some comparison.
- Show awareness of the effects of Shakespeare's language and stagecraft, with some analysis and use of technical language.
- Support all ideas with brief quotations.

Possible points on the first extract:

- Injustice is linked to a lack of reason (Frederick is acting out of anger and paranoia).
- Injustice is linked to stubbornness (Frederick will not change his mind).
- Frederick's unjust actions are a surprise as Rosalind is innocent, creating sympathy for her from the audience.

- Frederick's unjust actions are extreme: Rosalind is threatened with death.
- Frederick refuses to listen to Rosalind's defence of herself, nor to Celia's interventions.
- Frederick is unjustly cruel to his own daughter.

Possible points on the second extract:
- Injustice is linked to supposition (guesswork) rather than fact.
- Oliver is seen as guilty because of his relation to Orlando, rather than something he has done.
- Frederick doesn't appear to believe he is unjust.
- Frederick's unjust actions are extreme: he wants Orlando dead or alive, he seizes all of Oliver's assets.
- Frederick will not listen to Oliver's defence of himself.
- The audience may be less sympathetic to the injustice against Oliver as he has been unjust to Orlando.

Pages 196–197 – Shakespeare: *Romeo and Juliet*

An excellent answer (16–18 marks) will:
- Focus on the how language shows different ideas about Romeo's feelings for Juliet.
- Present a range of ideas, appreciating how the two extracts show similar and different aspects of Romeo's feelings for Juliet.
- Feature a balanced coverage of both extracts, with regular comparisons drawn between the two.
- Offer concise analysis of the effects of Shakespeare's language and stagecraft, making use of a range of technical terms such as adjective and simile.
- Successfully integrate regular, skilfully selected quotations into a well-developed discussion.

A good answer (12–15 marks) will:
- Display a general focus on the topic of Romeo's feelings for Juliet.

- Present a number of ideas, appreciating how the extracts show different things about Romeo's feelings for Juliet.
- Feature a balanced coverage of both texts, with some comparison.
- Show awareness of the effects of Shakespeare's language and stagecraft, with some analysis and use of technical language.
- Support all ideas with brief quotations.

Possible points on the first extract:
- Romeo is already in love with Juliet after their first meeting and hopes she feels the same.
- He sees her as a source of happiness and goodness.
- He thinks she is beautiful and wants to be close to her.
- He worships her.
- He sees her as pure and perfect.

Possible points on the second extract:
- Romeo is grieving for Juliet's death.
- He still loves and worships her.
- He marvels at her beauty, despite her death; he can hardly believe she is dead.
- He doesn't want to leave her and decides to die alongside her.
- He feels that life is over without Juliet.

Pages 198–200 – Shakespeare: *Macbeth*

An excellent answer (16–18 marks) will:
- Focus on the how language shows different ideas about Macbeth's character.
- Present a range of ideas, appreciating how the two extracts show similar and different aspects of Macbeth's character.
- Feature a balanced coverage of both extracts, with regular comparisons drawn between the two.
- Offer concise analysis of the effects of Shakespeare's language and stagecraft, making use of a range of technical terms such as adjective and simile.
- Successfully integrate regular, skilfully selected quotations into a well-developed discussion.

A good answer (12–15 marks) will:

- Display a general focus on the topic of Macbeth's character.
- Present a number of ideas, appreciating how the extracts show different things about Macbeth's character.
- Feature a balanced coverage of both texts, with some comparison.
- Show awareness of the effects of Shakespeare's language and stagecraft, with some analysis and use of technical language.
- Support all ideas with brief quotations.

Possible points on the first extract:

- Macbeth is troubled.
- He is ambitious but has some morality: he is considering killing the King but is worried by the consequences of damnation. His thoughts can be seen as self-interest rather than morality.
- He is fearful of corruption and evil; he is God-fearing.
- He has a conscience, realising there are many reasons why it is wrong to kill the King.
- The audience are reminded that Macbeth is well-respected, having recently fought well for the King in battle.
- Although Lady Macbeth will convince him otherwise, at this point he decides against killing the King and chooses good over evil.

Possible points on the second extract:

- Although he sees himself as in control, Macbeth is being manipulated by the witches: they make him simultaneously over-confident and paranoid.
- His association with the witches suggests he is also evil.
- Macbeth seems unstable.
- He begins to act on instinct rather than reason.
- His plan for violent revenge against Macduff is shocking.

ACKNOWLEDGEMENTS

The authors and publisher are grateful to the copyright holders for permission to use quoted materials and images.

P34 'Sea-fever' from 'Sea-Fever: Selected Poems of John Masefield' by John Masefield (Fyfield Books, 2005, edited by Philip Errington). Reprinted by permission of the Society of Authors.

P43 ©2009 Jupiterimages Corporation. All other images are ©Shutterstock.com

Every effort has been made to trace copyright holders and obtain their permission for the use of copyright material. The authors and publisher will gladly receive information enabling them to rectify any error or omission in subsequent editions. All facts are correct at time of going to press.

Published by Collins
An imprint of HarperCollins*Publishers*
1 London Bridge Street
London SE1 9GF

HarperCollins*Publishers*
Macken House, 39/40 Mayor Street Upper,
Dublin 1, D01 C9W8, Ireland

© HarperCollins*Publishers* Limited 2022

ISBN 9780008551469

This edition published 2022

10 9 8 7 6 5 4

British Library Cataloguing in Publication Data.

A CIP record of this book is available from the British Library.

Authors: Paul Burns and Ian Kirby
Commissioning Editors: Daniel Dyer and Clare Souza
Project Managed by Cambridge Publishing Management Ltd and Katie Galloway.
Cover Design: Kevin Robbins
Inside Concept Design: Sarah Duxbury and Paul Oates
Text Design and Layout: Jouve India Private Limited
Production: Emma Wood
Printed in India by Multivista Global Pvt. Ltd.

MIX
Paper | Supporting responsible forestry
FSC
www.fsc.org
FSC™ C007454